DISCARDED

A Comparative Political Economy of Industrial Capitalism

Also by R. C. Mascarenhas

COMPARATIVE POLITICAL ECONOMY OF EAST AND SOUTH ASIA:
A Critique of Development Policy and Management

GOVERNMENT AND THE ECONOMY IN AUSTRALIA AND NEW ZEALAND:
The Politics of Economic Policy Making

PUBLIC ENTERPRISE IN NEW ZEALAND

A STRATEGY FOR RURAL DEVELOPMENT:
Dairy Cooperatives in India

TECHNOLOGY TRANSFER AND DEVELOPMENT:
India's Hindustan Machine Tool Company

To my parents, Charles and Alice Mascarenhas

© R. C. Mascarenhas 2002

All rights reserved. No reproduction, copy or transmission of this publication may be made without written permission.

No paragraph of this publication may be reproduced, copied or transmitted save with written permission or in accordance with the provisions of the Copyright, Designs and Patents Act 1988, or under the terms of any licence permitting limited copying issued by the Copyright Licensing Agency, 90 Tottenham Court Road, London W1T 4LP.

Any person who does any unauthorized act in relation to this publication may be liable to criminal prosecution and civil claims for damages.

The author has asserted his right to be identified as the author of this work in accordance with the Copyright, Designs and Patents Act 1988.

First published 2002 by
PALGRAVE MACMILLAN
Houndmills, Basingstoke, Hampshire RG21 6XS and
175 Fifth Avenue, New York, N.Y. 10010
Companies and representatives throughout the world

PALGRAVE MACMILLAN is the global academic imprint of the Palgrave Macmillan division of St. Martin's Press, LLC and of Palgrave Macmillan Ltd. Macmillan® is a registered trademark in the United States, United Kingdom and other countries. Palgrave is a registered trademark in the European Union and other countries.

ISBN 0-333-99846-4

This book is printed on paper suitable for recycling and made from fully managed and sustained forest sources.

A catalogue record for this book is available from the British Library

Library of Congress Cataloging-in-Publication Data
Mascarenhas, R. C.
  A comparative political economy of industrial capitalism / R.C. Mascarenhas.
  p. cm.
  Includes bibliographical references and index.
  ISBN 0-333-99846-4
  1. Capitalism. 2. Comparative economics. 3. Comparative government.
  I. Title.
HB501 .M519 2002
330.12'2—dc21   2002072315

10 9 8 7 6 5 4 3 2 1
11 10 09 08 07 06 05 04 03 02

Printed and bound in Great Britain by
Antony Rowe Ltd, Chippenham and Eastbourne

A Comparative Political Economy of Industrial Capitalism

R. C. Mascarenhas
Principal Fellow
Department of Political Science
University of Melbourne

Contents

Preface	xi
Introduction	1

Part I Historical, Institutional and Philosophical Foundations of Capitalism

1 Comparative Political Economy: An Institutionalist Approach — 9
- Introduction — 9
- Developments in political economy — 10
- Importance of comparative studies — 17
- Comparative institutional approach — 20
- Post-Fordism — 24
- Conclusion — 26

2 Developments in Modern Industrial Capitalism — 30
- Introduction — 30
- Philosophical foundations of modern capitalism — 31
- From classical political economy to rational capitalism — 33
- Critics of rational capitalism — 37
- Transformation of capitalism — 40
- Conclusion — 42

3 State and the Economy — 45
- Introduction — 45
- Role of the state in mixed economies — 47
- Postwar developments in the role of the state — 49
- Critique of state intervention — 57
- Conclusion — 60

Part II Recent Developments and Changes in Industrial Organization

4 Changing Nature of Capitalism: Large-Scale Enterprises — 67
- Introduction — 67
- Role of large-scale industrial organization — 68
- Private power and the public interest — 71

The institutions of capitalism	76
The golden age of capitalism	83
Economic decline of the 1970s	85
A critique of Fordism	86
Conclusion	90

5 Globalization and Its Effects on Capitalism — 96
Introduction	96
Focus from national to global economy	98
Distinctive or changing nature of globalization	101
Changing role of the state	102
Was globalization voluntary or involuntary?	107
Conclusion	110

6 Alternative Models of Capitalism — 113
Introduction	113
Historical evolution	115
Comparing types of industrial production	119
Characteristics of industrial districts	122
The functioning of industrial districts	125
Industrial districts: unique or universal?	127
Conclusion	130

Part III Comparative Studies of Modern Capitalism

7 Types of Capitalism: Anglo-American — 135
Introduction	135
The historical background	137
Origins of the corporate device	142
Government and business in Anglo-American capitalism	147
Performance of Anglo-American economies	150
Response to the crisis of Fordism	154
Response: deregulation, liberalization and privatization	159
Conclusion	162

8 German Capitalism: The Social Market Model — 167
Introduction	167
Historical background	168
The institutional framework	172
Evaluating economic performance	185
The economic miracle: could it last?	191
Conclusion	194

9	**Japan: The East Asian Developmental State**	**199**
	Introduction	199
	Historical background	200
	Japanese industrial enterprise	202
	Role of the state	213
	Evaluation of economic performance	219
	Conclusion	223
10	**Comparative Perspective of Industrial Capitalism**	**226**

Bibliography	234
Index	237

Preface

My interest in the role of the state in the economy began with my early studies of public enterprise and development. Extensively adopted as a postwar strategy of development by developed and less developed countries, public enterprise captured the interest of economists who focused on economic and financial aspects. As investment in such enterprises was considerable, their performance understandably became the subject of much scrutiny. The gap in achievements when compared to expected promise was attributed to quality of decisions, failure of management and the absence of appropriate institutional mechanisms for control and accountability. As a political scientist, I felt that a comparative approach with an interdisciplinary focus would lead to a better understanding of the issues. From there I gradually moved to research and teaching in development studies.

As one who adopts a political science perspective, I view the role of the state in the economy as central, although debatable. In recent years, that debate has become increasingly polarized between those who attributed the economic crisis of the 1970s to excessive state intervention and those champions of the 'developmental state' who attributed the success of East Asian economies to appropriate state intervention. Thus kindled, my interest in comparative political economy resulted in two studies: *Government and the Economy in Australia and New Zealand: The Politics of Economic Policy Making* (San Francisco, Austin & Winfield, 1996), and *Comparative Political Economy of East and South Asia: A Critique of Development Policy and Management* (London, Palgrave Macmillan, 1999).

I regard this study of comparative industrial capitalism as a continuation of my interest in the state and economy. While reading Albert Hirschman's *Rival Views of Market Society and Other Essays* (1986), I began to ask why state intervention in the economy in the United States had differed from that in other mixed economies (Mascarenhas, 1992). To answer that question I turned to Louis Hartz's *The Liberal Tradition in America* (1955) and to the work of business historian, Alfred Chandler Jr. This interest led me to offer a graduate level seminar on 'State and the Economy', in which I used the work of Hirschman, Lindblom, Lane, Dore and others. From there I was gradually led to this study. While working on it, a series of studies on comparative modern capitalism

published in the late 1990s provided a sound base for developing the themes covered herein.

This study is a product of my extensive involvement as an academic in understanding the relationship between the economy and the polity. From my initial interest in the comparative development of the Third World, I have gradually moved to the study of industrialized capitalist economies. In the process of writing this, I have learnt so much that I cannot identify particular sources, apart from the anonymous reader of the manuscript, whose valuable suggestions were useful in my revision of the study. Despite my efforts, the limitations of time and the restriction of the word limit has meant that I have been unable to cover all the literature brought to my attention.

Much of this work was undertaken while I was a Senior Associate at the School of Business and Public Management at Victoria University Wellington, New Zealand. Apart from the provision of physical facilities, the presence of friendly colleagues and help from library staff, this study is entirely my own. As usual, no work of mine reaches completion without the support of my family and particularly the meticulous editing carried out by my wife, Iris. My thanks to her and our daughters, Arati Ann and Antara Paula, for their support. Ms Brenda Bongiovanni of the School of Business and Public Management (VUW) has willingly and cheerfully helped to compensate for my inadequate computer skills and I hereby express my gratitude to her. Finally, my thanks go to Jean Lyon of the Governance and Government Unit of Monash University and to the Department of Political Science at the University of Melbourne for administrative support.

R. C. MASCARENHAS

Introduction

This study of comparative industrial capitalism analyses the role of the state in Anglo-American, German and Japanese economies. In focusing on these industrialized economies, I examine underlying commonalities and differences between them. Most studies appear to have categorized industrial economies into capitalist market economies as opposed to centrally planned economies. In making such comparisons, such studies assume considerable convergence within the industrialized capitalist economies. As an interdisciplinary study that attempts to understand the role of the state in industrialized economies, this study is firmly based in the emerging field of comparative political economy and offers a different perspective from the government and business studies emanating from business schools.

The recent interest in comparative studies of industrialized economies suggests growing acceptance of convergence and recognition of the divergence within capitalist economies. However, these trends differ in the countries studied. The trend towards convergence within the Anglo-American group of countries appears to coincide with a trend towards divergence in another type of industrial capitalism, identified as Rhenish and Developmental state. Such divergence is of interest, and, indeed, is central to this study of the comparative political economy of industrial capitalism.

Unlike critics who view governments and markets as alternative institutions, in this study I take the position that the state and its institutions are a vital ingredient of market economies, and the degree of interaction between markets and states varies between countries. In other words, market economies are plural, ranging from the more interventionist German and Japanese economies to the less interventionist American or British. While the first type is identified with the developmental or

consensual state, the latter is identified with the adversarial model of government and the economy. The type and effectiveness of the state's role in the economy has been debated, particularly in the 1980s with differing experiences being well documented. Underlying such differences however are institutional capabilities, both constitutional and administrative, which enable the state to play an effective role.

In this study of industrial capitalism, I examine the institutional basis necessary for effective state intervention, assuming that the functioning of markets is linked to state authority or capacity. That is, in its role of governance, government provides the public order for market transactions to take place and intervenes when such transactions result in imbalances or structural variations. In adopting this approach, both state autonomy from vested interests and state capacity for intervention become crucial. If it is suggested that state intervention in the 1970s led to economic decline in some countries, then we need to examine the nature of state–society relations, that is, the various institutional links that influence the political process, the ensuing policies and the agencies responsible for their implementation. Accordingly, this study adopts the new institutionalist perspective to understand the autonomous role of the state in the economy.

The institutionalist approach enables this study to take the view that the state and market are complementary and not adversarial and the relationship between the two is constantly changing, that is, adapting to the changing context. In shaping or understanding that relationship, one has to compare the historical evolution of that relationship within and between countries. In order to study both convergence and divergence of the relationship between the state and the economy, this study focuses on three distinct politico-economic systems: the Anglo-American, the Rhenish or German social market and the Japanese developmental state. In choosing these three as distinct types for comparison, my objective is to analyse: (a) the adversarial Anglo-American state–business relationship, (b) the cooperative state–business relationship in Germany and (c) the Japanese state guidance model of capitalism.

All three types have adopted the technology of the first and second industrial revolutions using the medium of large-scale organization. However, there is an alternative type, identified with small and medium-scale enterprises using flexible technology for production of specialized products, which has survived for two centuries. Identified as an alternative system of capitalism in this study, it adopts distinctive cooperative strategies across public and private sector institutions such as banks, local government, training institutions and enterprises for

capital, research and development and marketing of products. Although identified with the recent success of Italy and Germany, this type of capitalism exists in all three systems referred to above. With the current dominance of large-scale industrial organizations based on competitive markets and standardized products, it has become particularly important to identify such specialized flexible production. Emerging as a response to the rigidity of mass production, flexible specialization has had a large impact on academic thinking, resulting in a number of studies, the most significant of which is that undertaken by the French regulationists during the 1970s.

The third industrial revolution, predominantly in transportation and communication technology, has added a new dimension to this study, that is, globalization. It is a transformation in which technology has in some industries overtaken the social systems of production, resulting in a considerable change in the role of the state. Similar changes in the state's role occurred with the decline of industrialized economies in the mid-1970s which followed the golden age of capitalism (1950–73) when private enterprise functioned within the framework of rules and regulations laid down by governments. Referred to as 'embedded enterprise' or 'bounded capitalism', this consensus broke down in the 1970s when industrialized economies experienced decline with increasing inflation, low growth, high unemployment and adverse balance of payments problems. Such widespread decline had a differential impact, generating varying responses in terms of government policies. While the Anglo-American economies attributed decline to state intervention and responded with deregulation, liberalization and privatization, Germany and Japan were less affected and avoided neoliberal policies.

In analysing postwar changes in the role of the state in the economy, I identify two phases. The first is the mixed economy or bounded capitalism phase that can be attributed to the postwar consensus, leading to the golden age of capitalism (1950–73). The second phase is identified with the energy crisis of the 1970s which led to the economic crisis and the emergence of Germany and Japan as competitors of the Anglo-American model of capitalism. Here we see the emergence of national types of capitalism whereby the Anglo-American economies reverted to neoliberal policies while Germany and Japan continued with their policies of state involvement in the economy.

As the study covers post-Second World War developments in industrial capitalism in selected countries, their underlying similarities and differences have to be studied in a historical context. As each country has evolved its own systems of production drawing from its unique

experience, such systems differ considerably. To understand these characteristics, I have grouped industrial capitalist countries into three categories based on the extent of state intervention in the economy. Following this, I proceed to develop a framework to understand patterns of similarities and differences which are then studied within each group as well as over a period of time: that is, by the adoption of a comparative historical approach.

Having explained the theme and the approach adopted, the following is a brief chapterization of the study. The ten chapters are categorized into three parts. Part I comprises three chapters. Chapter 1 covers the conceptual argument for the adoption of a comparative political economy approach, incorporating the significance of adopting the institutionalist approach. Chapter 2 provides a background to the study of industrial capitalism and looking critically into the philosophical foundation of capitalism and reviewing the contribution of classical political economists such as Adam Smith, Karl Marx and Friedrich List, followed by the work of Max Weber, Karl Polanyi, Joseph Schumpeter and later critics of modern capitalism such as Shonfield, Galbraith, Hirschman and Hirsch. The central argument of the study, the role of the state in mixed economies, is discussed in Chapter 3, where a distinction is made between state as political authority and state as economic agent. In so doing, the study attempts a clarification of the role of state intervention in the economy in different industrialized economies: Anglo-American, German and Japanese.

Part II of the study comprises three chapters. Chapter 4 analyses the organization of manufacturing industries identified as products of the second industrial revolution. Covering the first half of the twentieth century, this period is dominated by the Anglo-American concept of large-scale organization developed for the efficient manufacturing of mass standardized products for consumer markets. The model was later adopted by other industrialized economies like Germany and Japan.

Most studies of industrialized economies seem to focus on large-scale organizations. While this study also analyses them, it acknowledges their limitations when markets become diversified. To meet these limitations, two developments have emerged in industrialized economies, namely globalization and small-scale industrial units called 'districts'. Although not entirely new, the current phenomenon of globalization is a product of the third industrial revolution in communication and information technology and is a distinct development to meet the demands of changing financial markets. It has raised some fundamental

questions about the role of the state in modern capitalist economies and these are discussed in Chapter 5. Amid the debate on the role of the state in the era of globalization, one observes the survival and now the revival of 'industrial districts' identified with quality small-scale flexible production, seen as crucial to the resurgence of both German and Italian economies. Known for the production of specialized quality goods identified with traditional skills, these enterprises adopt closer public and private sector cooperation in providing credit, training, research and development. Termed 'alternative capitalism' this is discussed in Chapter 6.

Part III of the study focuses on three distinct types of capitalism: Anglo-American, the German and the Japanese, each discussed in separate chapters. Chapter 7 is a detailed coverage of the Anglo-American form in which the United States deservedly enjoys a prominent place as a leader of twentieth-century manufacturing enterprise. Like other chapters that follow, this chapter includes a historical background to the development of industrial capitalism in Anglo-American countries and examines the role of the state in the economy, organizational developments and recent policy changes, concluding with an analysis of the performance of the economy.

Chapter 8 titled 'German Capitalism: The Social Market Model' takes a look at the historical background and the institutional framework within which industry associations, banks and co-determination work and highlights the close cooperation between government, business and labour in Germany. As in the chapter on the Anglo-American type, the overall performance of the German economy is evaluated, highlighting the postwar recovery, the response to the energy crisis of the 1970s and the effects of reunification.

Chapter 9 focuses on Japan whose historical background, like that of Germany, has had an impact on the fundamental institutions of capitalism. Although Japan's industrial developmental model allows the state a prominent role, there appears to be a greater similarity with the German system in terms of postwar recovery and the closer relations between government, business and labour. By the 1970s, their remarkable economic performance saw them emerge as competitors to the Anglo-American dominance in manufacturing.

Chapter 10 attempts an integration of the study by trying to weave together some of the themes covered in the earlier chapters. In so doing, I focus on the role of the state in the economy in the Anglo-American, German and Japanese systems, highlighting the underlying commonalities and differences attributed to historical, cultural and contextual factors.

Part I
Historical, Institutional and Philosophical Foundations of Capitalism

1
Comparative Political Economy: An Institutionalist Approach

Introduction

Since the publication of Adam Smith's *The Wealth of Nations* (1776), academics have constantly debated the relationship between the state and market in industrialized economies. This relationship assumed greater importance after the historical compromise between business, labour and governments following the Second World War described variously as 'embedded liberalism' (Ruggie, 1982) or 'bounded capitalism' (Gourevitch, 1986). A significant outcome was the 'golden age of capitalism' (1950–73), whose end can be identified with the breakdown of the Bretton Woods agreement and the subsequent energy crisis of the 1970s (Marglin and Schor, 1990; Ikenberry, 1986). For some countries, the energy crisis was traumatic and resulted in economic decline, high inflation, increasing unemployment and growing balance of payments problems. In effect, it was a setback for the Keynesian consensus. The very survival of the 'welfare state' came into question resulting in a reordering of the relationship between the state and the economy. This however varied from country to country. The Anglo-American group's response to the crisis, based on the assumption that the economic decline was caused by extensive state involvement, was a move towards a distinctly market-oriented approach to the economy. Others like Germany and Japan weathered the economic crisis better, avoiding dramatic political and economic changes. This resulted in one group, the Anglo-American (Australia, Britain, Canada, United States and New Zealand), distancing itself from other capitalist economies. Following a long history of authoritarianism and a metamorphosis in the postwar period under Allied and other internal influences, Germany and Japan had emerged with liberal market economies and democratic political

systems. In both countries, the government–business relationship that had evolved was instrumental in helping them weather these crises.

The distinctive response to the end of the 'golden age of capitalism' (Marglin and Schor, 1990) generated much academic and policy debate on the role of state and markets as alternative systems of coordination. While questioning the claims of the convergence theorists of the 1960s, the events of the 1970s and the intense ongoing debate have encouraged discourse on the comparative political economy of industrial capitalism. Occurring mainly in Australia, Britain, Canada, New Zealand and the United States (Anglo-American), this reaction extended the debate on government's role in the economy, prompting studies which highlight convergence as well as divergence between countries (Crouch and Streeck, 1997; Chandler *et al.*, 1997; Hollingsworth and Boyer, 1997; Hall and Soskice, 2001). That debate about the likely form of capitalism that might eventuate has prompted this study. In this chapter I intend to explore various aspects of the comparative political economy approach and examine the importance of adopting the institutionalist approach to understanding the distinctive role of political and economic institutions in studies of comparative political economies.

Developments in political economy

Political economy refers to the study of the functioning of the economy with special emphasis on the effects of government policy. Adopting the political economy approach assists in studying their interaction and interdependence, that is, knowing how power and production are organized. That human beings seek to engage in voluntary exchange (economic) presupposes the fact that exchange takes place within a framework of rules determined by governments (political). The reference to the political alludes to the science of government, whereby political decisions allocate value by authority or command while economic decisions are made through voluntary exchange. The interrelationship of those two aspects of societal functioning, the political and the economic, is seldom recognized in everyday operations. It was recognized however by Weber who categorized supply and demand relations in the market as social relations that are maintained by reciprocity of expectations, distinguishing them from other relations that are maintained through orientation towards an exercise of authority (Bendix, 1969, p. 16). The network of social relations arising out of the exercise of authority differs qualitatively from the social relation-

ships arising out of Weber's 'coalescence of interests'. Thus social relations arising out of market exchange, in addition to kinship and custom, can sometimes limit the autonomy of those responsible for exercising authority. Likewise, designated people responsible for overseeing the exercise of authority also engage in social relations and are affected by affinities of interest that characterize these relations. Pervasive as such relations are, the exercise of authority requires some element of neutrality. Bendix's thesis is that 'from an analytical standpoint, authority and association constitute interdependent but autonomous spheres of thought and action which coexist in one form or another in all societies. These general considerations provide the basis for formulating the recurrent issues of legitimation involved in the exercise of private and public authority' (Bendix, 1969, p. 17).

Such a network of interrelationships that distinguishes one social structure from another raises doubts over the adoption in social science of artificial conceptual distinctions. To 'maintain this balanced approach, comparative studies should not only highlight the contrasts existing between different human situations and social structures, but also underscore the inescapable artificiality of conceptual distinctions and the consequent need to move back and forth between the empirical evidence and the benchmark concepts which Max Weber called "ideal types"' (Bendix, 1969, p. 18). The close interrelationship between government's exercise of authority and the subordination to that authority by other associations such as the market, by agreement and consent, in return for the right to operate freely in the exchange of goods and services, is, in effect, the acknowledgement of a political community. Walzer (1983) extends the concept of the political community as an important good that is distributed. Membership of that community is through physical admission; it is politically received and hence not handed over by an external agency (p. 29). Such intangible foundations of a political community are rarely doubted if government can successfully handle or adjust to situations perceived as important or critical. The continued existence of a stable political community is an automatic assumption of the existence of the nation-state. Its emergence in the eighteenth century led inevitably to the gradual separation of the two relatively autonomous spheres of authority and social relations, resulting in a nation-wide market economy, based on the capacity of individuals to enter into legally binding agreements. 'Both the growth of a market economy and the gradual extension of the franchise gave rise to interest groups and political parties which mobilized people for collective action in the economic and political spheres, thus transforming

the social structure of modern society' (Bendix, 1969, p. 23). Public authority, once affected by overlapping social interests, is gradually being governed by impersonal rules and influenced decisions.

It is from such transitions that one now uses concepts in social science such as economy, society and state. The purpose of reiterating the interrelationship of the polity and the economy has been necessitated by post-1970s neoliberal developments which have overlooked this in their desire to promote laissez faire or free market economy, suggesting that economies can operate independent of political authority. State intervention in the market economy has been and remains seriously contended (Lindberg et al., 1987), particularly by economists who employ the theoretical orthodoxy of methodological individualism (p. 349). In advocating greater dialogue between social science disciplines, Lindberg et al. advocate the development of an alternative research programme centred around collective action and organization theory. It is supported by O'Sullivan (2000) who also questions neoclassical economics as a foundation of corporate governance and prefers 'the nation state as primary unit of analysis' to examine the institutional foundations of organizational control of business enterprise (p. 67).

It is in such a context that the revival of interest in political economy has to be encouraged and applauded. Pleas for such integration or understanding between economics and politics are being constantly made with the hope of bringing about a better understanding of both the polity and the economy (Hirschman, 1970; Lindblom,1977; Etzioni, 1985). McGraw (1997) is critical of some studies of business, government and the economy, attributing the lack of understanding to a 'balkanization of disciplines' and advocating better communication between academic disciplines. 'The rigid lines separating disciplines would no doubt be unfamiliar to Smith and List who considered their subject to be political economy, not just politics or economics in isolation. We still have much to learn therefore from the old masters' (p. 545).

The term 'political economy' once implied a relationship between government and the economy wherein government promoted a competitive market within which efficient allocation of resources for the production of goods and services for profit could take place. The two components, the polity and the economy, although interrelated, signify different aspects of societal functioning. While polity encompasses both power and values, economy is a system for producing goods and services for exchange. Within countries their relationship varies and is often dictated by domestic and external factors, the latter becoming an in-

creasing feature of modern industrialized economies where the mobility of capital impacts on the working of political systems. Such changes have revived interest in comparative political economy, that revival being used to assess the 'effects on the performing of modern economics of the political systems with which they are enmeshed and, in turn, of the larger social structures and processes which comprehend economy and polity alike' (Goldthorpe, 1987, p. 1).

The revival of political economy is seen by some as an acknowledgement of the limitations of current social science research. These limitations have become evident with the emergence of policy studies which demands a holistic approach to socio-economic phenomena, in contrast to some disciplines which approach them in isolation. Such a narrow disciplinary focus is particularly noticeable in political science, which, since the Second World War, has been influenced by behaviouralism. Here the focus on studying individuals and groups has become increasingly technical. While such an approach is less illuminating in understanding economic and political systems where both historical and contextual factors are overlooked (Ashford, 1992), it has to be acknowledged that the limitations of current social science have certainly acted as a stimulant to the revival of political economy:

> One of the most distinguishing characteristics of the revised study of political economy is that it centres on an analysis of the interface that evolves over time between economic process and political institutions. For political economy with a liberal bent, this effectively means focusing attention on the interconnection between a dynamic market system and an evolving set of institutions such as political decision-making structures. For those with a Marxist orientation, this means investigating the relationship that exists between the mode of production and the superstructure. While most political economists do not limit themselves to a study of the interface between economic processes and political institutions, it is the place from which most investigators begin and to which most return.
> (Stone and Harpham, 1982, p. 16)

The concept of 'market' is thus broader than that of capitalism – the latter operates in a competitive market economy and survives by making profits, that is, accumulation. Market systems use relative prices for allocative decisions while capitalism is the private ownership of the means of production. In other words, a market system can operate with both public and private actors. The emergence of the mixed economy

reflects the increasing role of the state in market systems. As the state plays distinctive roles in various countries, we need to reckon with national systems of capitalism (Evans *et al.*, 1985; Mascarenhas, 1992).

These developments in political economy have led Charles Maier (1987) to distinguish between two related but differing approaches, each relying on a characteristic methodology and often associated with a political stance, one on the right, the other on the left (p. 2). Countries influenced by the public choice approach have adopted the model of the political economy on the right, leading to more market and less state. While the public choice approach considers that collective decisions are governed by self-interested politicians and bureaucrats rather than by the criteria of economic maximization, the school of political economy on the left analyses economic choice in terms of political forces. Analysts identified with this approach ask 'what power relations underlie economic outcomes.... The second approach to political economy, therefore, cannot take economic theory merely as a quasi-mathematical elaboration of deductive premises. It interrogates economic doctrines to disclose their sociological and political premises' (Maier, 1987, pp. 3–4).

Reviewing the work of Charles Maier, Longstrech (1990) differentiates the two approaches to the study of political economy into 'economics of politics' and 'politics of economics'. Widely referred to as the 'new political economy', the 'economics of politics' or public choice attempts to apply the methodology of analytical models of microeconomics to public policy. The 'new political economy' can be identified as a school of political economy whose origins are traceable to classical political economy dating back to the work of Adam Smith, John Stuart Mill and Karl Marx. In laying its foundations, they emphasized three aspects: practical discourse about policy, means of regulating and promoting the creation of wealth, and the relationship between state and economy. While the three aspects are interrelated, Smith combined them into one social vision: 'It was political economy because it was about improving government and the conduct of public policy in the light of theory about the way the economy worked' (Gamble, 1995, p. 518). However, in its revival it has taken several different directions: international political economy, state theory, comparative state–economy relations and public choice. Despite adopting different directions, there is still dissatisfaction with existing theoretical accounts of state–economy relations, indicating a desire to rethink basic concepts such as states and markets (Gamble, 1995, p. 516).

'Politics of economics' has, as its central concerns, 'the relations of power that shape economic choices, its main actors collective rather

than individual and its arguments concentrated in the structural and institutional contexts in which policy is made. Adherents of this approach deny any strict segregation between state and market and tend to prefer some form of regulation to free market solutions for economic problems' (Longstrech, 1990, p. 97).

Academics identified with the latter approach adopt a historical political economy approach wherein there are no boundaries between state and markets as power pervades the economic arena as well as the political (Etzioni, 1985). Academics and policy-makers have, over the years, battled over an appropriate mix of state and market. As Lindblom (1977) and Hirschman (1970) acknowledge, such a mix remains elusive and changes constantly. While the former identifies the strengths and weaknesses of authority and market systems, the latter advocates greater flexibility in adopting either the market (exit) or the polity (voice). The importance of the state in modern mixed economies is now being widely acknowledged, prompting calls for 'bringing the state back in' (Evans *et al.*, 1985). Underlying this is a belief in the state's independent role as an actor in industrial transformation, a subject that has generated research ranging from society-centred to state-centric theories. Comparative historical studies reveal underlying variation between countries in their concept of the state. In the context of this study, the state is seen as diffused in Anglo-American political systems but concentrated in Japan and Germany.

In response to the nature of state–market mix posed earlier, it would be pragmatic to recognize the interdependence between the economy and the polity and thereby encourage a shift from disciplinary to interdisciplinary studies. However, the problem with interdisciplinary studies is the question of compatible perspectives – one emphasising power, the other, markets. One discipline cannot easily accommodate the other owing to conceptual and methodological differences. Though political economy is intended to be interdisciplinary, we encounter inherent obstacles in its functioning. One important hurdle relates to the place of values such as freedom, choice and democracy.

Disagreements between political economists of different persuasions focus on such differences in values. Libertarians identified with the new political economy adopt an aggressive posture and seek to apply the assumptions, language and logic of neoclassical economics to political behaviour. For those adopting such a perspective, 'political economy involves the application of the methods and techniques of economics to the subject matter of politics'. The growing influence of public choice and principal–agent theories based on the precision and rigour of economic analysis affirms this position (Gamble, 1995, pp. 516–17).

Such thinking has been applied to a range of public and private decision-making with the support of conservative regimes in Anglo-American countries. While the 'new political economy' gained ascendancy in the 1980s, those adopting the 'politics of economics' approach, having recognized the importance of power in the working of state and market, continue to enjoy considerable influence in some countries.

Political economy, as we now understand it, attempts to examine interconnections between state and market. Nineteenth-century liberals, had, according to Maier (1987), analytically separated the two. Economics was seen as the study of the production and exchange of goods and services and political science as being concerned with the exercise of authority and allocation of values.

The need to understand the interrelationship between the economy and the polity has arisen in recent times because of the variation in response (divergence) of countries to the decline in economic performance during the 1970s. Examining such variation in response of government and market institutions as instrumental to economic performance of countries has renewed interest in the comparative political economy of capitalism. As a result it has opened up the debate between types of capitalism so far ignored by the neoclassical or unitary industrialization model.

The two approaches to public policy issues have become contentious, especially in the context of neoliberal reforms focusing on efficiency and enterprise at the cost of socio-economic values of equality and welfare. Governments have favoured policies that advanced the needs of capital (incentives), discouraging those that hinder the interests of business and help the underprivileged (Stone and Harpham, 1982, p. 20). Such neoliberal influence has been less prevalent in other industrialized economies such as Germany and Japan, resulting in the growing acknowledgement of divergent national types of capitalism – the Anglo-American, the Alpine or European and the East Asian or Developmental state. Such variation in types of capitalism is seen by Cox (1995) as a product of the weakness of hyperliberalism and its contradictions.

That political and economic activities are organized differently in industrialized economies is a product of their history, system of beliefs and the nature of political institutions. Such differences have become issues for political debate, precipitated in the 1970s by a neoliberal view which promoted the laissez faire principle. According to this view, what is produced, how it is produced and the incentives associated with such production should be left to market forces. As such an ideal market economy capable of self-regulation has not and is not likely to exist in

the real world, we need to recognize the usefulness of the political economy approach which acknowledges government's overriding role in promoting the broader public interest.

In this debate about the role of the state in the economy, Lindberg *et al.* (1987) believe that democracy is a collective quest for the general welfare assigning a pre-eminent position to the roles and institutions through which citizens and public officials consider and define what the public interest shall be. In this quest, policy professionals have explicit responsibility to clarify the ethical and empirical perspective of their respective disciplines, and, at the same time, 'acknowledge that the perspective of each discipline is by itself incomplete. Thus, policy analysis has a necessary and natural affinity for interdisciplinary dialogue and discourse.' By adopting such an approach, scholars from different disciplines can select strands that will enhance understanding of the relationship between state and market (p. 353).

Importance of comparative studies

The divergence in the response to the economic crisis of the 1970s in advanced capitalist economies has encouraged greater academic interest in comparative studies of capitalism. Such comparative studies offer a realistic understanding of societies, their history, political systems and economies and also examine the recent revival within capitalist economies of small-scale flexible production competing with standardized mass production (Fligstein, 1990; Sabel and Zeitlin, 1997). Accordingly, Anglo-American economies are shaped by market forces while those of Germany and Japan attempt to shape market forces. Germany's economic policy model and Japan's, to some extent, has been developed over a period of time drawing on a historical legacy of policy experiences which have gradually been institutionalized within the structure and operating processes of the state. Insofar as industrial economies operate within their distinctive political and social context, one ought to adopt a comparative historical institutional approach to understand the political economy of industrial capitalism.

Comparative historical studies received a significant boost with Barrington Moore Jr's (1966) *The Social Origins of Dictatorship and Democracy: Lord and Peasant in the Modern World*. Moore sees comparisons 'as a rough negative check on accepted historical explanations. And a comparative approach may lead to new historical generalizations. In practice these features constitute a single intellectual process and make such a study more than a disparate collection of interesting cases' (p. x). Of the

three main historical routes he traces from the pre-industrial to the modern world, the first is the bourgeois revolutions that occurred in England, France and the United States en route to their transformation into modern industrial democracies. The result was a combination of capitalism and western democracy. The second route, also capitalist, culminated in the twentieth century in fascist Germany and Japan. The third, a peasant revolution, resulted in communism in Russia and China. Moore Jr (1966) then provides a comparative historical basis to explain why similar class relations resulted in democracy in one setting (France, Britain and the United States) and in fascism in others (Germany, Japan). Historical context, according to Moore Jr, is crucial in tracing the direction (path dependence) in the evolution of capitalism, democracy and dictatorship. His analysis, based on economic classes, is useful in understanding the role of politics in market societies (Lindblom, 1977) and the divergence in modern capitalism.

Moore Jr's thesis of the anti-democratic nature of the landed interests or aristocracy provides some evidence as to why feudal remnants acted as an obstacle to the development of *doux commerce* as markets emerged (Hirschman, 1986). In the course of economic and political change, the power of the aristocracy was destroyed by the emerging industrial and commercial middle classes (the bourgeoisie) eventually leading to the development of democracy and capitalist economic relations. Comparative historical studies offer a different insight into the development of capitalism from Smith, Mill or Marx whose work, being based largely on England, was not universal (Bates, 1987–88). Such variations also illustrate the significance of institutional factors, which were later highlighted by the relative response of industrialized economies to the energy crisis (Gourevitch, 1986; Ikenberry, 1986). Emphasizing the importance of historical and social context, Ashford (1992) expresses his amazement at the simple models of man adopted by economists to build a 'formidable body of useful economic theory' without calling on contextual knowledge, an issue that concerns the regulationists who are critical of economic theory for not accounting for historical facts and the inability to express the social control of economic relations (Aglietta, 1979, p. 9). The use of aggregate data and statistical methods to erase differences overlooks underlying contextual influences upon decisions or actions. Evans (1995) therefore suggests that 'a comparative analysis that starts with contextual differences and then looks for underlying regularities is the only way to proceed' (p. 29).

While Moore Jr (1966) offers a historical route to compare countries in their journey towards capitalism, democracy and dictatorship, Hirsch-

man (1986) explains why expected behaviour in the form of gentleness, probity and social manners (Montesqui's 'Doucier or Doux Commerce') did not eventuate when markets replaced feudalism. Concluding that this was due to a tendency to self-destruct, he uses Hirsch's 'decline of moral legacy' and Schumpeter's view of the inability of capitalism to control itself – that is, alluding to the Sorcerer's Apprentice to support his argument (Hirschman,1986).

Hirschman (1986) offers two alternative explanations based on historical development to understand variation among capitalist economies. While his 'feudal shackles thesis' explains capitalist development in Europe, his 'feudal blessings thesis' explains capitalist development in the USA. In the former, the development of the market did not result in the complete overthrow of feudalism, the remnants developing into seeds of self-destruction. In the latter, the very absence of feudal experience created a society that lacked ideological diversity. This argument is supported by Louis Hartz (1955) who believes that the absence of feudalism resulted in the lack of a genuine conservative tradition in the USA (p. 133). The latter explanation is interesting in terms of the direction taken by capitalism in the United States as opposed to Europe. The continued existence of feudal remnants in Europe suppressed the positive values of the market. By contrast, the exceptionalism, active capitalism and healthy pluralism of the United States is explained by the absence of that heritage, referred to by Hirschman as 'feudal blessings'. While the shackles of feudalism have resulted in ideological diversity in Europe, the absence of feudal blessings has denied the United States that ideological diversity referred to by Louis Hartz (1955) as the liberal tradition.

Both Moore Jr and Hirschman, by contrasting the historical development of various countries, offer a comparative approach that combines detailed analysis of specific cases with a broad causal analysis of macrostructures that can assist in developing general themes such as democracy or capitalism. In terms of this study of convergence and divergence of capitalism, Moore Jr's comparative historical approach meets up with what Skocpol (1994) describes as Mill's 'method of agreement' and 'method of difference'.

We see two distinct phases in the academic studies of capitalism which compared the responses of advanced economies to the 1970s economic crisis. The first, represented by Goldthorpe's *Order and Conflict in Contemporary Capitalism*, highlighted the success of neocorporatism. As identified earlier, this helped to overcome the energy crisis and was attributed largely to systems of government–business coordination,

known as social democracy. The second is represented by countries that had moved from mixed economies with state intervention towards more market-oriented approaches in an attempt to overcome the crisis of the 1970s. In recognizing the two distinctive approaches and their outcomes, Goldthorpe questioned 'industrialism' which had postulated the convergence of industrial societies.

The combined effects of globalization, decline of industrial production and the shift from Fordist towards flexible specialization left the advanced capitalist economies confronted by different policy issues. The ascendance of neoliberalism with consequent deregulation and privatization challenged the underlying rationale of state intervention. Greater internationalization, it was expected, would lead to a shift of power towards capital and gradual loss of power to labour. While this trend did not actually eventuate in countries like Germany and Japan, the Anglo-American countries did move substantially in that direction placing greater importance on shareholder value (Fligstein, 2001).

That move within the Anglo-American group towards a market-oriented model contrasted with the firm neocorporatist stance of Germany and Japan and resulted in a 'second wave' of scholarship recognizing the importance of decentralized production and flexible specialization. While this was essentially a response from small-scale units to changing technology and markets in their search for alternative ways of industrial organization, it was also a post-Fordist response to the rigidities of mass production anticipated by Piore and Sabel (1984). While these issues are explored in depth in later chapters, a brief résumé of the post-Fordist critique follows later.

To complete the 'second wave' (Hall, 1999), one other type of research termed varieties of capitalism attempts to confirm the overwhelming evidence against the convergence thesis (Hall and Soskice, 2001, pp. 143–5). Focusing on the nation-state, such research builds on the neocorporatist and neoinstitutionalist work of the 1980s. By acknowledging the competitive advantage of institutions, the varieties approach distinguishes liberal market economies (Anglo-American) from coordinated market economies (Japan and Germany). While the former lack coordinating organization, the latter possess coordinating agencies which enable them to establish relations with relevant interests to the economy.

Comparative institutional approach

In the comparative political economy of industrial capitalism my interest lies in studying the relative capacity of institutions, that is, in under-

standing the variation in the response of countries to economic crises. In the 1970s, such response in the form of liberalization by some countries regenerated interest in comparative studies of the interrelationship of the economy and polity. Evans (1995) advocates the comparative institutional historical approach to the study of industrial transformation, thus overcoming the weakness of the neoutilitarian model of the state as an aggregation of individual interests. In rejecting reductionist logic for enduring patterns which differ across economic, political and social systems, social scientists have recognized the utility of the comparative institutional approach to the study of political economy. Such an approach shifts the emphasis of studies from a narrow, disciplinary focus to a comprehensive broad-based interrelationship between the economy and polity.

The institutionalist approach adopted in this study helps to understand the role of the state in capitalist economies, thus answering critics who claim that economic institutions receive insufficient attention from historical institutionalists (Pontussan, 1995, p. 120). In making a case for the adoption of a comparative institutional approach, I hope (a) to provide a clearer perspective on the role of the state in the economy and (b) to examine the variation of that role between different industrial capitalist countries. While the first aspect provides an understanding of the interrelationship between the state and the economy, the second suggests the usefulness of a comparative approach in understanding the variation among countries with regard to the relationship between state and economy. States, like markets, are embedded and their functioning cannot be isolated from their social and economic context. This context helps to explain why states perform functions differently in the context of their respective economies. Ashford (1992) emphasized the importance of the historical context in explaining the working of institutions. His work, with that of Hall (1986), March and Olsen (1989) and Steinmo *et al.* (1992), among others, has generated considerable interest in 'new institutionalism'. New institutionalism, which presents an answer to conventional comparison in social science research, can be viewed more particularly as a response to the influence of behaviouralism in post-Second World War political science. March and Olsen (1984) critique the direction of political science research as overly reductionist, utilitarian, functionalist and instrumentalist (p. 735). Such critics have found that modern political science has overlooked the role of the state, prompting calls to 'bringing the state back in' (Evans *et al.*, 1985). New institutionalism (March and Olsen, 1984) is a response to the overly society-centred approach to the study of political science differing from

the old in that it extends the concept of institution beyond the legal and constitutional to include both the economy and the polity, while also being cross-national in analysis (Hall, 1986, p. 20). For Steinmo *et al.* (1992), the institutionalist approach offers comparativists a 'new angle through which to better understand policy continuities within countries and policy variation across countries' (p. 13); while for March and Olsen (1996), the institutional rules, duties, rights, and roles define acts as appropriate or inappropriate. The logic of appropriateness represents the abstract concept of institution (rules, operating procedures) while their actual functioning is the manifest institution (Pierre and Park, 1997).

In adopting the institutionalist approach, I recognize the importance of linkages the state has to establish with dominant elements like private capital in order to promote social and economic objectives without being captured by special interests. It is also a recognition of the influence of institutional factors such as sectoral networks, policy communities and strong and weak states (Mascarenhas, 1996). A growing body of such work has earned for its proponents the label 'new institutionalists' (distinct from old or classical institutionalists) and comprises two variants – the rational choice and the historical interpretive institutionalists (Steinmo *et al.*, 1992; Hall and Taylor, 1996).

The growth of institutionalism has necessitated attempts to distinguish between its differing schools (Hall and Taylor, 1996). Before exploring such developments, it is appropriate to acknowledge the significance of the comparative historical approach in the quest for answers to explain why some countries are more successful at adjusting to international economic conditions than others. In modern industrial capitalism, we observe greater interaction between public institutions and private enterprise in Japan and Germany when compared to Anglo-American systems. Analysts adopt the corporatist to least corporatist distinctions when comparing capitalist political systems. Distinguishing them as liberal market economies (LMEs) and coordinated market economies (CMEs), Hall and Soskice (2001) explore the institutional complementarities found in such economies.

Dosi (1997) questions the extent to which one can go in interpreting the links among organizational forms, competences and collective economic performance without bringing the broader institutional structure defining each 'political economy' into the picture. In adopting the historical institutionalist approach, it is appropriate for us to identify what is meant by institutions. While Dosi (1997) defines it as 'the formal and customary forms of governance of markets for labor, finance and

products, and the relationship between state and firm' (pp. 471–2), Hall (1986) includes 'the formal rules, compliance procedures, and standard operating practices that structure the relationship between individuals in various units of the polity and economy' (p. 19). The definitions incorporate electoral systems, the structure of party systems and the relationship between different branches of government (Steinmo et al., 1992, p. 2). A significant development in 'new institutionalism' is the concept of the veto, which has been built into institutions and is seen as a constraint in making policy changes or as protection against arbitrary use of power. The concept of veto has been helpful in comparing political systems such as presidential and parliamentary, unitary versus federal systems, two party versus multi-party systems, legislative –executive relations and in studying types of democracies (Steinmo et al., 1992; Weaver and Rockman, 1993; Mascarenhas, 1996, 1999).

I adopt a position that attributes to the state (government) a crucial role in a mixed economy. The effectiveness of the state in promoting the growth and development of the economy, both public and private, rests on appropriate institutions. Adopting such an approach helps to 'develop a conception of political action that puts particular stress on the critical role played by institutions in the definition and articulation of interests, the dissemination of ideas, the construction of market behaviour, and the determination of policy' (Hall, 1986, p. 5). Differences in the role of the state in industrialized capitalist economies are explained in terms of differences in institutions – that is, the success of some countries in implementing appropriate policies and the inability of others. Such variation in response becomes important due to the demands and the constraints placed on industrialized economies. This discrepancy between growing societal demands and institutional capabilities is central to the work of new institutionalists (Steinmo et al., 1992; Immergut, 1998).

Public institutions in industrialized capitalist economies are to be judged in terms of both responsiveness and efficiency in conducting public business. However it is not assumed that institutions of state are mere reflections of public demands; they should also act autonomous of societal actors in countries where power is not equally distributed and where public interest demands they act independent of special interests. 'Within an institutional framework, "choice", if it can be called that, is based more on a logic of appropriateness than on the logic of consequence that underlies conceptions of rational action' (March and Olsen, 1996, pp. 251–2). Thus the institutional theorists' concern for the common good as its distinguishing characteristic differs from exchange

theories of politics. Closely identified with economic theories of organization, the latter 'downplay the significance or meaning of virtue in the values of the citizenry and doubt the relevance of social investment in citizenship' (March and Olsen, 1996, p. 253). While duties, rights, rules and roles define what is appropriate, interpretation rests on how individuals translate them into actual behaviour in specific situations. While exchange theories, which form the basis of the neoliberal resurgence, promote the virtues of self-interest, institutional theories of politics view humans as 'able to share a common life and identity, and to have a concern for others' (March and Olsen, 1996, p. 253). In that context one witnesses the growing importance of political economy and the significance of the autonomous state and its role in the economy. Strongly identified with the political scientist view of institutions, this approach differs from that of the economist in which the individual is the focus (opportunistic behaviour), and that of the sociologist, in which culture and society are dominant. While all fall under the rubric of new institutionalism, these are then categorized into rational choice, sociological and historical institutionalism, the last being the approach adopted in this study. Hall and Soskice (2001) adopt the concept of the comparative institutional advantage: that is, that the institutionalist structure of a particular political economy provides firms with advantages for engaging in specific types of activities (p. 37).

Post-Fordism

Recent studies of industrial districts involving closer cooperation between public and private organizations at local and decentralized levels have prompted Immergut (1998) to identify new avenues for the adoption of the historical institutionalist approach. Based on close cooperation between economic, social and political elements, these models of industrial organization raise questions about the assumptions of the neoclassical and neoliberal concept of economic behaviour emphasizing competition and overlooking cooperation. Essentially they offer an alternative model to the Anglo-American model of capitalism (discussed in Chapter 6).

The resurgence of industrial districts identified with craft-based production has led to the growth of post-Fordist literature, where the emphasis is on flexible specialization (Piore and Sabel, 1984). As an answer to the limitation of vertically integrated corporations geared to mass production of standardized products, the post-Fordist response has attracted a range of critics drawing inspiration from Marxist theories

and Polanyists. The most important of these are the regulationists (Aglietta, 1979) and the 'social systems of production' school (Hollingsworth and Boyer, 1997).

If the postwar arrangements referred to as embedded liberalism (Ruggie, 1982) provided the stability that partially explains the 'golden age', its underlying contributions came from the Fordist mode of production. Based primarily on the use of semi-skilled labour for the production of standardized products for mass consumption, this form of production was supported by Keynesian policies and organized labour. Together they provided the social conditions that reduced the uncertainties facing high-volume producers (Hall, 1999, p. 140). The strengths of 'flexible specialization' – production systems possessing features capable of overcoming the rigidities of Fordism – were identified as a viable alternative to the crisis of the 1970s by social scientists. Underlying that shift was the acknowledgement that rapid changes in technology and markets demand greater diversity in production systems. An important outcome of such analysis is the increasing emphasis on the working of firms where micro-level understanding of relations with suppliers, competitors, public authorities and the workforce is considered to be as important as macro-level structures (Hall, 1999, p. 140).

The French 'regulation school' interpreted the pressures faced by capitalism in the 1970s as a structural crisis of the Fordist–Keynesian 'regime of accumulation'. They believed that the capitalist mode of accumulation relies on government policies, social institutions and norms of behaviour and that modes of regulation such as Keynesianism had enabled the emergence of Fordist regimes (Arrighi,1994). A structural crisis is basic to the regulation approach when periods of relative dynamic stability reach limits and leave room for change. 'In structural crisis (unlike small cyclical crises), the very process of accumulation becomes less and less compatible with the stability of institutional forms and the regulation which sustains it.... High levels of unemployment in industrialized countries are for this approach the manifestation of structural crisis which appeared in the early 1970s' (Delorme, 2001, p. 7).

Regulation theory arose out of dissatisfaction with macroeconomic theorizing which had overlooked institutions. Such dissatisfaction led researchers to investigate the past and to identify the basic institutional forms operating in a market capitalist economy. According to Delorme (2001), 'what makes the theory of regulation original in economic theory is its attempt to include institutions in macroeconomic theorizing and to build a framework in which institutions play an explicit and important role' (p. 3). Further, he states, 'Regulation theory subscribes to

plurality of institutions and rejects the dichotomy between market and state. It oversimplifies issues when it is used to support state intervention as a necessary consequence of market failure and vice versa.... Simply it does not reflect the role played by other institutional and organizational forms in modern economies' (Delorme, 2001, pp. 11–12).

Conclusion

The importance of understanding the relationship between the economy and polity in a comparative study of industrial capitalism has been examined in this chapter. While disciplinary boundaries between economists and political scientists have made the task difficult, there is now an awareness of the need to adopt a political economy approach. Attributable in part to the emergence of policy studies, such a development has demonstrated that policy problems cannot be analysed or solved without closer interrelationship between economics and political science.

References

Aglietta, Michel A., *A Theory of Capitalist Regulation: The US Experience* (London: NLB, 1979).

Arrighi, Giovanni, *The Long Twentieth Century: Money, Power and Origins of Our Times* (London: Verso, 1994).

Ashford, Douglas E., *History and Context in Comparative Public Policy* (Pittsburgh: University of Pittsburgh Press, 1992).

Bates, Robert H., 'Lessons from History, or the Perfidy of English Exceptionalism and the Significance of Historical France', *World Politics*, vol. 40 (1987–88), 499–516.

Bendix, Reinhard, *Nation Building and Citizenship* (New Delhi: Wiley Eastern Publishers, 1969).

Chandler Jr, Alfred et al. (eds), *Big Business and the Wealth of Nations* (Cambridge: Cambridge University Press, 1997).

Cox, Robert W., 'Critical Political Economy', in Bjorn Hettne (ed.), *International Political Economy: Understanding Global Decline* (London: Zed Books, 1995).

Crouch, Colin and Wolfgang Streeck (eds), *Political Economy of Modern Capitalism: Mapping Convergence and Diversity* (London: Sage, 1997).

Delorme, Robert, ' Regulation as an Analytical Perspective: The French Approach', in Atle Midttun and Eirik Svindlund (eds), *Approaches and Dilemmas in Economic Regulation: Politics Economics and Dynamics* (Basingstoke: Palgrave Macmillan, 2001).

Dosi, Giovanni, 'Organizational Competences, Firm Size, and the Wealth of Nations: Some Comments from a Comparative Perspective', in Alfred Chandler Jr et al. (eds), *Big Business and the Wealth of Nations* (Cambridge: Cambridge University Press, 1997), 465–79.

Etzioni, Amitai, 'The Political Economy of Imperfect Competition', *Journal of Public Policy*, vol. 5 (1985), 169–86.
Evans, Peter, *Embedded Autonomy: States and Industrial Transformation* (Princeton: Princeton University Press, 1995).
Evans, Peter *et al.* (eds), *Bringing the State Back In* (Cambridge: Cambridge University Press, 1985).
Fligstein, Neil, *The Transformation of Corporate Control* (Cambridge, Mass.: Harvard University Press, 1990).
Fligstein, Neil, *The Architecture of Markets: An Economic Sociology of Twenty-First Century Capitalist Societies* (Princeton: Princeton University Press, 2001).
Gamble, Andrew, 'The New Political Economy', *Political Studies*, vol. 63 (1995), 516–30.
Goldthorpe, John, *Order and Conflict in Contemporary Capitalism*, Oxford, Clarendon Press, 1984).
Goldthorpe, John, 'Problems of Political Economy after a Postwar Period', in Charles Maier (ed.), *Changing Boundaries of the Political* (New York: Cambridge University Press, 1987), 363–407.
Gourevitch, Peter, *Politics in Hard Times: Comparative Responses to International Economic Crises* (Ithaca: Cornell University Press, 1986).
Hall, Peter A., *Governing the Economy: The Politics of State Intervention in Britain and France* (Oxford: Polity Press, 1986).
Hall, Peter A., 'The Political Economy of Europe in the Era of Interdependence', in Herbert Kitschelt *et al.* (eds), *Continuity and Change in Contemporary Capitalism* (Cambridge: Cambridge University Press, 1999).
Hall, Peter A. and Rosemary C. R. Taylor, 'Political Science and the Three New Institutionalisms', *Political Studies*, vol. 64 (1996), 936–57.
Hall, Peter A. and David Soskice (eds), *Varieties of Capitalism: Comparative Institutional Advantage* (Oxford: Oxford University Press, 2001).
Hartz, Louis, *The Liberal Tradition in America* (New York: Harcourt Brace, 1955).
Herrigel, Gary, *Industrial Constructions: The Sources of German Industrial Power* (Cambridge: Cambridge University Press, 1996).
Hirschman, Albert O., *Exit, Voice and Loyalty: Response to Decline in Firms, Organizations and States* (New York: Free Press, 1970).
Hirschman, Albert O., *Rival Views of Market Society and Other Recent Essays* (New York: Viking, 1986).
Hollingsworth, Rogers J. and Robert Boyer (eds), *Contemporary Capitalism: The Embeddedness of Institutions* (Cambridge: Cambridge University Press,1997).
Ikenberry, John, 'The Irony of State Strength: Comparative Response to the Oil Shocks', *International Organization*, vol. 40 (1986), 105–37.
Immergut, Ellen M., 'Theoretical Core of the New Institutionalism', *Politics and Society*, vol. 26 (1998), 5–34.
Lindberg, Leon N. *et al.* (eds), *Comparative Policy Research: Learning from Research* (New York: St Martins Press, 1987).
Lindblom, Charles E., *Politics and Markets* (New York: Free Press,1977).
Longstrech, Frank H., 'Historical Political Economy and Liberal Democratic Capitalism', *Economy and Society*, vol. 19 (1990), 95–120.
Maier, Charles S., *In Search of Stability: Explorations in Historical Political Economy* (Cambridge: Cambridge University Press, 1987).

March, James G. and Johan P. Olsen, 'The New Institutionalism: Organizational Factors in Political Life', *American Political Science Review*, vol. 78 (1984), 734–49.
March, James G. and Johan P. Olsen, *Rediscovering Institutions: The Organizational Basis of Politics* (New York: Free Press, 1989).
March, James G. and Johan P. Olsen, 'Institutional Perspectives on Political Institutions', *Governance*, vol. 9 (1996), 247–64.
Marglin, Stephen and Juliet B. Schor, *The Golden Age of Capitalism: Reinterpreting Postwar Experience* (London: Clarendon, 1990).
Mascarenhas, Reginald C., 'State Intervention in the Economy: Why is the United States Different from Other Mixed Economies', *Australian Journal of Public Administration*, vol. 52 (1992), 385–97.
Mascarenhas, Reginald C., *Government and the Economy in Australia and New Zealand: The Politics of Economic Policy Making* (San Francisco: Austin & Winfield, 1996).
Mascarenhas, Reginald C., *Comparative Political Economy of East and South Asia: A Critique of Development Policy and Management* (Basingstoke: Palgrave Macmillan, 1999).
Mcgraw, Thomas K., 'Government, Big Business and the Wealth of Nations', in Alfred D. Chandler Jr et al. (eds), *Big Business and the Wealth of Nations* (Cambridge: Cambridge University Press, 1997).
Moore Jr, Barrington, *Social Origins of Dictatorship and Democracy: Lord and Peasant in the Making of the Modern World* (London: Penguin, 1966).
O'Sullivan, Mary, *Contests for Corporate Control: Corporate Governance and Economic Performance in the United States and Germany* (New York: Oxford University Press, 2000).
Pierre, Jon and Sang-Chul Park, 'The Dynamics of Abstract and Manifest Institutional Change: MITI and the Japanese "Economic Miracle" Reconsidered', *Governance*, vol. 10 (1997), 351–76.
Piore, Michael J. and Charles F. Sabel, *The Second Industrial Divide: Possibilities for Prosperity* (NY: Basis Books, 1984).
Pontusson, Jonas, 'From Comparative Public Policy to Political Economy: Putting Political Institutions in Their Place and Taking Interests Seriously', *Comparative Political Studies*, vol. 28 (1995), 117–47.
Remmer, Karen L., 'Theoretical Decay and Theoretical Development: The Resurgence of Institutional Analysis', *World Politics* (1997).
Ruggie, John Gerald, 'International Regimes, Transactions and Change: Embedded Liberalism in Postwar Economic Order', *International Organization*, vol. 36 (1982), 379–415.
Sabel, Charles and Jonathon Zeitlin, *World of Possibilities: Flexibility and Mass Production in Western Production* (New York: Cambridge University Press, 1997).
Skocpol, Theda, *Social Revolutions in the Modern World* (Cambridge: Cambridge University Press, 1994).
Steinmo, Sven et al. (eds), *Structuring Politics: Historical Institutionalism in Comparative Analysis* (New York: Cambridge University Press, 1992).
Stone, Alan and Edward J. Harpham (eds), *The Political Economy of Public Policy* (London: Sage, 1982).

Walzer, Michael, *Spheres of Justice: A Defence of Pluralism and Equality* (Oxford: Martin Robertson, 1983).

Weaver, Kent R. and Bert A. Rockman (eds), *Do Institutions Matter? Government Capabilities in the United States and Abroad* (Washington, DC: The Brookings Institution, 1993).

2
Developments in Modern Industrial Capitalism

Introduction

The history of modern industrialized economies centres around the relationship between the state and organized business which has evolved gradually between countries, reflecting elements of convergence and divergence across industrialized economies. Recent studies of comparative capitalism have brought about greater understanding of such variation. Whilst such studies have enriched our understanding of industrial capitalism, two recent developments associated with the 1970s have been particularly crucial in encouraging comparative studies: first, internationalization or globalization of the economy, and second, flexible specialization with the re-emergence of industrial districts. While the former has brought about a change in the relationship of state with business, the latter is an example of the distinctive role that the state can play in cooperation with the public and private sectors.

In analysing postwar changes in the role of the state in the economy, I identify two phases: first, the mixed economy or bounded capitalism phase attributable to the postwar consensus leading to the golden age of capitalism (1950–73), and second, the energy crisis of the 1970s followed by the economic crisis, when Anglo-American countries reverted to neoliberal policies while Japan and Germany continued with their policies of active state involvement in the economy. This led to the emergence of national types of capitalism.

In exploring the role of the state in the development of industrial capitalism, my purpose in this chapter is to trace its historical development and to provide a philosophical background to modern capitalism. In the next section I critically review various studies that provide a background to the philosophical foundations of modern industrial cap-

italism. The third section builds from the philosophical foundations to evaluate later contributions with emphasis on Weber, Polanyi and Schumpeter. The fourth section reviews more recent critics including Galbraith, Shonfield, Hirsch and Hirschman. A conclusion sums up in the final section.

Philosophical foundations of modern capitalism

Early developments in political economy can be traced to the writings of Adam Smith, Karl Marx and Friedrich List, whose influence is reflected to a great extent in the libertarian and neo-Marxist schools. Their work provides a useful background to a comparative study of industrial capitalism.

Libertarian philosophy centres around freedom of choice, individual liberty and the right to property, which together contribute to enterprise, initiative and self-interest. '*The Wealth of Nations* so intriguingly titled and coming as it were, from the horse's mouth, seemed to provide the answer: the economy was ascendant because of man's natural and rational propensity to truck, barter, and exchange, and the British economy was ascendant because of free competition' (Greenfeld, 2001, p. 33). Viewed as the source of laissez faire ideas, Adam Smith in *The Wealth of Nations* (1776) stated that economic freedom increases an individual's desire to maximize wealth. This allowed individuals rather than governments to be better judges as to the maximization of wealth and resulted in individual well-being. National wealth was the sum of individual wealth (Rashid, 1998, p. 47). Competitive capitalism was, according to Smith, 'if not the best of all economic systems, at any rate the best of all possible systems.... Do away with most, if not all, monopolies and restrictions on internal and external trade; allow each man to do as he wants with his own (and in particular with his own capital); give "the obvious and simple system of natural liberty" its head, and the famous invisible hand will automatically maximize the rate of growth of the national product and promote the diffusion of the increasing opulence among the populace' (Meek, 1977, p. 4). Smith's theory that humans make rational choices based on individual preferences, for which one needs individual freedom, has earned him recognition as the founder of modern economics and a strong proponent of classical individualism.

Influenced by such theories, conservatives established a connection between the economic system and freedom. The concept of specialization and the self-interest of the butcher, baker and brewer is central to Smith's theory of the development of entrepreneurial or liberal

capitalism. As specialization through the division of labour led to economic growth, factors such as improved technology, machines and improved organization gradually led to organized capitalism. The classical school based its preference for limited state involvement on its belief that individual achievements and economic growth are beneficial to the national economy. Debate within the disciplines of economics and political science since then has centred around the appropriate role of the state in the economy (discussed in Chapter 3).

While disapproving of Smith's competitive market, Marx described capitalism as monopolistic capital with inbuilt contradictions displaying a tendency towards replacing labour with machinery, decreasing profit and deterioration of the working class. In fact, he went so far as to predict the end of capitalism and its replacement with socialism (Meek, 1977, p. 4). Like Smith, Marx investigated relations of production and regarded them as representing classical political economy and capitalism as incapable of delivering a just and equitable society. The profit-driven motive of capitalism based on private property, he felt, was an obstacle to the emergence of such a society. 'Marx's theory of capitalism, however, clearly went beyond a purely economic analysis, and even beyond what could be adequately encompassed by the term "political economy". It was, in fact, a broad socio-historical theory which treated capitalism as a "total society" involved in a distinctive process of development' (Bottomore, 1985, p. 2). Marx showed how capitalism could generate vast and unprecedented productive power, thus transforming material conditions in industrialized capitalist economies. Taking this further, he examined the dynamic development of capitalism and the human and class relationships associated with production. It was the relationship between labour and capital that concerned him most, a relationship which continues to influence the nature of contemporary capitalist societies discussed in this study. 'Historically, the capitalist phenomenon in its full-blown form coincided with the phenomenon of industrialism. Together, the new economic institutions and the new technology (in Marxian terms, the relations and the means of production) transformed the world' (Berger, 1986, pp. 19–20). Marx's critique of capital, based on historical materialism, offered a sound methodological basis for understanding internal contradictions, which increased as capitalism matured. The period 1885–1920 is regarded as the high-water mark of political economy characterized by balanced debate which proved beneficial to intellectual advancement.

According to Greenfeld (2001), Marx's reason for turning his attention to economic and social life was the 1841 publication by Friedrich List of

his work *National System of Political Economy*. Apparently, for both List and Marx, Adam Smith's *The Wealth of Nations* was a central point of reference (p. 6).

In his *National System of Political Economy* (1841), Friedrich List proposed protection for German industry and opposed the theory of free trade advocated by Smith. He formulated his justification for protection through the creation of a constructivist doctrine of national development:

> Smith's political economy, List asserted, was devoid of political because it considered the political economy 'ought to yield to universal economy' of free trade. The real reason for the absence of the political and policy in 'English' doctrine was that, for England, the cosmopolitan and national principle were one and the same thing. Since the two principles were so different for mid-century Germany, the ideal German state had to intend the development of productive powers through tariffs and other means to promote and protect domestic manufacture.
>
> (Cowen and Shenton, 1996, p. 163)

His advocacy of protection, in order to promote indigenous industry, was intended to assist a backward economy to catch up with advanced economies, with strategies adopted to preserve their advantage. List was particularly concerned about building local capabilities through training, education and, most importantly, innovation. Such advocacy is a plausible explanation for the development of an excellent technical education system in Germany (Archibugi and Michie, 1997). While his writing appears to have been overlooked by traditional economists, his ideas have certainly influenced policy-makers in Europe and Japan and can be seen as a precursor of divergent capitalism (Fallows, 1994, p. 63).

From classical political economy to rational capitalism

In the *Protestant Ethic and the Spirit of Capitalism*, Max Weber discussed the origin and nature of capitalism in the West (Zeitlin, 1981, p. 127). 'Weber referred to the orientation of the economy toward growth as the "spirit of capitalism" and he called the economy oriented to and capable of growth "capitalism"' (Greenfeld, 2001, p. 11). To understand the impact of religious values on economic conduct, he analysed differences in education and occupation between catholics and protestants and found pronounced economic rationalism among protestants. Studying the various

protestant groups, Weber observed commitment to industry, frugality, hard work and punctuality among Calvinists and concluded that the ethical elements that foster the capitalistic spirit are to be found in Calvinism (Zeitlin, 1981, p. 132). 'Hard work is the morally dutiful pursuit of a worldly calling and absolute avoidance of anything which detracts from an ascetic way of life – that was the Protestant ethic.... it had the greatest significance for the development of the spirit of capitalism' (Zeitlin, 1981, p. 133). However, once the capitalist system was established, the protestant ethic was no longer found to be necessary for its maintenance (Zeitlin, 1981, p. 134). 'Capitalism, Weber argues, combines the protestant idea of "calling" with a traditional, puritan emphasis upon moral personal conduct. The combination of these two ethical principles finds expression in hard work, the development of surpluses from that hard work (capital), and the investment of these surpluses for purposes of greater productivity' (Dobelstein, 1980, p. 105). The protestant ethic advocates a religious and cultural explanation for the birth of capitalism, that is, ascetic protestantism – that helped to create a new type of economic mentality, namely rational capitalism (Swedberg, 1998, p. 7). 'The Puritans introduced a stern and honest morality into economic life. They detested the aristocracy for its idleness and luxuries, and they deeply disapproved of everything that came close to adventurer's capitalism. The hostility of the Puritans to monopolies and political capitalism undoubtedly helped a competitive and private kind of capitalism to emerge. The viewpoint that money-making and religion could very well go together also helped to legitimise capitalism' (Swedberg, 1998, p. 126).

While the protestant ethic explains the existence of capitalism in the West, its rationality is manifested in the pursuance of interests through exchange in markets, the use of money (price) to transact such exchanges, in the means of accounting, and the use of specific technology to produce goods through rational organization of labour within a legal framework that guarantees contracts and private property. Its salient feature is its rationality (Bottomore, 1985, pp. 23–5): 'What is distinctive about modern, large-scale, "rational capitalism" – in contrast to earlier, partial forms – is that it is methodical and predictable, reducing all areas of production and distribution as much as possible to a routine. This is also Weber's criterion for calling bureaucracy the most "rational" form of organization' (Collins, 1980, p. 927). Capitalism in this context is defined as 'production for a market by enterprising individuals or combines with the purpose of making profits' (Berger, 1986, p. 19). Collins (1980) views Weber's thesis as offering the institutional foundations of the neoclassical concept of the market, whereby individual entrepre-

neurs calculate their outcomes. The state was key to the institutional structure of rational capitalism through professional administrators, who applied law, eliminating pre-capitalist barriers such as feudalism (pp. 928–32).

Weber followed his explanation of the foundations of modern capitalism with an analysis of the modern bureaucratic state, providing insights into the management of large-scale capitalist enterprise. Here Weber saw an intimate relationship between bureaucracy and capitalist enterprise. Extending the idea of specialization (Smith's repetitive tasks) to bureaucratic organization, Weber felt that a typical competitive modern capitalist enterprise would, through bureaucratization, achieve efficiency and cost reduction. That process in public and private organizations, in addition to achieving efficiency, would materialize in power (Zeitlin, 1981, p. 165). While recognizing the value of Weber's contribution in identifying the type of public institutional structure needed to counter private entrepreneurial groups, Evans (1995) is critical of his lack of exploration into its role in promoting private enterprise.

The social systems of production approach to studies of comparative capitalism (Hollingsworth and Boyer, 1997) owes its influence to the work of Karl Polanyi, author of *The Great Transformation* (1944). Polanyi viewed the institutional framework of industrial capitalism as being based on self-regulating markets and the gold standard, both of which were to be supported by a liberal state. He viewed the economy as a system for mobilizing resources, involving forms of interaction other than market exchange. Polanyi introduced obligation and power based on reciprocity and redistribution into economic relationships. Questioning the liberal view of non-intervention in markets, Polanyi stressed the essential role of the state in a market society.

The free market, or doctrine of laissez faire, is an institutional structure which was planned and did not emerge spontaneously (Scott, 1996, p. 96). Scott attempts to compare Weber's bureaucratic organization with Polanyi's free market as forms of social order, creating a structure of rewards with a degree of predictability. Despite the differing logics, Scott (1996, p. 97) asserts that bureaucracy and market are compatible and complementary forms of organization.

Polanyi's argument is founded on the assumption that most economies are embedded in society (Holton, 1992). The development of a market society however occurs through a process of differentiation from an embedded economy (reciprocity, redistribution and household). Although laissez faire or free markets were influential in mid-nineteenth-century

economic affairs, they were unable to function successfully as self-sufficient institutions free from political or cultural regulation (Holton, 1992, p. 37). If the change from embeddedness to differentiation did take place, its direction was not uniform across countries (Barrington Moore Jr, 1966). In other words, embeddedness and differentiation do exist in different economies in varying proportions.

Polanyi's 'great transformation', as a disjunction from an embedded to a disembedded economy, triggered an interesting debate on the morality of markets, leading to the emergence of the communitarian or moral economy school (Booth, 1994). Moral economists concerned with the pervasiveness of market institutions use the logic of calculation and maximization to explain human activity. One measure of this transformation is the array of perverse effects attributed to the pervasive market, such as effects on subsistence, labour, and the environment (Booth, 1994, p. 657).

Gershenkron (1962), like List, recognized the state's inherent role in late industrialization. In *Economic Backwardness in Historical Perspective* (1962), Gershenkron viewed industrialization as helpful in understanding the relationship between the economy and polity. In his view, the process of advancement through political and institutional adaptation was essential for the development of backward countries which lacked an industrial infrastructure. While List was influenced by the United States of Alexander Hamilton, Gershenkron appears to have been persuaded by Saint Simon's advocacy of investment banks in France's development. 'Although the extent of the bank as an instrument of industrialization was limited by the extent of backwardness, Gershenkron's argument was that it was belief in intended development which formed the pervasive ideology of a common policy of late industrialization' (Cowen and Shenton, 1996, p. 392). In effect, it was the state that played a crucial role in late industrialization through the organization of financial markets. That state intervention in the economy need not always be obstructive (a view held by anti-statists or neoliberals) has been supported by Hirschman, Shonfield, Galbraith, Evans, Johnson and others. Recent experience of the Rhenish model and the East Asian developmental state confirms Herrigel's (1996) claim, that, based on the German experience, 'political and institutional innovations make it unnecessary for all industrializing countries to follow the exact same path to sustained industrial growth' (p. 13). That the state can play a variety of roles in industrialization is evident in light of recent studies (Evans, 1995; Herrigel, 1996; Sabel and Zeitlin, 1997).

Critics of rational capitalism

A different perspective to our understanding of modern capitalism is offered by Hirschman, Hirsch, Schumpeter and others. A brief analysis of their critique follows. The types of capitalism (rational, political and adventurist) enunciated by Weber can be adopted to critique the divergence of present-day capitalism. It is appropriate at this stage to start with the two contradictory arguments enunciated by Hirschman in *Rival Views of Market Society and other Essays* (1986). The first of these is the 'Doux Commerce' thesis attributed to Montesquieu, wherein commerce naturally leads to gentleness. The virtues likely to be enhanced through capitalism are 'industriousness and assiduity, frugality, punctuality and, most important perhaps for the functioning of market society, probity' (Hirschman, 1986, p. 109). According to him, capitalism creates a set of compatible attitudes and moral dispositions which replace pre-capitalist mentalities. But, according to the second thesis, that of self-destruction, this has not occurred. Capitalism has not fostered *doucier*. On the contrary, because of its inheritance of the remnants of the feudal order it has exhibited a pronounced proclivity to undermining the moral foundations of society. Inevitably, self-interest, typical of capitalism, has made it difficult to promote cooperative or collective values, which are increasingly necessary for its functioning. 'Doux Commerce' became a victim of the industrial revolution and, with increasing competition, all classes of society developed a wild, unbridled passion for enrichment. Such failure of *doucier* and its self-destruction is attributed to the persistence of feudal remnants. The pre-capitalist institutions and attitudes of the previous social order were left intact, thus restraining the free development of markets. Capitalism was weak in playing the 'progressive' role allegedly assigned to it by history. 'Until now it was presumed that advanced capitalist countries... suffered from contradictions that arose from capitalism's strengths and not its weaknesses' (Hirschman, 1986, pp. 126, 131). However, the United States, in the absence of feudalism, was able to engage in both a vigorous development of capitalism and sturdy political pluralism. It must be asked whether the existence of democracy and equality without enduring a democratic revolution is a blessing or a misfortune. According to Louis Hartz, the United States suffers from a lack of ideological diversity, that is, a 'prime constituent of genuine liberty' so abundant in Europe (Hirschman, 1986).

In *Passions and the Interests* (1977), Hirschman notes Smith's belief that *doucier* would result in corruption and decadence. By suggesting that the material welfare of society as a whole is advanced by allowing

everyone to follow their own interests without hindrance, Smith, in effect, treated passions and interests as synonyms. Hirschman, on the other hand, considers them to be antonyms (1977, p. 111). The reality of capitalist development with its cyclical fluctuations is that it has enriched some and impoverished many: 'Those caught in these violent transformations would on occasion become passionate – passionately angry, fearful and resentful' (Hirschman, 1977, p. 126).

The two sides to this debate evident in Hirschman's *Passions and the Interests* (1977) are also seen in Hirsch's *Social Limits to Growth* (1976). Subscribing to Polanyi's view that a self-regulating market is a utopia, Hirsch believes that market liberalism emerged from special historical conditions, a view disputed by present-day neoliberals who attribute its emergence to the natural framework of liberal capitalist societies. Smith's 'invisible hand' which linked individual self-interest with social need survived, according to Hirsch, with the help of favourable conditions from an earlier socio-economic system resulting in the development of liberal capitalism. Such conditions cannot be relied on to persist or be maintained by deliberate action (Hirsch, 1976, p. 11). The principle of self-interest as a social organizational device is, according to Hirsch, effective only if supported by a social principle. This reliance on social orientation or social responsibility increases as correctives to laissez faire, through public policy, are gradually introduced:

> Market capitalism has never been the exclusive basis of the political economy in any country at any time. That has been its strength. It was the marriage of market capitalism with state regulation that produced a hybrid politico-economic system with the necessary resilience and plasticity to survive. But the new skin grafted on to western capitalism to provide it with stability and support appears to have papered over a continuing and perhaps growing stress in the foundations of the system.
>
> (Hirsch, 1976, p. 118)

In Hirsch's view, attempts to reconcile the public interest with Keynesian economic controls while leaving individual self-interest intact would not work. Such Keynesian guidance was unlikely to succeed because the moral legacy that supported the pre-capitalist foundation and promoted values celebrated by the invisible hand had disappeared (Hirsch, 1976, p. 119). State controls were expected to protect the weaker sections from the burden of market forces, make market forces

efficient and encourage forms of social behaviour needed for the operation of markets (Hirsch, 1976, pp. 120–1).

While acknowledging the depletion of the moral legacy fundamental to the development of capitalism, commentators like Kumar (1988) fear that a mere statement of the importance of non-economic factors is sociologically and historically inadequate (p. 43), a point emphasized by Schumpeter.

Schumpeter emphasized the role of the entrepreneur as the principal agent in capitalist development. Capitalist development, he wrote, rested on innovation wherein competitors constantly entered the market with new combinations of materials to replace existing products. More often than not, this could be a new producer rather than an existing one. To do this, one required command over the means of production, achievable only through the availability of credit. Materials had to be combined to manufacture a new product and the task of production required entrepreneurial ability. Capitalist entrepreneurs were seen as distinctive with not all cultures being conducive to their emergence. A specific trait identified with entrepreneurs and the development of capitalism is individual autonomy, and this, in Weberian thinking, is more likely to be developed in a Calvinist environment. Berger's (1986) narration of Calvinist practices of child-rearing explored their encouragement of strong-willed and self-directed individuals (p. 102).

The emergence of the modern corporation led to the decline of the entrepreneurial function associated with early capitalism. In his analysis of these changes, Schumpeter in *Capitalism, Socialism and Democracy* (1942) states that the tendency of capitalism to 'destroy itself' resulted in the emergence of socialism. A slump, he wrote, is an essential process of technological innovation involving creative destruction, whereby inefficient firms are bankrupted. This phenomenon, although tamed by the stabilizing feature of a large organization, is an inherent feature of violent or volatile markets (Shonfield, 1965, p. 53). Private property, the other feature that sustains capitalism, is undermined in two ways: first, through large-scale monopolies which threaten medium-sized enterprises, and second, the transformation of owner-proprietor into salaried executive whose attitudes may be at variance with that of shareholders (Bell, 1974, p. 66). While acknowledging the shift from the competitive capitalism of the innovative entrepreneur to that of managed or organized capitalism, Schumpeter recognized the role of the large corporation in the process of creative destruction. Emphasizing the importance of corporate organizations in the innovation process, he pointed out that capitalism was an evolutionary process (Lazonick,

1991, pp. 125–9). While Schumpeter's entrepreneur who developed new products and searched for markets as a form of personal capitalism was succeeded by managerial capitalism, the entrepreneur identified with personal capitalism has survived in craft-based industry associated with industrial districts. This in itself is an acknowledgement that personal and managerial capitalism are compatible (see Chapter 6).

While most commentators acknowledge the changing nature of modern capitalism, Shonfield observes that Schumpeter's characterization of market volatility overlooks the important role played by postwar governments. He acknowledges therein differences between the United States and Europe in utilizing government resources to combat the business cycle. Belief in the automacity of economic processes held by economists of the classical tradition has had an important influence on governments in the Anglo-American world (Shonfield, 1965, pp. 53–4, 57). In his analysis of the decline of capitalism, Bottomore summarizes the reasons thus: (1) the obsolescence of the entrepreneurial function resulting from the growth of large corporations, (2) the creation of an environment in which economic change is accepted as a matter of course, and (3) the depersonalization and automatization of economic progress (1985, p. 37).

Transformation of capitalism

Postwar growth and expansion in industrialized economies has resulted in increasing incompatibilities and inner contradictions. The pressures caused by such inconsistencies have in turn led to growing tensions within society. Hence, the collective power of the state has become an inevitable complement to the success of capitalist enterprise. Galbraith (1967) characterized the modern industrial system as one in which the individual is subordinate to the productive organization. While power rests with managers, the role of the capitalist remains suppressed. However, according to Galbraith, the capitalist still lurks behind the puppets, the powerful managers, who continue to manipulate the levers (pp. 16–7).

In identifying changes that have taken place within the capitalist system, Galbraith challenges conventional wisdom regarding the assumption that the competitive capitalist system identified with modern industrialized economies still exists. Once identified with railroads, steelmaking, petroleum production and well-known names such as Carnegie, Rockefeller and Ford, corporations are now more diversified and located worldwide, headed by relatively unknown men and women who own no

appreciable share in the enterprise. The state has gradually enhanced its role in economic activity – in the US this rose from 8 per cent in 1929 to 25 per cent in 1967. In addition, the state, through regulatory controls, influences a range of activities once regarded as fairly commonplace in socialist countries. We are also witness to less fluctuations – the business-cycle, once regarded as routine in the form of recession or depressions, is a less common occurrence in industrialized economies. Other important changes identified by Galbraith as important are the increasing investment in business promotion through persuasion, the stabilization or decline of union membership and the expansion in enrolment in higher education. With the cumulative effects of these changes has come the need and opportunity for the large corporation to determine what to produce and how to persuade consumers to use their products. No longer does the consumer influence the producer (1967, pp. 21–6). Power in *The New Industrial State* has moved to the 'techno-structure', which has replaced capitalism. As the technostructure is interested in advancing goals somewhat similar to that of the state's, it becomes an extension of government bureaucracy. Accordingly, the ideology of market capitalism identified with competitive free enterprise, consumer sovereignty and limited government does not reflect social and economic reality as it exists today. The reality is that large industrial corporations seldom make a loss and the majority of executives continue to work for the same firm that they began their career with. In the world of the techno-structure, stability is attained through planning for a negotiated environment in which large corporations are guaranteed profits with minimal risk (Galbraith 1967, pp. 96–108). Galbraith's populist depiction of American industrial capitalism, although realistic, has come under attack from academic economists (Reisman, 1980).

In acknowledging the changing balance of public and private power in *Modern Capitalism*, Shonfield (1965) was, in effect, extending Galbraith's view of American industrial capitalism to a worldwide perspective. While governments have always played a more active role in managing the economy in Europe when compared with the United States, the role of government in Europe has become politically acceptable and constructive. Writing at the time of a full employment economy with rapid technical progress, Shonfield expressed his belief that progress could be maintained only through an active public policy which assisted the quick transfer of people from jobs in which they had been established to new forms of employment (1965, p. 67). The changing balance of public and private power is reflected in the changes one observes in private enterprise in the second half of the twentieth

century. It is a steadier employer of labour, more amenable to the influence of public authority and more sensitive to the public view of its behaviour. Being large, it is influenced by its long-term future and sees itself as a permanent institution. Gradually the state has assumed the role of taming the market, realizing it was no longer acceptable in a civilized society to encounter sudden market fluctuations (Shonfield, 1965, p. 377). This taming of the market differs from Schumpeter's concept of the role of innovations in the process of creative destruction whereby inefficient enterprises are bankrupted. Shonfield comments that Schumpeter did not foresee the importance of 'authoritative calculations made by postwar governments, whose activities as entrepreneurs have become much the most important single force in the whole system' (1965, p. 53).

Conclusion

While analysing the intellectual foundations of modern capitalism, I have in this chapter discussed the theories of classical political economists like Smith, List and Marx, advocates of Rational Capitalism represented by Weber, Polanyi and Gershenkron, followed by critics of capitalism such as Hirschman, Hirsch and Schumpeter, and concluded with recent commentators on capitalism like Galbraith and Shonfield. In the interest of brevity, the choice has been selective, according to their relevance to this study. Their categorization into sub-sections could be questioned as arbitrary. While being open to such criticism, my purpose has been to explain the intellectual foundation which has sustained the edifice of capitalism and to trace how later thinkers have viewed the changes to the institution on which western industrial economies have been built and sustained.

Central to the institution of capitalism is the concept of private property which, when used for productive purposes by individuals to meet demands of consumers, creates what we refer to as the market. The use of private property for production gradually transforms into capital, from which we derive the term 'capitalism'. Classical political economists were divided on the outcome of such use of capital. While some saw it as encouraging unfettered self-interest through the invisible hand of the free market, others were concerned about the exploitation of labour by capital.

Marx adopted a broader historical view and predicted the decline of capitalism and its replacement with socialism. Weber, like Marx, adopted a historical approach to understanding the origin and nature

of capitalism and explained why it emerged first in the West. Viewing the state as the key to the institutional structure of rational capitalism, Weber was nonetheless particularly interested in the influence of religious values on economic conduct and concluded that capitalism was a combination of the protestant idea of calling with the traditional puritan emphasis upon moral personal conduct. Polanyi, like Weber, emphasized the role of the state in the economy and considered the self-regulated market to be a utopia, insofar as most economies are embedded and not differentiated in society. List, Weber, Polanyi and Gershenkron advocated an active role for the state in the economy.

That the market is not self-regulatory but self-destructive due to the pre-capitalist institutions of feudalism, proved, according to Hirschman, to be an obstacle in generating the gentleness and the discipline expected of a market society. Using the relative influence of pre-capitalist influences on the development of capitalism in Europe as against the US, Hirschman offered an interesting clue to the diversity in the development of modern capitalism. Supporting his self-destructive thesis, he used Schumpeter's theory to explain capitalism's undoing and Hirsch's theory of depleting moral legacy. The sound basis provided by Galbraith and Shonfield for an analysis of the role of the state in modern capitalism is discussed in subsequent chapters.

References

Archibugi, Daniele and Jonathan Michie, *Technology, Globalisation and Economic Performance* (Cambridge: Cambridge University Press, 1997).
Bell, Daniel, *The Coming of Postindustrial Society: A Venture in Social Forecasting* (London: Heinemann, 1974).
Berger, Peter, *The Capitalist Revolution: Fifty Propositions About Prosperity, Equality and Liberty* (New York: Basic Books, 1986).
Booth, William James, 'On the Idea of the Moral Economy', *American Political Science Review*, vol. 88 (1994), 653–67.
Bottomore, Tom, *Theories of Modern Capitalism* (London: Allen & Unwin, 1985).
Collins, Randall, 'Weber's Last Theory of Capitalism: A Systemetization', *American Sociological Review*, vol. 45 (1980), 925–42.
Cowen, M. P. and R. W. Shenton, *Doctrines of Development* (London: Routledge, 1996).
Doblestein, Andrew W., *Politics, Economics and Public Welfare* (Englewood Cliffs: Prentice Hall, 1980).
Evans, Peter, *Embedded Autonomy: States and Industrial Transformation* (Princeton: Princeton University Press, 1995).
Fallows, James, 'How the World Works', *Atlantic Monthly*, January (1994), 61–87.
Galbraith, John Kenneth, *The New Industrial State* (Harmondsworth: Penguin, 1967).

Gershenkron, Alexander, *Economic Backwardness in Historical Perspective* (Cambridge, Mass.: Harvard University Press, 1962).
Greenfeld, Liah, *The Spirit of Capitalism: Nationalism and Economic Growth* (Cambridge, Mass.: Harvard University Press, 2001).
Herrigel, Gary, *Industrial Constructions: The Sources of German Industrial Power* (Cambridge, Mass.: Cambridge University Press, 1996).
Hirsch, Fred, *The Social Limits of Growth* (Cambridge, Mass.: Harvard University Press, 1976).
Hirschman, Albert O., *Passions and the Interests: Political Arguments for Capitalism Before its Triumph* (Princeton: Princeton University Press, 1977).
Hirschman, Albert O., *Rival Views of Market Society and Other Recent Essays* (New York: Viking, 1986).
Hollingsworth, Rogers J. and Robert Boyer (eds), *Contemporary Capitalism: The Embeddedness of Institutions* (Cambridge: Cambridge University Press, 1997).
Holton, Robert J., *Economy and Society* (London: Routledge, 1992).
Kumar, Krishan, *The Rise of Modern Society: Aspects of the Social and Political Development of the West* (Oxford: Basil Blackwell, 1988).
Lazonick, William, *Business Organization and the Myth of the Market Economy* (Cambridge: Cambridge University Press, 1991).
Meek, Ronald L., *Smith Marx and After* (London: Chapman & Hall, 1977).
Moore Jr, Barrington, *Social Origins of Dictatorship and Democracy: Lord and Peasant in the Making of the Modern World* (London: Penguin, 1966).
Rashid, Salim, *The Myth of Adam Smith* (Cheltenham: Edward Elgar, 1998).
Reisman, David, *Galbraith and Market Capitalism* (London: Palgrave Macmillan, 1980).
Sabel, Charles and Jonathan Zeitlin, *World of Possibilities: Flexibility and Mass Production in Western Industrialisation* (New York: Cambridge University Press, 1997).
Scott, Alan, 'Bureaucratic Revolutions and Free Market Utopias', *Economy and Society*, vol. 25 (1996), 89–110.
Shonfield, Andrew, *Modern Capitalism: The Changing Balance of Public and Private Power* (Oxford: Oxford University Press, 1965).
Swedberg, Richard, *Max Weber and the Idea of Economic Sociology* (Princeton: Princeton University Press, 1998).
Zeitlin, Irving M., *Ideology and the Development of Sociological Theory* (Englewood Cliffs: Prentice Hall, 1981).

3
State and the Economy

Introduction

Alfred Chandler Jr (1990) in *Scale and Scope: The Dynamics of Industrial Capitalism* categorized the United States, Great Britain and West Germany into three distinct types of capitalism – competitive, personal and cooperative. In adopting such a classification, Chandler recognized the dominant characteristics of each country and acknowledged at the same time the presence of common underlying characteristics of modern industrial capitalism. The unique experience of each country in the development of industrial capitalism, within a broadly accepted model of a mixed economy, has encouraged comparative studies. Such studies in comparative political economy have helped to identify both convergence and divergence in the development of modern capitalism (Crouch and Streeck, 1997; Hall and Soskice, 2001). While recognizing such variations, I have explored the differences between state intervention in the United States and other mixed economies (1992). This exploration into the role of the state in the economy has led me to view the interrelationship between polity and economy as essentially complementary or synergistic (Mascarenhas, 1992, 1996, 1999; Evans, 1995).

In adopting the synergistic or complementary view of the relationship between the polity and economy, I depart from the 'new political economy' identified with the pro-market, anti-state school of public choice/neoliberalism which, essentially, endorses the libertarian view of individual freedom of choice in a laissez faire economy and a minimalist state. This model gained ascendancy in the early 1980s with the decline of industrial economies in the aftermath of the energy crisis which had

caused stagflation, declining growth and high levels of unemployment. Policies associated with the new political economy such as public choice and monetarist prescription were actively encouraged by Ronald Reagan in the United States and Margaret Thatcher in Britain as a solution to the ills of industrialized economies. They were also advocated by international agencies such as the World Bank and the IMF and by others in the economic profession (in the English-speaking countries) who espoused and taught generations of students the neoclassical concept of the market based on specialization and the market mechanism first popularized by Adam Smith (Rashid, 1998).

In promoting the 'new political economy', which allows a greater role for private enterprise, governments in Anglo-American countries have shown a commitment to rolling back the state, whose post-Second World War role had, according to them, crowded out the private sector. To promote the private sector and reduce the role of the state in the economy, such countries adopted programmes of liberalization, deregulation, privatization, tax reform, labour market reform and public sector restructuring. The objective of these policies was to restrict the legitimate exercise of power by political authorities, described as 'government action at a distance'. Rose and Miller (1992) comment:

> At a rhetorical and programmatic level, neoliberalism also embodies a profound transformation in the mechanisms for governing social life. In place of collective provision and social solidarity the new rationality of government proposes notions of security provided through the private purchase of insurance schemes, health care purchased by individuals and provided by the health industry, housing offered through the private sector and efficiency secured through the discipline of competition within the market. The public provision of welfare and social security no longer appears as a vital part of a programme for political stability and social efficiency. (p. 200)

While domestic economic and political change led to neoliberal policies and, with it, a decline in the role of the state, the conservative resurgence of the 1980s also led to a questioning of the state's relevance in the context of internationalization and globalization (Evans, 1997; Mascarenhas, 1998). Weiss lamented that 'across the social sciences, the state is being weakened, hollowed out, carved up, toppled or buried. We have entered a new era of "state denial"' (1998, p. 2). Even while such questioning and policies of liberalization led to the 'hollowing of the state' in the Anglo-American countries, the state maintained a signifi-

cant role in the East Asian model of the 'developmental state' (Johnson, 1982) and in the 'Alpine model' (Albert, 1993). Such differences in response to the energy crisis and the economic decline within advanced industrial economies has led to growing interest in studies of comparative capitalism (Ikenberry, 1986; Crouch and Streeck, 1997; Hollingsworth and Boyer, 1997; Kitschelt *et al.*, 1999; Hall and Soskice, 2001), encouraging me to adopt a political economy approach in order to understand the variations in institutional structures between societies.

Amid attempts by monetarists and public choice theorists to discredit or question the relevance of the state, I maintain that its role is fundamental to the functioning of markets. That this role varies between countries is increasingly evident and is discussed in this study.

In the next section of this chapter I discuss the role of the state in mixed economies. I then critique methods of state intervention. The fourth section reviews changes arising from the decline of industrialized economies and the consequent shift in thinking on the role of the state in mixed economies.

Role of the state in mixed economies

Traditionally, the rationale for an active state in mixed economies was based on market failure arguments. That is, there are certain functions which are uneconomical or infeasible for markets to undertake and such functions should generally be left to the state. They are categorized into public goods and externalities: the former because their enjoyment cannot be excluded from those who do not bear the cost, the latter identified as costs or benefits that cannot be accounted for by economic actors or agents. In the neoclassical sense, the state is expected to play a minimalist role of protecting the freedom of the individual and private property by providing a set of rules and regulations for the conduct of individuals (a system of justice) and to protect citizens from external threat (defence, police). Adam Smith regarded any activity beyond this minimalist role as unproductive as it would interfere with the system of natural liberty and was justifiable only in the public interest. However, the liberal or laissez faire defence of competitive markets was justified by Smith on the grounds that it reconciled liberty with efficiency. 'Liberty meant the absence of constraints and since governments constrained the market when they interfered and the market was voluntary to its participants, economic freedom from government interference could not but enhance political freedom' (Helm, 1986, p. x). In Smith's view, the state's role should be to protect society from invasion by other

independent societies, from injustices or oppression by other citizens and to erect and maintain certain public works or public institutions which individuals are incapable of erecting. All three functions are categorized as public goods which no market can offer. The doctrine of free enterprise economic management was intended to create an economic order whereby self-interested individuals and privately-owned firms would be enabled to produce results superior to that produced by any alternative system.

This, it was thought, would result in greater individual freedom and a liberal constitutional and political system with opportunities for personal advancement. Large sections of the population in western industrialized economies subscribe to the view that government intervention harms if not destroys such values. However, evidence to support such a claim is insufficient (Dahl, 1998). Such a role for the state, advocated by the late-eighteenth-century concept of private enterprise, was termed the capitalist state. As the moral foundations of that era had until then acted as constraints on the owners of property, it was deemed unnecessary to develop a political theory of capitalism which would separate rights to property from notions of moral worth. While moral constraints were regarded as a constraint on capitalism, there was, however, no equivalent core of beliefs relating to the appropriate role of the state such as that advocated by economic liberals in political science, sociology or institutionalists (Lindberg *et al.*, 1987, p. 350). My own analysis has persuaded me to consider the actual role of the state in the economy as an empirical question, since that role, while varying within countries, is continuously evolving. In adopting a political economy approach, I advocate a distinct role for the state in modern capitalist systems, where private enterprise can perform effectively in a stable economic environment based on predetermined rules and regulations, implemented by appropriate economic and political institutions (Mascarenhas, 1992, 1996).

While Adam Smith's *The Wealth of Nations* (1776) continues to inspire policy-makers and academics of the minimalist state perspective, Friedrich List, his contemporary, appears to have inspired 'state interventionists' in East Asia and Germany. Smith wrote 'the market will suffice to almost all things, so the role of government is to create the minimal facilitative conditions, then step back. Treat market imperfections on an adhoc basis as they arise' (McCraw, 1997, p. 522). List questioned this view. 'Everywhere [the Smithian system] seeks to exclude the action of the power of the state.... Statistics and history, however, teach on the contrary, that the necessity for the intervention of legislative power and

administration is everywhere more apparent, the further the economy of the nation is developed' (McCraw, 1997, p. 524). As an advocate of an active role for the state in development, List commented that 'for the "particular people" of a nation, the uniting of labour to enhance productive powers, through the development of the ideal social and moral conditions had to be governed by "government" or "Policy". History was what made possible the reconciliation of philosophy and policy' (Cowen and Shenton, 1996). In taking this position, List recognised the dominance of manufacturing in Britain. Others, like Germany, being predominantly agricultural, required a more active role on the part of the state. This role is recognizable in the German 'social market' (Haucup, 1998, pp. 11–28) and the East Asian 'developmental state' (Johnson, 1982). Interestingly, the contribution of List as a critic of Adam Smith has received renewed attention in recent years in reaction to the overemphasis placed on markets by neoliberals in the 1980s (Greenfeld, 2001).

Postwar developments in the role of the state

The derivative approach to the role of the state under market failure advocates intervention whenever the market is unable to undertake a task which is considered critical or when it must correct its malfunctioning to protect the public interest. In Chapter 2, I refer to Polanyi's emphasis on the embeddedness of markets, thus acknowledging that its role as a social institution may require guidance. Such guidance can come only from the state. Events such as the emergence of communism and fascism and the two world wars confirmed the suspicion that the market is not self-regulating. Perceived as a crisis of capitalism, these events led to an active debate between Keynesians and socialist planners, ultimately resulting in 'the three pillars of postwar consensus' – the welfare state, nationalization or national planning and macroeconomic coordination of economic policy by the state (Helm, 1986). This response, sustained through the 1950s and 60s, was instrumental in upholding the capitalist system through to its golden age.

Ruggie (1982) claims that regimes which aim to serve the market in money and trade try to restrict the state from meddling in markets. For such regimes to survive without the erosion of their authority, we note how power and legitimate social purpose fuse to project political authority into the international system:

> Applied to post-World War II context, this argument leads us to characterize the international economic order by the term 'embedded

> liberalism'.... In sum, this shift in what we might call the balance between 'authority' and 'market' fundamentally transformed state–society relations, by redefining the legitimate social purposes in pursuit of which state power was expected to be employed in the domestic economy. The role of the state became to institute and safeguard the self-regulatory market.
>
> (Ruggie, 1982, p. 386)

To do this and to tide their citizens through the inter-war period, governments assumed responsibility for domestic social security and economic stability. Marking a transformation in the mediating role of the state between market and society, such liberalism, termed 'embedded liberalism' by Ruggie, differed from the previous version (1982, p. 392). Prior to this, control over high finance had been retained by private bankers for profit. With the Bretton Woods arrangement, this was taken over by government organizations, thus making world money a byproduct of state activity. Power thus shifted from London and New York to Washington as the seat of the 'production' of world money (Arrighi, 1994, p. 278).

Gourevitch (1986), unlike Helm and Ruggie, interprets this changing relationship between state and market arising out of the trauma of the depression and the Second World War, as a 'historic compromise' between countries of Western Europe and North America:

> Bitter enemies had worked out a truce built around a mixed economy, a kind of bounded capitalism, where private enterprise remained the dynamo but operated within a system of rules that provided stability, both economic and political. Demand management to promote full employment, the welfare state, an extensive system of economic regulation, institutionalized industrial relations, free trade – these were the policy approaches of this bounded capitalism, and they departed strongly from the market orthodoxy of pre-depression days. Political power was shared as well, and to a far greater degree than before the war. (p. 18)

The historic compromise centred around (1) labour's acceptance of capitalist management of the economy, (2) retention by agriculture of extensive market stabilization in exchange for support for programmes of business and labour, and (3) acceptance by business of these conditions in return for retaining the regulatory mechanism that stabilizes markets and control over investments and management. The outcome of this compromise was prodigious economic growth that continued

until the 1970s economic crisis. The post-1945 policy mix created state activism in economic management that differed from the classical and the protectionist policy patterns that had predominated in earlier decades (Gourevitch, 1986, p. 29). The final outcome was the mixed economy which became the accepted form for postwar economic regimes in industrialized countries.

As advanced capitalist economies become more complex, the role of the state becomes more important despite claims by globalists to the contrary. According to Helm (1986), the enhanced role emerged because 'Capitalism is an imperfect system which may need careful guidance and control to save it from itself' (p. ix). In fulfilling that role, it relies on a proper mix of fiscal and monetary policies, providing a conducive environment for business to function effectively.

As the state used its resources and skills to rebuild economies in postwar Western Europe and Japan, it became increasingly difficult to maintain the separation between state and market, leading to the modern industrial state (Shonfield, 1965; Galbraith, 1967), a variant of which is the 'developmental state' (Johnson, 1982). Identified with the Keynesian welfare state, the period from the 1940s to the 1960s witnessed a response to the demands for redistribution and social welfare benefits caused by the competitive risks of an international economy. Government response through a variety of policy instruments such as social security, unemployment benefits, subsidies and the encouragement of investment through incentives led to the expansion of the public economy which 'dramatically enlarged the scope of the tax state in contemporary advanced capitalist society' (Cameron, 1986, p. 1260). Such increases in capital expenditure became the target of neoliberal economic policies during the 1980s.

Thus in industrialized countries, the institutions of government and the market play a significant role in the economy, albeit varying among nations. Where there is greater support for freedom of enterprise, governments play a minimal role. Where governments are expected to promote the collective interest by restraining markets, they play a more active role. Whichever way the balance tilts, in as much as the functioning of markets relies on a set of political institutions responsible for providing the legal framework, then, irrespective of government's role in the economy, such economies, for purposes of this study, are best described as mixed economies. In such mixed economies, governments play a distinct role and both public and private sectors of the economy are entrusted with distinct decisional and operational roles within the framework of the market. The government's primary responsibility is to

govern and maintain public order so that citizens can act freely while transacting in the market. Secondly, governments intervene when such markets function imperfectly. The first function is essential to a civilized society and is referred to as the universal role of the state (Nelson, 1989). The second role, relative to the nature of market malfunctioning, dictates the nature of the public–private mix. While this varies between countries, they are generally categorized as industrialized capitalist economies or mixed economies. Accordingly, it ranges from controls and regulation such as licensing, pricing and tariffs, the promotion of industry through incentives and subsidies, through to the production of goods and services through public ownership. The choice of policy instruments to assist economic and industrial development is influenced by historical, political and economic factors.

Evans (1995) categorizes the state's role in industrial transformation of information technology into custodial, the dimiurge, midwifery and husbandry. 'The first two, "custodian" and "dimiurge" represent variations on the conventional roles of regulation and producer. The second pair which Evans calls "midwifery" and "husbandry" focus more on the relation between state agencies and private entrepreneurial groups in the process of setting up new industries and tending to the growing industries' (1995, p. 13). Weiss (1998) distinguishes the state's extractive capacity from its transformative capacity, emphasizing that the latter is not synonymous with state intervention. Recognizing the existence of relative domestic capacity for industrial transformation, Weiss is hesitant to adopt state capacity in general terms, preferring to use it in context. Such a position is in line with the caution against using strong-state weak-state analysis when such capacity varies across sectors, types of policies and institutional constraints (Mascarenhas, 1996). For Weiss, this depends on the depth (insulation) and breadth (embeddedness) of institutionalization which is a product of historical and geopolitical influences. Accordingly, she considers that the domestic capacities of states to respond to economic change is determined by historically formed regime disposition to government coordination and public–private cooperation. The author concludes that while the Anglo-American countries adopt a limited role for the state, Germany and Japan adopt an active one (Weiss, 1998, pp. 18–20).

Governments of different complexions (conservative or liberal/labour) adopt a mix of these interventions to meet a variety of situations. Lacking apparent consistency, these interventions are dictated by ideological preferences, historical influences, pressure groups and regime characteristics. Within the group of countries generally identi-

fied as advanced capitalist or industrialized economies, states play a variety of roles and are thus categorized as mixed economies. Governments may introduce policy initiatives to compensate victims of market malfunctioning or to promote the market, which, without such intervention, is unlikely to respond. Essentially, a co-evolution of state and market in varying proportions takes place in most capitalist economies.

Accordingly, states/societies are categorized into individualistic or communitarian. In individualistic societies, the role of government is limited to protecting property, enforcing contracts and assisting market competition. Government intervenes only in times of crisis. An individualistic society such as the United States is suspicious of government and concerned about centralized power, preferring to leave most decisions to the play of interest groups. In communitarian societies such as Japan and, to some extent, Germany, government defines the needs of the community over the long term as well as the short term. It sets visions for society; it defines and ensures the rights and duties of the community. The actual task of government is entrusted to a prestigious bureaucracy which adopts a cooperative approach towards business which itself is organized into influential industrial groups (Lodge and Vogel, 1987; Lodge, 1990; Accordino, 1992).

While these are ideal types, countries may adopt a mix of strategies in response to circumstances. For example, the United States generally prefers regulation, while Western European governments prefer to adopt public ownership when the actions of big business are likely to contravene the public interest. The adoption of a regulatory model in the US to counteract big business must be understood in a historical context. In contrast to Europe, business preceded the public service in the United States. This attracted political opposition to big business. Early links between manufacturers and the privately owned railroads, which were developed primarily for the distribution of goods through nation-wide outlets, further contributed towards an anti-state attitude. Other features which characterize the US are the absence of an ideological debate explained by the lack of feudal influences as well as the lack of political organization of labour. Together, such factors have contributed to the distinctiveness of government–business relations in the United States (Chandler Jr, 1980; Mascarenhas, 1992).

There is one other anti-state phenomenon that one observes in the United States. This is the feeling that business, while holding a privileged role, views the state with contempt (Lindblom, 1977; Vogel, 1996). Despite this strong anti-state phenomenon, which in the 1980s extended to the Anglo-American group of countries, the state has played

an active role within the corporate model of capitalism. This was seen during the New Deal, the postwar military industry complex, the space programme, the energy crisis and through several attempts to bail out businesses during industrial crises.

To dispel the notion that the United States is non-interventionist, it may help to adopt Spulber's (1995) classification of state intervention, into:

> (a) regulatory processes to promote effective competition and effective allocation
> (b) supervisory processes affecting specific phases of a business operation
> (c) allocation processes concerning the attribution of certain rights and privileges and the rationing of certain scarce resources
> (d) promotional processes aimed at assisting the growth and development of business; and finally
> (e) activities involving the government as a large buyer in various markets and as producer and owner of certain business enterprises.
> (p. 49)

The underlying contradictions, more pronounced in the United States than in Britain, appear in the differing position among corporate liberals and democratic collectivists, both identified with American New Liberalism:

> Corporate liberals looked on the modern corporation, with its rational, bureaucratic structure, its phenomenal productivity, and its capacity to administer markets, as a product of institutional evolution, justified by its superior efficiency and its capacity for providing new avenues of mobility to replace those foreclosed by the decline of proprietary capitalism.... Whereas corporate liberals identified the public interest with the long-term interests of capital, democratic collectivists rejected the identification of *any* private interest with the public good. In the early stages of this discourse, many of them held back on libertarian grounds from expanding *federal* power, but they considered the state, and not the corporation, the appropriate instrument for transcending selfish interests, on the grounds that voluntary associative arrangements would ordinarily favor the wealthy, whereas promoting social justice, equality, democracy, and balanced development would require increased state intervention, often redistributive in intent.
> (Furner, 1990, pp. 244–5)

In discussing the different approaches to government–business relations adopted by countries, one must bear in mind their varying conceptions of the state. While in continental Europe the concept of state is identified with unified authority, in the Anglo-American context the state has usually been regarded operationally. 'In this interpretation, the state is not monolithic or poised over civil society, but diverse, and composed of elements that interact more or less independently with the changing structure of private groups and institutions, differing from them mainly by virtue of the monopoly of coercion and authoritative control it possesses over all sorts of resources' (Furner and Supple, 1990, p. 26). Constitutional differences between the United States and Britain must also be considered when explaining the differences among the Anglo-American countries. A greater degree of policy unity is evident among political institutions in Britain, reflecting the wishes of the party in power. Such unity is not possible in the United States due to federalism and the separation of powers.

With fragmentation and an underlying conflict between agencies, the role of the state in the economy in the United States can result in untoward consequences. Firstly, the dispersal of information regarding the functioning of the economy in several agencies renders coordination difficult. Secondly, such dispersion can encourage special interests to exploit the system to their advantage at the cost of the public interest. Indeed business in the United States is seen as enjoying a privileged position, while simultaneously adopting an anti-state posture. According to Etzioni (1985), critics of state intervention overlook the power that private business groups exercise to meet their own economic ends. He terms it interventionist power. 'Thus corporate interventionist power refers to the use of government by corporations to interfere in the economy in line with their goals' (p. 173).

In analysing the relationship between the state and the economy, some studies seek to establish a close link between big business and the state. Lindblom (1977) argues that, as a result of the privileged position that business holds, the state often pursues policies that favour business. As business undertakes vital functions in the economy which may otherwise have to be undertaken by government, Lindblom tends to view such business executives as public officials in a market system. Therefore, business must be induced and not commanded. The responsibilities that market systems place on businessmen lead to a need for government officials to grant them a privileged position. 'He simply understands, as is plain to see, that public affairs in market-oriented systems are in the hands of two groups of leaders, government and

business, who must collaborate and that, to make the system work government leadership must often defer to business leadership. Collaboration and deference between the two are at the heart of politics in such systems. Businessmen cannot be left knocking at the doors of the political systems, they must be invited in' (Lindblom, 1977, p. 175). This does not, however, suggest that governments will not exercise their authority under certain circumstances. US government intervention was seen during the Justice Department's case of anti-competitive behaviour brought against Microsoft in 1999.

Business, once accustomed to inducements and privileges, does not tolerate intrusions in the form of state intervention. This ambivalence towards state intervention arising from a 'distrust' of the state is rooted in history. 'What is striking about American business ideology is the remarkable consistency of business attitudes toward government over the last one hundred and twenty-five years' (Vogel, 1996, p. 46).

While Lindblom's (1977) analysis explains why business enjoys a privileged position vis-à-vis other interest groups, the configuration in the relationship between capital, labour and the state varies considerably in different countries and during different periods. The success of different industrial sectors in different countries is linked to such alignments, varying in Japan, the United States, the United Kingdom, France and Germany (Hart, 1992).

In making a case for state intervention, one must consider the conditions under which such intervention can be effective. This involves differences in capacity of institutions of state, and the possibility of them becoming instruments of domination by powerful groups as anticipated by Marxist analysis and pluralists like Dahl (1998) and Lindblom (1977). When considering this situation, one cannot overlook internal structures, rules and regulations that determine relations between state and society. In the institutionalist complexity of modern mixed political economies, Nelson (1989) claims that we have yet to come up with a satisfactory normative theory regarding the appropriate roles for government. Deeming the market failure approach unsatisfactory, he writes, 'Government sets the basic ground rules that define and delimit how other institutions are to operate. And governmental means are the natural ones to employ to achieve purposes widely regarded as public purposes. Government is not there so much because other institutions occasionally fail, but to set the stage so that they can work decently well in their assigned arenas of action, or as a chosen instrumentality in its own right for getting a job done' (p. 544). Other factors to consider are internal divisions among policy-makers whose political

or personal goals may differ. While such roles may result in conflict, Weber, in an effort to distinguish them, advocates the need to separate the 'coalescence of interests' from the legitimate exercise of authority (see Chapter 1). The need to acknowledge underlying tensions, conflicts and contradictions within the state apparatus prompted Rueschmeyer and Evans (1985) to make a case for an effective bureaucratic apparatus combined with relative state autonomy for effective state intervention (pp. 46–9). They comment:

> The state offers, in the context of a capitalist economy, a contribution that is both unique and necessary – unique because it transcends the logic of the competitive market and necessary because a capitalist economy requires for its development as well as its maintenance in the face of changing conditions, the supply of 'collective goods' that cannot be provided by the competitive actors in the economy. (p. 61)

Critique of state intervention

In the 1980s, the welfare state, a product of the postwar consensus, became a target of critics who sought to dismantle it. To counter the growth of state intervention and its consequences, critics offered the government failure argument which questions the capacity of governments to adjust market failures. Basing their argument on the self-interest of individuals, public choice theorists concluded that all actions by politicians, bureaucrats and voters would be in their own and not in the public interest. Broadly identified with the 'new political economy', this line of argument sought to replace state action with a market-like mechanism to achieve public purpose. This took the form of economic liberalization, deregulation, privatization, user pays and contracting, effectively replicating market incentives to achieve greater public sector efficiency.

In their attempts to restore a laissez-faire political economy as a solution to the problems of industrialized economies, critics of state intervention sought to promote the disciplines and incentives of free markets. In seeking to install the market model, they sought a redefinition of the role of government in the economy. This was a repudiation of Keynesianism, that is, disavowing responsibility for the overall level of economic activity, and rejecting the objective of full employment, while at the same time controlling inflation. Such exponents of the new laissez faire share with their nineteenth-century predecessors a concept

of the capitalist market economy as a quasi-natural system. Such a market system which supposedly possesses powerful self-regulatory properties, is, however, easily exposed to external pressures. In presenting this view, Goldthorpe (1987) contends:

> From such a conception, a distinctive view of economic policy derives. Governments should be concerned primarily with sustaining an institutionalist context within which the economy may freely operate according to its own inherent logic and should modify their claims to be 'in control' or even 'in charge' of the economy itself. (p. 367)

In the context of growing public expenditure, the neoliberal argument appealed to governments in Anglo-American countries at a time when economies were experiencing serious decline. While the remedy appealed to policy-makers in societies historically inclined towards ideologies such as liberalism and individualism, it unfortunately was ahistorical and asocial to the point of focusing exclusively on the individual (methodological individualism) at the cost of the collective wellbeing of society. Moreover, its overbearing and prescriptive approach as a universal remedy for the supposed ills of state intervention suffered a setback with the emergence of left-of-centre governments in Europe and across the Atlantic. Such developments failed to impact on governments in West Germany and Japan whose economic performance, based on state–private sector cooperation (collective capitalism), proved as good, if not better. Observing the Anglo-American countries in their promotion of competitive markets based on individualism, there were some who felt that their current insecurity and income inequalities could be addressed by adopting stakeholder principles (Hutton, 1995; Plender, 1997) as in West Germany and Japan. However, in Plender's view, advocacy of stakeholding as a workable alternative to the narrow and abrasive Anglo-American version of capitalism threatens to turn its only strength of creative destruction into mere destruction (1997, p. 16).

Evans (1995) terms this philosophy neo-utilitarian and sums up its tenets thus:

> Neo-utilitarian political economy is both cynical and utopian: cynical in denying the practical importance of the 'public spirit'... and utopian in assuming that the 'invisible hand' offers an easy substitute. Its utopian side gave it charisma but also burdened it with positions that were hard to defend, logically or empirically. Its ex-

treme view of the state, however elegant, was, in the end, logically untenable. Its utopian belief in the power of the market to reconstruct society was equally so. (p. 25)

Even if the 'new laissez faire' is a coherent doctrine, Goldthorpe (1987) doubts if it is politically feasible to restore such a free enterprise economy (p. 368). In other words, the prevailing neoutilitarian ideology is not in harmony with the choices confronting countries with different values and contexts. This recognition has led to the questioning of the relevance of neoliberal prescriptions for industrialized economies (Lodge and Vogel, 1987). Even in the heyday of neoliberal thinking, academics such as Fligstein (1990) endeavoured to correct the misconception that had existed about corporate functioning by emphasizing the role of the state. According to him, the state

> defines the rules by which actions in the economy are carried out. It is one thing to say you are in favor of freemarkets, and quite another to actually define what free market is. That definition has shifted over time and the dispute has primarily been between firms and the state. Laws regarding incorporation, antitrust, and the regulation of various industries are important aspects of state definitions. The state also affects the economy by consuming products, intervening in the business cycle, and providing for the redistribution of income through taxation and social expenditures. (p. 8)

In exercising this role, the real issue rests on the level of autonomy enjoyed by the state in relation to business. Distinguishing despotic power from infrastructural power of the state, Mann comments that 'all infrastructurally powerful states, including the capitalist democracies, are strong in relation to individuals and to weaker groups in civil society, but capitalist democratic states are feeble in relation to dominant groups – at least in comparison to most historical states' (1988, p. 7). Unlike the methodological individualism advocated by public choice and monetarism, the individualism advocated by the early liberals was a protection against the exercise of arbitrary power by the sovereign state. The role of the state has since moved from direct production of goods and services to a social partnership under collective capitalism (Lazonick, 1991; Mascarenhas, 1996). Today's development states are characterized by Evans (1995) as 'embedded autonomy' where states are embedded in domestic business. To ensure that development goals are central to national objectives, close relations between state and business

are maintained by a classic Weberian bureaucracy. The dominance of neoliberal orthodoxy in the former has increased the divergence between Anglo-American economies and other industrialized capitalist economies while the ability of the latter to achieve economic stability and enhance communitarian values through growth has regenerated interest in the comparison of types of capitalism.

Conclusion

Essentially, the understanding of a modern industrial economy rests on whether one views the state as derivative to the market (market failure) in a predominantly capitalist economy or whether one adopts a positive theory of state intervention in which the role of the state is more central to the functioning of the economy. In a political economy approach, the state, despite the dominance of the neoclassical market model, provides the environment within which markets function, intervening when necessary with a variety of fiscal, monetary and industrial policy instruments. It appears, then, that the problems faced by Anglo-American countries have been brought about by their failure to develop proper institutions for effective state intervention.

The success of economies like Japan, West Germany, France and Italy in the 1980s has raised fundamental questions regarding the policies of Anglo-American countries and their attempts to liberalize, deregulate and privatize. In analysing the role of the state in the economy, one needs to acknowledge the changing nature of capitalist economies from entrepreneurial (personal capitalism) to managerial (competitive) capitalism (Shonfield, 1965; Galbraith, 1967). In that transformation one cannot overlook the unique historical and cultural factors that have shaped the nature of the relationship between government and business.

In other words, the state is fundamental to the functioning of markets and plays different types of roles governed by historical, cultural, political and economic factors. Accordingly, the focus of comparative analysis must change with the changing context, which is reflected in the following comment:

> The competitive battle senior managers now face is not some kind of factory-to-factory combat with mirror-image rivals in other parts of the world. Rather it is deeper struggle among different capitalist systems, each with its own distinctive set of values, priorities, institutions, and goals. In this context of competing systems, the measure of success should not be limited to trade flows, exchange rates, or

productivity improvements, significant as those measures are. Instead, the most important question is: Which of the three capitalist systems can give its people the best standard of living and most fully prepare them for the future?

(Ohmae, 1995, p. 4)

References

Accordino, John J., *The United States in the Global Economy: Challenges and Policy Choices* (Chicago: American Library Association, 1992).
Albert, Michael, *Capitalism vs. Capitalism* (New York: Four Walls Eight Windows, 1993).
Arrighi, Giovanni, *The Long Twentieth Century: Money, Power and the Origins of Our Times* (London: Verso, 1994).
Cameron, David R., 'The Expansion of the Public Economy: A Comparative Analysis', *American Political Science Review*, vol. 72 (1986), 1243–61.
Chandler Jr, Alfred D., 'Government versus Business: An American Phenomenon', in John T. Dunlop (ed.), *Business and Public Policy* (Cambridge, Mass.: MIT Press, 1980).
Chandler Jr, Alfred D., *Scale and Scope: The Dynamics of Industrial Capitalism* (Cambridge, Mass.: Harvard University Press, 1990).
Chandler Jr, Alfred D. *et al.* (eds), *Government, Big Business and the Wealth of Nations* (Cambridge: Cambridge University Press, 1997).
Cowen, M. P. and R. W. Shenton, *Doctrines of Development* (London: Routledge, 1996).
Crouch, Colin and Wolfgang Streeck (eds), *Political Economy of Modern Capitalism: Mapping Convergence and Diversity* (London: Sage, 1997).
Dahl, Robert, *On Democracy* (New Haven: Yale University Press, 1998).
Etzioni, Amitai, 'The Political Economy of Imperfect Competition', *Journal of Public Policy*, vol.5 (1985), 169–86.
Evans, Peter, *Embedded Autonomy: States and Industrial Transformation* (Princeton: Princeton University Press, 1995).
Evans, Peter, 'The Eclipse of the State? Reflections on Stateness in the Era of Globalisation', *World Politics*, vol. 50 (1997), 62–113.
Fligstein, Neil, *The Transformation of Corporate Control* (Cambridge, Mass.: Harvard University Press, 1990).
Furner, Mary O. and Barry Supple (eds), *The State and Economic Knowledge: The American and British Experiences* (New York: Cambridge University Press, 1990).
Galbraith, John K., *The New Industrial State* (Harmondsworth: Penguin, 1967).
Goldthorpe, John H., 'Problems of Political Economy after the Postwar Period', in Charles S. Maier (ed.), *Changing Boundaries of the Political* (New York: Cambridge University Press, 1987), 363–407.
Gourevitch, Peter, *Politics in Hard times: Comparative Responses to International Crises* (Ithaca: Cornell University Press, 1986).
Greenfeld, Liah, *The Spirit of Capitalism: Nationalism and Economic Growth* (Cambridge, Mass.: Harvard University Press, 2001).

Hall, Peter A. and David Soskice (eds), *Varieties of Capitalism: The Institutional Foundation of Comparative Advantage* (Oxford: Oxford University Press, 2001).

Hart, Jeffrey, 'The Effects of State-Societal Arrangement on International Competitiveness: Steel, Motor Vehicles and Semi-Conductors in the United States, Japan and Western Europe', *British Journal of Political Science*, vol. 22 (1992), 255–300.

Haucap, Justus, 'Institutions, Development, and the Human Factor: The German "Miracle"', in Senyo B-S. K. Adjibolosoo (ed.), *International Perspectives on the Human Factor in Economic Development* (London: Praeger Press, 1998).

Helm, Dieter, 'The Assessment: The Economic Borders of the State', *Oxford Review of Economic Policy*, vol. 2 (1986), i–xxiv.

Hollingsworth, Rogers J. and Robert Boyer, *Contemporary Capitalism: The Embeddedness of Institutions* (Cambridge: Cambridge University Press, 1997).

Hutton, Will, *The State We're In* (London: Jonathan Cape, 1995).

Ikenberry, John, 'The Irony of State Strength: Comparative Response to the Oil Shocks', *International Organization*, vol. 40 (1986), 105–37.

Johnson Chalmers, *MITI and the Japanese Miracle* (Stanford: Stanford University Press, 1982).

Kitschelt, Herbert et al. (eds), *Continuity and Change in Contemporary Capitalism* (Cambridge, Cambridge University Press, 1999).

Lazonick, William, *Business Organisation and the Myth of the Mixed-Economy* (Cambridge: Cambridge University Press, 1991).

Lindberg, Leon et al., 'Economic Policy Research: Challenges and a New Agenda', in Heinhoff Dierkes et al. (eds), *Comparative Policy Research: Learning from Experiences* (New York: St Martins Press, 1987).

Lindblom, Charles E., *Politics and Markets* (New York: Free Press, 1977).

Lodge, George C., *Perestroika for America: Restructuring U.S. Business–Government Relations for Competitiveness in the World Economy* (Boston: Harvard Business School Press, 1990).

Lodge, George C. and Ezra F. Vogel, *Ideology and National Competitiveness: An Analysis of Nine Countries* (Boston: Harvard Business School Press, 1987).

Mann, Michael, *States, War and Capitalism: Studies in Political Sociology* (Oxford: Basil Blackwell, 1988).

Mascarenhas, Reginald C., 'State Intervention in the Economy: Why is the United States Different from other Mixed-Economies?', *Australian Journal of Public Administration*, vol. 51 (1992), 387–97.

Mascarenhas, Reginald C., *Government and the Economy in Australia and New Zealand: The Politics of Economic Policy Making* (San Francisco: Austin & Winfield, 1996).

Mascarenhas, Reginald C., 'Managing Globalization: The Role of the State', Paper presented to the Australia New Zealand International Business Conference, November 13–14, 1998.

Mascarenhas, Reginald C., *The Comparative Political Economy of East and South Asia: A Critique of Development Policy and Management* (Basingstoke: Palgrave Macmillan, 1999).

McCraw, Thomas K., 'Government, Big Business and the Wealth of Nations', in Alfred D. Chandler Jr et al. (eds), *Big Business and the Wealth of Nations* (Cambridge: Cambridge University Press, 1997).

Nelson, Richard R., 'Role of Government in a Mixed Economy', *Journal of Policy Analysis and Management*, vol. 6 (1989), 541–7.

Ohmae, Kenichi (ed.), *The Evolving Global Economy: Making Sense of the New World Order*, (Boston, A Harvard Business Review Book, 1995).
Plender, John, *A Stake in the Future: The Stakeholding Solution* (London: Nicholas Brealey, 1997).
Rashid, Salim, *The Myth of Adam Smith* (London: Edgar Elgar, 1998).
Rose, Nikolas and Peter Miller, 'Political Power Beyond the State: Problematics of Government', *British Journal of Sociology*, vol. 43 (1992), 173–205.
Rueschemeyer, Dietrich and Peter B. Evans, 'The State and Economic Transformation: Toward an Analysis of the Conditions Underlying Effective Intervention', in Peter Evans *et al.* (eds), *Bringing the State Back In* (Cambridge: Cambridge University Press, 1985), 44–77.
Ruggie, John Gerard, 'International Regimes, Transactions and Change: Embedded Liberalism in Postwar Economic Order', *International Organization*, vol. 36 (1982), 379–415.
Shonfield, Andrew, *Modern Capitalism: The Changing Balance of Public and Private Power* (Oxford: Oxford University Press, 1965).
Spulber, Nicolas, *United States: The Struggle for Supremacy in the 21st Century* (Cambridge: Cambridge University Press, 1995).
Vogel, David, *Kindred Strangers: The Uneasy Relationship Between Politics and Business in America* (Princeton: Princeton University Press, 1996).
Weiss, Linda, *The Myth of the Powerless State* (Ithaca: Cornell University Press, 1998).

Part II
Recent Developments and Changes in Industrial Organization

4
Changing Nature of Capitalism: Large-Scale Enterprises

Introduction

The gradual transformation of capitalism, from its identification with individualism or laissez faire to a position more closely aligned to that of a mixed economy, clearly acknowledges the crucial role played by the state in the functioning of modern industrial economies. This acknowledgement recognizes the changes that have occurred within capitalist enterprise and appreciates the importance of the state in society. As industrialized economies have become powerful, they have also become vulnerable to external influences such as fluctuations which have immediate impact on their respective societies.

In critiqueing modern industrial capitalism, John Kenneth Galbraith (1967) and Angus Maddison (1991) focused largely on the large-scale corporation which dominates western industrial economies, particularly the United States. While covering the largest segment of the economy in terms of volume, their analysis failed to present the total picture and, in fact, overlooked its diversity. In this and subsequent chapters of this study, while acknowledging the dominance of the large corporation, I will attempt to portray contemporary capitalism as diverse and constantly undergoing change. This chapter offers a panoramic view of postwar developments in modern industrial capitalism by firstly examining the role of the large-scale corporation and then proceeding to discuss the development of the balance of power in the public–private mix. This development of the mixed economy has led to organizational relationships in which the state has played a coordinating role, albeit differing between countries. Such variations notwithstanding, postwar government–business relations ushered in the golden age of capitalism. However, a variety of factors in the 1970s led to the decline of capitalist

economies, resulting in a dramatic response from governments in the form of neoliberal policies. The differing responses to such decline, while accentuating the divergence between countries, were further fuelled by the phenomena of globalization and flexible specialization. While this chapter focuses on the adjustment of different countries to the postwar consensus, Chapters 5 and 6 discuss globalization and flexible specialization respectively.

This chapter is divided into the following sections. The next section builds on the themes of previous chapters by tracing the development of the corporate organization. The third section analyses components of modern industrial economies, showing how large-scale organization and some elements of specialized production contributed to the growth of the public sector. The fourth section comments on how governments adjusted their economic regimes to suit postwar changes by examining the institutions of capitalism, while the fifth section reviews the achievements of the golden age of capitalism and the reasons for its decline. The sixth section traces the neoliberal response to decline in the form of new laissez faire, and the last section provides a conclusion.

Role of large-scale industrial organization

Modern industrial enterprises employ different types of technology to manufacture a variety of products demanded by domestic and international markets. That process, while becoming increasingly sophisticated with the advancement of technology (such as communication, transportation and computers) has, owing to increasing pressure towards economic and political liberalization, resulted in the disappearance of economic borders. Referred to as globalization, modern industrial capitalism is seen to be converging towards one large enterprise, a world economy. This has been brought about partly by the breakdown of the Bretton Woods agreement and its replacement by a regime of free floating exchange rates encouraging voluminous transactions in international capital. Rapid changes in communication and transportation technology facilitate free movement of physical capital across borders, in response to promotional incentives and the availability of low-wage non-unionized labour in developing countries.

Although largely attributed to advancement in technology and its management, such developments had been anticipated and were, in fact, preceded by historical occurrences during previous periods, notably the first and second industrial revolutions. Often overlooked in the earlier analysis of capitalism is the influence of the large-scale organiza-

tion, a product of improved technology and managerial competence that emerged in order to meet increased demand. The large-scale organization, a distinct product of twentieth-century capitalism, has, while making an immeasurable contribution to economic growth, changed the very nature of capitalism (Shonfield, 1965; Galbraith, 1967; Chandler Jr, 1990). The reasons for its existence are best summed up by Edward S. Mason (1973) thus:

> Given the technologically determined need for a large stock of capital, the managerial requirements set by the problem of administering the efforts of many men, and the area of discretion demanded for the effective conduct of an entrepreneurial function, the corporation, or a reasonable facsimile thereof, is the only answer. (p. 1)

Briefly, large industrial enterprises have contributed by (1) lowering the cost of production by investing in manufacturing facilities to exploit economies of scale, (2) establishing input and output linkages to take advantage of large-scale production, (3) developing human resources which then became the primary source of technological advances, and (4) initiating, developing and enhancing product specific intangible organizational assets (Chandler Jr *et al.*, 1997, p. 26). In other words, the modern corporation represents the successful integration of land, labour and capital through large-scale organization and technical progress.

The analysis thus far highlights how the growth of the large corporation has placed limits on market forces resulting in a gradual increase in the power of managers. Such managerial power in effect constitutes economic power. While it can be used favourably for the benefit of the corporation particularly in a negotiated environment of administrative competition, it is increasingly being used to influence public policies (Lindblom, 1977; Vogel, 1996). To sustain such economic power, organizations seek to acquire interventionist power (Etzioni, 1985). Tracing the gradual shift of power from the property or shareholder to the corporate technostructure, Galbraith (1967) comments that the 'annual meeting of the large American corporation is, perhaps, our most elaborate exercise in popular illusion' (p. 99). He then makes a crucial distinction between corporations: those that maintain simplicity in their operations and accord power to individuals such as control over capital (entrepreneurial corporations), and those in which the technostructure has taken over (mature corporations) (1967, p. 105).

The corporation has played a special role in the development of modern capitalism. The American version, in particular, has had an

impact so widespread that any change in public policy or other economic or political influence affects society as a whole. With globalization, the corporation as an organizational device has become universal, although its functioning continues to be a cause of ambivalence for Americans (Vogel, 1996). Whether viewed as a virtue or a vice, no one doubts the continuing influence of the corporation in the economic development of the modern capitalist economy. By their very nature corporations are best suited to large-scale operations. However, their control of the largest component of the economy has enabled them to acquire considerable power, raising several uncomfortable questions in supposedly pluralist democracies (Lindblom, 1977; Vogel, 1996). In the real world of modern industrial capitalism, the only safety valve available against such power is the set of rules and regulations established and implemented through state machinery. That role is crucial because:

> The problem arises approximately where 'individual possessory holdings' give way to 'systems of power' – that is, at the point at which corporate size divorces control from ownership and converts owners essentially into *rentiers*. In Berle's terms, 'The capital is there and so is capitalism. The waning figure is the capitalist.'
> (Mason, 1973, p. 15)

Chandler Jr's (1990, p. 1997) studies in the development and working of large corporations has generated interest from other disciplines such as organization theory, economics of organization and public policy. Each of these disciplines adopts a particular perspective to the analyses of business organizations. For example, the neoclassical theory of the firm emphasizes the narrow production function while public policy analysts adopt a restrictive approach to vertical integration and to conglomerates. It is in this light that Williamson (1986) and O'Sullivan (2000) advocate the importance of studying the governance structure of the firm. In advocating a transaction-costs economic approach, Williamson (1993) recognizes the influence of the institutional environment (macro) as well as the role of the individual (micro) in the comparative efficacy of designing alternative modes of governance (pp. 112–13). O'Sullivan (2000) adopts the organizational control theory of corporate governance to analyse the question of who makes investment decisions, what type of investment decisions they make and how returns from investments are distributed. She regards such an approach to corporate governance as preferable to market control of resource allocation (p. 1). In this study of comparative capitalism which looks

at the significant role played by large-scale corporations, one cannot overlook the importance of governments in promoting stable relationships between various elements like firms and workers to produce growth (Mascarenhas, 1992, 1996; Fligstein, 2001).

Private power and the public interest

Post-Second World War economic growth of industrialized economies was a product of the extraordinary dynamism of the corporate sector, which, with the judicious support of governments, responded to the changing environment of business. Known as the golden age of capitalism (Marglin and Schor, 1991), this era (1950–73) witnessed the ability of business to work within the framework of government rules and regulations and was described as 'embedded enterprise' (Ruggie, 1982) or 'bounded capitalism' (Gourevitch, 1986). That arrangement also spawned the postwar consensus and the welfare state.

Pre-Second World War capitalist enterprise operated with limited restraints from public authorities. Insofar as the consequences of its actions were internal to its operations, the enterprise could function without restraint from public authorities. However, as the power and influence of the private corporation increased to a point where private interests could harm the public interest, the state's authority came into play against possible excesses. As the private sector of the economy became more complex and powerful, this role gradually expanded.

The role of the state as protector against market excesses is distinct from its role as a public authority (see Chapter 3). However it should not be concluded that prior to the Second World War the term 'free enterprise', or 'laissez faire', meant that the state had no role to play. In my view a market does not exist without the state's provision of the basic framework of rules and regulations for the protection of private property, a fundamental of a free market economy. The free enterprise system therefore does carry the label 'made by government' (Schultz, 1977, p. 30) while the post-Second World War phenomenon is best referred to as state intervention in the economy through the use of a range of instruments like controls, regulations, incentives and ultimately public ownership. The extent and nature of that intervention resulted in what I categorize as a mixed economy, that is, an economic system where both public and private sectors of the economy enjoy distinct decisional and operational roles within the framework of the market (Mascarenhas, 1992).

The state intervenes to direct a type of behaviour which would otherwise not be forthcoming. Such intervention has to be viewed from

different perspectives. The first is the need to protect or promote the public interest against possible excesses such as arbitrary pricing, quality of product, concentration of monopoly power in certain sectors and working conditions through labour laws and environmental degradation. The second is when the state intervenes to promote the private sector through incentives, tariffs, subsidies and government procurement. In the first category we observe a distinctive pattern. While the US opted to regulate business, Europe preferred to extend intervention to include public ownership (Mascarenhas, 1992). The second category, state intervention through promotion of private enterprise, emerged in the US and is described as the 'military industry complex', a product of the cold war. Evocative of the close association between big business and state, some critics viewed this development as dangerous, reminiscent of the 'iron and rye' phenomenon in pre-war Germany. Galbraith (1967) cautioned against the 'new industrial state' – the close working relationship between private enterprise and the state, where large private and public organizations become virtually indistinguishable, operating like large bureaucracies controlled by a managerial elite. Their functions become so complex and technical that neither elected representatives nor shareholders have a say in their actual functioning.

The picture painted above differs from the general notion of a capitalist mixed economy associated with private enterprise competing for markets and funded through private capital traded on sharemarkets. Investors in such markets are assumed to have overall control of their property in the form of land and shares, protected through a variety of institutional rules and regulations. Described by Polanyi (1944) as utopian, this popular notion, perpetuated in economics and business texts and taught to millions of undergraduate and graduate students, has undergone a transformation.

Modern industrial capitalism is a co-evolution of state and market, the actual mix differing from country to country. The domestic economy is generally a combination of a competitive sector comprised of small and medium sized industries and a large segment which is non or less competitive, generally referred to as big business. Other developments that have had significant impact are the multinational or transnational corporation and the emergence/continuation of flexible quality production in industrial districts which produce specialized products for international markets. In recent years, the influence of the 'new economy' has brought about a dramatic transformation in the composition of the domestic economy, particularly in the United States (see Chapter 7).

While confining my analysis to the competitive and the non-competitive components of the economy, I observe that the competitive sector is largely associated with local or regional markets organized as small businesses such as groceries, drug stores, restaurants, service stations and light manufacturing industries such as clothing and industrial accessories. Constituting a small segment of the economy, such enterprises are on the decline, attracting low-skilled, low-paid workers interested in part or short-term employment. Unlike the large-scale or non-competitive sector, which is geared for production for national and export markets, employment in this sector is unstable with high mobility. The large-scale or non-competitive sector includes capital goods industries such as steel, aluminum and electrical equipment, consumer goods like automobiles and appliances, and transportation industries such as railroads and airlines.

Owing to complex technology, large capital investments and the need for stability, management is required to maintain regular production and hire a skilled workforce on high wages. Further, management has to establish durable linkages with suppliers of raw materials and establish outlets for finished products. In the large-scale sector, both prices and wages are administered and not determined solely by forces of the market. With the emergence of the 'new economy', however, we see further divisions within the workforce. The development of a two-tiered economy, where the income of the top third has increased with declining wages for the remaining two-thirds, has exacerbated income inequalities.

In looking at modern industrial economies as co-evolution of state and market, few commentators realise how the private sector has, in the process of playing a variety of roles, not only been transformed but has also contributed to the gradual development of the state sector. While state intervention in the form of rules and regulations is a direct outcome of an industrialized capitalist economy, the indirect demands placed on the state sector in the form of technical and higher education, science and technology infrastructure, industrial health, environmental pollution, safety in the work place, unemployment benefits and the provision of roads, water and power, have contributed to the growth of the state sector. Its emergence as a significant component of the economy is not often recognized as a consequence of industrial capitalism. This area of state activity, the welfare state, which has expanded since the postwar consensus, does not include direct production of goods and services like public enterprises (Mascarenhas, 1992).

As large private corporations increasingly rely on government contracts or are consumers of bulk inputs like power, they operate in

negotiated environments. That is, they prefer to operate in an environment of stability and certainty without having to constantly adapt to changing demands and input prices (Galbraith, 1967). Demand and supply, the traditional concepts of market functioning, are inoperative in the real world of big business. Evidence of this is the steady growth, profitability and stability of the majority of large industrial enterprises between 1950 and 1973. That notion of perfect competition has been overtaken by what Gardiner Means (1979) described as 'administrative competition'. 'The great evolution from private capitalism has given us a new form of free enterprise system which may be called Collective capitalism. It is a form of capitalism lying entirely outside the conception of John Stuart Mill and Karl Marx, and, of course, outside the conception of Adam Smith' (pp. 126–7). Such close cooperation between government and business is seen as an unusual phenomenon and sits uncomfortably in a relationship of distrust between business and the state (Vogel, 1996), contributing to the distinctive character of American individualism (Mascarenhas, 1992).

While the above analysis is more applicable to the developments of industrial capitalism in the United States of the 1970s, in other industrial economies, particularly in Western Europe, the state adopted regulation and public ownership to promote the public interest. Surprisingly, Britain, generally associated with the Anglo-American blend of industrial capitalism, nationalized major industries following the election of a Labour government in 1948. France followed suit causing that nation more than any other western industrial economy to become identified with dirigisme. By contrast, West Germany sought to promote a unique blend of state and market in the form of the 'social market' now labelled Rhenish or Alpine capitalism. In promoting the 'social market', Germany successfully retained its small and medium-sized industries, thereby raising doubts about the necessity of equating modern industrial capitalism with large-scale organization. In response to the rigidity of such corporations to market changes, one notes the revival of industrial districts where public and private sector organizations collaborate, a development described by Piore and Sabel (1984) as the 'second industrial divide' (discussed in Chapter 6). Essentially it is the recognition of the existence of craft-based production on a small scale in specialized industrial districts.

The concept that the market is a universal institution as propounded by classical liberalism and revived by the neoliberals is questionable because, as Polanyi (1944) observed, societies protect themselves from markets through organized intervention. One cannot overlook the ten-

sions experienced by former centrally planned economies as they go through liberalization and restructuring, or the difficulties experienced in transforming former planned centralized economies into decentralized market economies, and finally the uncertainty of the Third World as it moves from a protected economic regime to a competitive one (Gourevitch, 1998). This just confirms that markets are not completely autonomous and the distinctive characteristics they have acquired serve to exacerbate the obstacles in transplanting economic and political institutions from one social setting to another.

Amid the confusion of moving from one regime to another, one senses the need for complex systems of coordination. Such systems of coordination, while not autonomous, are socially embedded, generating interesting analysis into comparative 'social systems of coordination'. 'More generally each form of market is completed by or embedded in a series of other coordinating mechanisms, which are based either on obligation (and not only self interest) and/or vertical coordination, alliances, hierarchies, communities, networks, or public authorities' (Hollingsworth and Boyer, 1997, p. 70). Subsequent studies of comparative capitalism have explored varieties of capitalism based on forms of coordination. Hall and Soskice distinguish these as liberal market economies (LMEs) and coordinated market economies (CMEs) (Hall and Soskice, 2001). Interestingly, the decline of Anglo-American capitalism is attributed by Weiss and Hobson (1995) to the failure of economic coordination. They feel that 'the longer a political economy relies primarily on markets to achieve structural change, the greater, eventually the need for a "strong" coordinating intelligence able to institute change and arrest decline' (p. 199). Kester (1992) points out that the existence of layers of interlocking arrangements to monitor the interests of stakeholders in industrial groups in Germany and Japan helps to anticipate possible decline in firms – a feature noticeably absent in Anglo-American capitalism.

The ability of institutions in Germany like banks to intervene to stem possible decline is an effective recuperative mechanism, unlike the takeover or bankruptcy option in capital markets. The neocorporatist arrangements that are successful in managing business enterprises in West European countries offer a voice option for recuperation, avoiding unproductive use of resources from a stage of decline to ultimate exit (Hirschman, 1970). The absence of such central coordination intelligence in Anglo-American capitalism has led Weiss and Hobson (1995) to observe, 'A modern economy demands a corrective agency with strategic, think-tank, coordinating functions to make extensive reorganization

possible. And in many countries where the technological and organizational shifts are under way, this is precisely the enabling role that the state has come to play, in combination with organized industry and industrial finance' (p. 202).

Despite extensive evidence of the success of neocorporatist arrangements in Germany and Japan, the neoliberal drive of the 1980s influenced by principal–agent theory moved Anglo-American corporations from 'retain and invest' strategies to 'downsize and distribute' strategies. Driven by a new breed of investors, this shift in emphasis from managerial control to shareholder value resulted in a spate of mergers, takeovers and bankruptcies in order to meet predetermined rates of return on investment. According to Fligstein (2001), the finance conception that dominated large American corporations from the mid-1960s suffered a crisis in the 1970s. To counter this crisis (termed an accumulation crisis by Marxists when firms are not profitable enough for shareholders), an alternative emerged. Known as the shareholder value conception of the firm, this gained significant support within corporations. The rapid acceptance of a conception which claims that the only legitimate purpose of the firm is to maximize shareholder value can be explained only in terms of the 'organizational cultural' approach adopted by Fligstein (2001, pp. 147–8). The shift to shareholder value coincided with the emergence of the 'new economy' in the United States leading to unexpected sustained growth and a boom in the stock market. Interestingly, even economies like Japan and Germany, identified as successful due to their 'social systems of production' became targets for adopting the 'shareholder value' philosophy, generating further debate (O'Sullivan, 2000; Lazonick and O'Sullivan, 2000).

The institutions of capitalism

Looking beyond technical and economic issues, Shonfield, like Gershenkron, emphasized the character of political institutions (Shonfield, 1965, pp. 387–8). 'Among the most important, on which Gershenkron lays particular stress, is the marked divergence in the national institutions of the latecomers to industrial capitalism in the nineteenth and twentieth centuries from those of the pioneering Anglo-Saxon model' (Shonfield, 1960, p. 59). Gershenkron's belief that market forces alone were insufficient for economies to catch up was based on German experience and influenced the literature on political economy of industrial development in both developed and developing worlds. According to Gershenkron, the Germans circumvented the market by (1) acquiring

advanced technology with the assistance of the state, (2) constructing large efficient plants, and (3) financing their development by initiating a unique type of banking. 'This combination of technological and institutional innovation, in his view, ultimately affected both the structure and organization of industry' (Herrigel, 1996, p. 4). Gershenkron was preceded by Friedrich List, another powerful advocate of state support for industry to enable it to catch up with advanced economies (Cowen and Shenton, 1996). In addition to state support and innovative banking, German organized capitalism or cooperative managerial capitalism has consciously borrowed organizational principles from the states (*Lander*) (Herrigel, 1996, p. 5).

In mixed economies, governments play a variety of roles to counteract what Hirschman (1986) identified as the natural instinct for self-destruction. Recognizing the built-in under-utilization of resources when a declining economic enterprise proceeds towards bankruptcy in Schumpeter's volatile market, Hirschman (1970) advocates recuperative mechanisms. He questions the undue reliance in economic theory on 'exit' while there is still an opportunity to rescue a declining firm or organization through the mechanism of voice. In such a context, political institutions can play a more active role. The justification for institutional support is offered by Shonfield (1965): 'the taming of the market – in the sense that sudden movements of market forces are no longer permitted to disrupt the life of civilized society – is the condition for a style of private enterprise which tends to grow more like the behaviour of certain public institutions' (p. 377).

During the 'golden age of capitalism' (1950–73), the state and other public and private institutions played a significant role in protecting the markets from business cycles. Successful performance of the economy, which was pivotal for national survival, was probably helped by defence-related industries at the height of the cold war. Maddison (1991) attributes the 'productivity miracle' of the 1950–73 period to 'favourable concatenation of political and policy circumstances' (p. 131). High levels of skills, education and institutional capacity enabled Japan and the European countries to seize the opportunities. While the acknowledgement that ownership in itself is less important became more acceptable in the postwar period, Shonfield in *Modern Capitalism* (1965) alerted us to the significant role of governments in the development of postwar capitalism. This was reiterated by Lindblom in *Politics and Markets* (1977). As a result, we have several comparative studies of capitalism which show that the real difference between countries lies in the role of the state (Albert, 1987; Lodge and Ezra Vogel, 1987; Chandler *et al.*, 1997; Crouch and

Streeck, 1997; Hollingsworth and Boyer, 1997; Hall and Soskice, 2001). Such studies have brought home the importance of understanding the broader institutional structures defining each political economy. In other words, the performance of an organizational form such as the large corporation cannot be understood independent of the institutional context – for example, the relation between German firms and banks or the role of credit institutions in France (Zysman, 1983; Chandler Jr *et al.*, 1997; Streeck, 1997).

Adopting such a perspective leads one to describe the relationship between government and business in the United States as 'an American phenomenon' built on adversarial relationship dating back to the Sherman Anti-Trust Act 1890 (Chandler Jr, 1980). Chandler Jr (1980) asks why other countries did not develop similar anti-trust and regulatory policies. The answer lies in the role and attitude of the federal government towards business which had been defined well before the creation of a professional class of public administrators. In other words, business antipathy towards the state developed when the state was weak and small (Vogel, 1996, p. 48). The other explanation is the variation in the pattern of industrialization which, in the case of the United States, differed from other countries. While early industrializers relied on entrepreneurs, late industrializers, according to Gershenkron, needed support from government and banks to catch up. Therefore the relationship between government and business differs in the case of early and late industrializers (Zysman, 1983, pp. 289–90). 'As Giddens suggests, the conditions under which a nation industrializes leave a permanent legacy to its political and economic institutions and to the relationship between them. The pattern of industrialization not only affects a society's subsequent institutional arrangements, as Gershenkron argues; it also shapes the ideology of those who industrialize' (Vogel, 1996, p. 40).

With the decline in economic performance of industrialized economies in the 1970s, the importance of an institutional framework in support of industrial capitalism assumed relevance. An institutional framework capable of adapting to internally and externally induced crises became an issue for analysis. Zysman (1983) takes a distinctive approach to study the response of industrialized economies by examining their national financial structures. 'The particular arrangements of national financial systems limit both the marketplace options of firms and the administrative choices of government. That is, financial markets in each country are one element that delimit the ways in which business and the state can interact' (p. 16). Politics and political institutions become important when countries are going through an

economic crisis. 'Prosperity blurs a truth that hard times make clearer: the choice made among conflicting policy proposals emerges out of politics' (Gourevitch, 1986, p. 17). Therefore to understand the adjustments undertaken by countries to overcome economic crises, Zysman (1983) feels it is important to 'eliminate the artificial dichotomy that separates the study of markets from the study of politics' (p. 17).

Government–business relations in advanced industrial economies are governed by three types of financial systems. The first is the capital market which allocates resources by establishing prices competitively and by keeping the relationship between government and business at an arm's length. In such a system, prevalent in the United States, managers prefer to retain their autonomy and to adopt a company-led adjustment strategy to meet a crisis. The second is a credit-based financial system with government-administered prices which encourages government intervention in business. Such a system operates in Japan and France where the state promotes adjustments in private sector businesses. The third is a credit-based system where financial institutions influence the functioning of business. Prevalent in West Germany, it is described by Zysman as a negotiated type of modern capitalism. 'Each of these models represents a distinct way of resolving both the political and economic problems of growth and, not surprisingly, each has distinct advantages and identifiable weaknesses' (Zysman, 1983, p. 18).

These three types of financial systems establish a framework which can be used to analyse the relationship between the state and capital – from the indirect in the United States to the direct in Japan, France and Germany. The state's role is so important for some analysts that, in comparing it with capital, Heilbroner (1985) comments: 'Remove the regime of capital and the state would remain, although it may change dramatically; remove the state and the regime of capital would not last a day' (p. 105). With globalization and free floating exchange rates, capital-based markets are likely to be more vulnerable to external shocks than the credit-based type. Interestingly, neoliberal economic philosophy has permeated the capital-based more than the credit-based economies and to that extent the latter are more stable than capital market based economies. Other legal, organizational and cultural factors have led commentators to term the Anglo-American as the company law model and those like the Japanese as the community model (Dore, 1987; Lodge and Vogel, 1987).

In extending the comparison between them, one recognizes variations in social systems of production, that is, mass large-scale production from flexible specialization and diversified mass quality production. 'Both

social systems of flexible specialization and diversified quality mass production work best when transacting actors are embedded in institutional environments in which collective forms of coordination are highly developed. Broadly speaking, both of these social systems of production are basically incompatible with neoliberal regimes of unregulated economies' (Hollingsworth and Boyer, 1997, pp. 23–4).

Coordinated market economies recognize the limitations of markets and therefore try to balance virtues against vices such as increasing income inequalities, disregard for the environment, poor safety record and monopolistic tendencies. In adopting state intervention to overcome likely shortcomings, they ensure reciprocal relations between state agencies and various intermediaries representing firms and workers (Hollingsworth and Boyer, 1997, p. 128).

Like social systems of production, technology is influenced by the community and social organization from which it emerges. If technology is closely linked to state and society, certain types of state–societal arrangements are conducive to the creation and diffusion of new technologies (Hart, 1992, p. 274). To understand the importance of state–societal arrangements to industrial competitiveness, Hart examined the steel, semi-conductor and automobile industries in Britain, Germany, United States, France and Japan and observed a distinctive pattern of influence of government, business or labour in these countries. Studying the relationship between the three, he categorized as neocorporatist the set-up in which certain groups, business or labour, have access to the state; as coalitional, where policies emerge out of bargaining among influential groups; and as statist, where the state is relatively autonomous from groups like business or labour. Explaining that all three systems are limited, Hart expressed his preference for the state–societal arrangements because they focus on patterns of relationship among the three actors – state, business and labour (Hart, 1992, p. 295). From this, Hart concluded that the competitiveness of Germany and Japan is attributable to the harmonious relations between state, business and labour, while the decline in competitiveness is attributable to the adversarial relations that one sees particularly in Britain and the United States.

Streeck (1997) offers the concept of 'beneficial constraint' implying that the performance of an economy may be improved by surrounding society, thus overcoming what he considers the limitations of rational voluntarism. That is, the state takes the responsibility to govern 'its' economy (p. 198). In other words, an economy is not independent of its society and social institutions. A society that leaves the functioning of

an economy to market-rational economic actors is not optimally using its productive potential and ends up performing less well (1997, p. 199). Streeck (1997) claims:

> The notion of beneficial constraint draws on Polanyi's (1944) central proposition that a self-regulatory free market that makes the rational pursuit of economic gain the only maxim of social action, will ultimately destroy its own human, social, and natural conditions. In both theories, rational individualism is described, not just as socially destructive but as inherently destructive and unable to attain even narrow economic objectives unless properly harnessed by noneconomic social arrangements. (p. 207)

Social structures as instruments of beneficial constraint are not deliberately designed but are unintended consequences. To illustrate, Streeck (1997) cites the German apprentice system and the Italian artisanal family networks. Once condemned, they have now emerged as important social institutions contributing to Germany's economic performance and Italy's flexible production (p. 211) and demonstrating that 'turning institutional constraints into opportunities may in fact be one of the most important functions of Schumpeterian entrepreneurialism' (p. 212). Another case of a restraint converted into an opportunity is the Dutch horticultural industry, which, when faced with environmental protests regarding water pollution, responded with innovation resulting in enhanced productivity (Porter, 1995). In an era of neoliberal reform in industrialized economies, there is the danger that social structures, which indirectly act as beneficial constraints, may become victims of economic rationalization. Zysman's (1983) assertion that one cannot isolate the political from the economic is reiterated by Streeck (1997), who comments 'While letting politics operate on its own terms may sometimes go wrong economically, making politics subservient to economics always will' (p. 215).

Streeck's (1997) beneficial constraint to counteract or complement voluntary rationalism is, in some ways, equivalent to Dore's (1983) benevolence in questioning Adam Smith's self-interest of the baker, the butcher, and the brewer. Both Streeck and Dore offer a pragmatic view of society in answer to the economists' narrow view of market rationality. Dore prefers 'goodwill' to benevolence, borrowing from Hobhouse's principle of mutuality which, according to him, conveys 'the sentiments of friendship and a sense of diffuse personal obligation which accrue between individuals engaged in recurring contractual

economic exchange' (p. 460). In essence, it attempts to explain the impact of society on modern capitalist enterprise in Japan, which, in my view, offers another socially embedded model, that is, a type of 'moralized trading relationships of mutual goodwill' (p. 463). Questioning Williamson's hard-nosed profit-maximizer, Dore explains the reason for adopting such trading relations based on relational contracting thus:

> It is a calculation, perhaps, which comes naturally to a population which until recently was predominantly living in tightly nucleated hamlet communities in a land ravished by earthquake and typhoon. Traditionally, you set to, to help your neighbour rebuild his house after a fire, even though it might be two or three generations before yours was burnt down and your grandson needed the help returned... They most commonly say benevolence is a duty. Full stop. It is that sense of duty – a duty over and above the terms of written contract – which gives assurance of pay-off which makes relational contracting viable.
>
> (Dore, 1983, p. 470)

The argument offered by Streeck (1997) and Dore (1983) in support of historically established social structures confirms the thesis held by Hirsch (1976) that the success of capitalism is due to the existence of special conditions. The supporting social principle which worked in tandem with self-interest was ignored or taken for granted by the advocates of the invisible hand (Kumar, 1988, pp. 40–1).

The evidence now available on the role of public authority in the working of markets in modern economies raises questions on the continued influence of neoliberal thinking in Anglo-American countries. An ingredient often linked to markets in Anglo-American economies is the close link that exists between free enterprise ideology and the functioning of democracy. In the American concept of justice, 'the market is thought to be "fair and wise", but not the government' (Lane, 1986, p. 385). Capitalism identified with markets is closely linked to democracy as a form of government but that relationship is viewed as a 'kind of antagonistic symbiosis' (Dahl, 1998, p. 166). Market capitalism favours democracy because it relies on a middle class which invests in property, avails opportunities of education and employment and contributes to economic growth through individual decisions. Questions are being raised as to the effectiveness of democratic institutions in protecting weaker sections of society (Lindblom, in Shapiro and Reeher, 1988, p. 156). Research confirms that the degree of corporatization of interests in the political economy influences the nature of economic policy-

making. In 'most corporatist' political systems, policy-makers recognize greater interdependence of public policies and place importance on long-run costs and benefits. In 'least corporatist' political systems, policy-making is politicized. This is an outcome of fragmented systems, which have reduced capacity to plan or implement policy and a short-run single-issue focus (Lindberg *et al.*, 1987, p. 365). The type of democracy in neocorporatist countries is a reflection of their industrial capitalist system which relies on a mix of state and market coordination. Commenting on recent literature on corporatism, Panitch (1980) observes the lack of agreement on what the concept actually refers to because it is variously understood to be an economical system or mode of production, a state form and a system of interest intermediation (p. 159).

Independent of these factors which distinguish one political economy from another, one cannot overlook the fundamental difference between market and authority as coordinating mechanisms. To quote Lindblom (1977):

> For all that, a market system is a limited use institution. Some tasks no market system can attempt or achieve. In simplest and very rough form, the distinction between what markets can and cannot do is this: For organised social life, people need the help of others. In one set of circumstances, what they need from others they induce by benefits offered. In other circumstances, what they need will not willingly be provided and must be compelled. A market system can operate in the first set of circumstances, but not in the second. Its limitation is conspicuous with an authority system. Although authority is not required in the first set of circumstances, it can be used for both. (p. 89)

The golden age of capitalism

At the present time when most analysts of western industrialized economies are critical of state intervention, it may seem controversial to attribute the success of industrial capitalist economies between 1950 and 1973 to the 'historic compromise' of bounded capitalism when private enterprise operated within a system of rules that provided economic and political stability. This involved 'demand management to promote full employment, the welfare state, an extensive system of economic regulation, institutionalized industrial relations, free

trade – these were policy approaches of this bounded capitalism, and they departed strongly from the market orthodoxy of pre-depression days. Political power was shared as well, and to a far greater degree than before the war' (Gourevitch, 1986, p. 18). An understanding of the golden age of 1950–73 according to Marglin (1991) rests on an understanding of the key economic arrangements of that period. 'To apply the lessons of the golden age, we must understand not only what allowed capitalism to deliver the goods... but also the ways in which the very success of the system in the 1950s and 1960s undermined it and eventually led to the drift of the 1970s and the stagnation of the 1980s' (pp. 1–2).

Postwar economic arrangements worked smoothly. Internally, economies were able to combine high capacity utilization and stable profits through demand management based on the power of trade unions to raise wages and the welfare state. Maddison (1991) identifies special characteristics that were identified with economic performance of the 1950s and 1960s. They were:

- successful reapplication of liberal policies in international transactions
- government promotion of buoyant domestic demand and policies and circumstances that kept inflation low in conditions of very high demand. (p. 168)

The postwar compromise or embedded liberalism (Ruggie, 1982; Gourevitch, 1986) promoted liberalism in international transactions by devising a form of multilateralism that was compatible with requirements of domestic stability. Once postwar reconstruction through the Marshall Plan was achieved, there was greater cooperation and consultation between countries and freer trade was possible through postwar international payments system. With it, export volumes of these countries rose nearly sevenfold, and foreign direct investment from the United States to Europe increased from \$1.7 billion to \$40 billion. Such investment naturally led to technology transfer to Europe from the productivity leader. During the golden age the net migration of people into Western Europe was 9.4 million when compared with 3.7 million from 1914 to 1949 (Maddison, 1991, p. 169).

A significant influence on the economic performance of industrialized economies was the role of fiscal policy in macroeconomic objectives. It 'transformed the nature of the business cycle, which was dominated by swings in government policy rather than by movements in the private sector'. Predicted price increases with contemplated full

employment policy was less damaging. The average annual price increase for 1950–73 was 4.1 per cent, helped partly by fixed exchange rates and competition with removal of trade barriers. All these factors accounted for the economic performance of industrialized economies during 1950–73. 'The period thus brought a change of tempo, an unforeseen break with what past experience would have suggested as likely or even possible. In the light both of earlier history and of later developments, the period has become labelled as a golden age; and just as this golden age had been unanticipated, so the extent to which economic performance fell away in the succeeding period was greater than could reasonably have been foreseen' (Henderson, 1990, p. 278).

Economic decline of the 1970s

The steady economic growth with low levels of inflation achieved through postwar economic management based on Keynesian economic thinking, had, according to Goldthorpe, heralded 'a new era of capitalism in which stability and dynamism were reconciled and guaranteed' (1987, p. 363). This however did not last. By the early 1970s, the energy crisis, along with declining economic growth, increasing unemployment, growing balance of payments deficits and high rates of inflation, transformed the scene. The 'discomfort index' created by summing the rate of unemployment and the rate of inflation in seven major OECD countries rose from 5.5 percentage points for the decade 1959–69 to 17 percentage points for 1974–5 (Goldthorpe, 1987, p. 363).

An analysis of growth figures for the period 1973–87 confirms the decline from the golden age (1950–73). According to Henderson, this suggests that the golden age was an 'exceptional once-for-all interlude in economic history'. While such an interpretation appears logical, one cannot ignore the fact that both Japan and West Germany have had higher growth rates with new capital investments under postwar recovery programmes. However, the initial thrust shown in dramatic increases in the 1950s and 1960s, particularly in Japan, tapered off in the 1970s after the technology had reached a level of maturity. Further declining growth rates resulted in increasing unemployment and a rising rate of inflation. Together they contributed to stagflation (Henderson, 1990). Job losses combined with declining productivity forced wages up, placing pressure on existing rules of coordination between capital and labour. Steady growth in real wages had been a vital part of the postwar economic arrangements and union leaders were now under pressure to deliver, resulting in increased wages and lower profits. As

investment started falling, declining profits affected accumulation of capital. The effects of stagflation on the domestic economy were compounded by international developments when the United States unilaterally abandoned the Bretton Woods agreement in 1971. Thus the decline of the golden age, initiated by domestic factors such as capital–labour conflict, unemployment and increasing inflation, was accentuated by international developments. The collapse of the Bretton Woods fixed exchange rate, the defeat of the American forces in the Vietnam war and the timing of the APEC oil price hikes together finally ended the golden age (Marglin and Schor, 1991; Maddison, 1991).

The decline was particularly severe in the case of Anglo-American countries when compared to West European and East Asian economies. The patterns of response to the economic crisis in East Asia and Europe revealed not only the respective soundness of their economies prior to the crisis, but also the distinctiveness of their economic and political institutions. In the Anglo-American countries the narrow consensus of the postwar arrangement gave way to a debate on the relevant merits of market and state as coordinating mechanisms. Neoliberals sought to roll back the state to enable markets to function freely. The shift in the ideological debate between market and state was fuelled by changes in government, particularly the elections of Margaret Thatcher in Britain (1979) and Ronald Reagan in the United States (1980). Their anti-state stand on economic policies spread to other Anglo-American countries in the mid-1980s, despite the election of Labour governments in Australia and New Zealand. Thus the role of the state in the economy in Anglo-American countries underwent a dramatic transformation between 1980 and 1995 through economic liberalization, deregulation and privatization. While this was happening, European economies such as France moved towards increasing state intervention. Sweden adopted measures that incorporated unions known for their encompassing character, giving them a voice in combating economic pressures. While other industrialized economies underwent change, the German policy approach retained its postwar compromise (Gourevitch, 1986).

A critique of Fordism

The relative stability and growth enjoyed by postwar industrialized economies until the 1970s, described by some as a convergence around a model of industrial organization and known for mass production of standardized goods, earned for itself the term 'Fordism'. The postwar

model of accumulation that Fordism is identified with is mass production based on rigid division of labour for workers and machines influenced by the scientific management movement. Credited with contributing to the 'golden age of capitalism', Fordism reached its limits when markets became increasingly diversified and consumers sought quality products. Geared towards mass production of standardized consumer goods, the Fordist model was too rigid to adapt to changing demands. In other words, the contradictions of capitalism became apparent – that is, rigidity of long-term, large scale investments in mass production and labour markets.

There were those however who sensed increasing pressure for greater flexibility to meet changes in technology and markets (Piore and Sabel, 1984). That Fordism was unable to contain the inherent contradictions of capitalism became evident in the 1970s when it was faced by a recession, followed by increases in energy costs. As these crises evolved, signs of experimentation of a new regime of accumulation along with a system of political and social regulation became apparent (Harvey, 1990, p. 145). Pressures for such changes in industrial production indicated that 'It was no longer a question of competing through economies of scale in the production of standardized goods and services using dedicated production systems, but of competing through the capacity to introduce flexible manufacturing or service delivery systems and to exploit the resulting economies of scope' (Jessop, 1994, p. 110).

While the need for serious questioning of the mass production model arose from the economic crisis of the 1970s, Piore and Sabel (1984) believe the causes lie deeper, resulting from the limits of the model of industrial development. To overcome the crisis, the authors advocated the modification of technologies and operating procedures of modern corporations, forms of labour-market control, macroeconomic management of the economy and the international monetary and trading system (pp. 4–6).

Based on the above, Piore and Sabel (1984) developed a dichotomy between mass production and flexible specialization, the two approaches to technology, associated with distinct forms of economic organization at the micro and macro levels. Adopting the French regulationist approach of 'balancing mechanism' and 'equilibration', Piore and Sabel (1984) analysed the institutional circuits that connect production and consumption as regulatory mechanisms and identified the occurrences of disruption to these circuits as regulation crises. 'The two major regulation crises in the epoch of mechanized production are associated with the rise of the large corporation in the late nineteenth

century, and of the Keynesian welfare state in the 1930s (pp. 4–5) (see Boyer, 1988; Jessop, 1990; Arrighi, 1994).

Robert Boyer, a leading member of the 'regulation school', identifies reasons for the crisis facing Fordism:

- increased organization of work is becoming counter-productive
- that mass production requires world markets
- Fordism leads to growing social expenditure on housing, education and health and with changes in consumption patterns cannot be met through conventional means of standardized production. (Boyer, 1988, pp. 199–203)

According to the regulation school, the relationship between production and consumption was regulated by a variety of social norms and institutions described as modes of regulation. A viable economic regime derives from the compatibility of several institutional forms: wage labour nexus, a configuration for competition, a monetary (and credit) regime, a set of state interventions, and finally an international regime (Hollingsworth and Boyer, 1997, p. 192).

While Piore and Sabel (1984) proposed flexible specialization as the industrial model best capable of producing quality goods for specialized markets, Amin noted the success of Japan in combining rigidity with flexibility as well as quality and price competitiveness within mass production (1994, p. 22). This shift from the Fordist growth model based on mass production has led us to look towards Japan whose development can be attributed to the adoption of different 'technoeconomic paradigms and social modes of regulation which are deemed to have successfully challenged the mass production model' (Jessop, 1994, p. 110). The promotion of flexible specialization as a post-Fordist option has generated a polarized debate around the geography of industrial organization. Within one cluster of productive activity (industrial districts), proximity provides solidarity, cooperation and trust, thus replacing national and international hierarchies of command and control. The other direction of this debate is the globalization of production through mergers and acquisitions (Amin, 1994, p. 26) (explored in Chapters 5 and 6).

In this contestation for a post-Fordist regime, regulation theory has, according to Tickell and Peck (1995), a positive role to play in developing the political and social institutions needed to sustain an element of stability. However, the coincidental emergence of neoliberalism has led to controversy.

Tickell and Peck (1995) are concerned about the use by some theorists of regulation theory to prematurely bestow on neoliberalism the label of a post-Fordist regime. They comment: 'Used more positively and more progressively, the theory can provide a basis for making substantive politico-economic claims. It need not lamely endorse a neoliberal or neo-competitive agenda because that is the one – perhaps by default – which happens to be dominant at the time' (p. 365). According to them, it would be audacious to claim that flexible production and flexible labour systems are sufficient while little attempt has been made to develop a post-Keynesian mode of social regulation (MSR) to sustain it. Critics warn against reaching firm conclusions while developments and experiments are still in a state of flux.

In questioning Jessop's (1991) advocacy of the Schumpeterian workforce state as a possible successor to the Fordist–Keynesian state, Tickell and Peck (1995) worry 'that it is inappropriate to label the ensemble of regulatory practices as an MSR because it is internally crisis prone and therefore unstable' (p. 366). Their evidence for this is the *fragility* of the 1980s growth patterns and the emergence of flexible specialization which are incompatible with the neoliberal regime of unregulated markets and cut-throat competition (p. 367). By adopting Smith's utopia in which markets are self-regulating, neoliberals rejected state intervention. In the absence of a new institutional fix, 'neoliberalism, we want to argue, is capitalism's *"law of the jungle"*' (p. 369).

The post-Fordist response varied. Anglo-American countries sought the neoliberal route while West European and East Asian countries adopted a balanced approach in which the state continued to play an active role in the economy in partnership with the private sector. While encouraging the private sector to invest, this ensured that different constituencies such as managers and workers would work in cooperation. 'Europe's social balancing act, as we know it today, has no place in the anonymous, atomistic market environment envisioned by Adam Smith. Rather, it is the linchpin of a civic universe that also functions in economic terms. We have long understood that homelessness, illiteracy, and other social ills are not only morally unacceptable but also economically harmful' (Henzler, 1995, p. 8).

While governments produce reports on the quality of life, markets are not exclusively judged for their capacity for resource allocation and producing goods and services. The enormous impact that modern economies have on entire societies makes any separation of economy from society not just difficult but undesirable as well. Some of the policies adopted by governments to promote the market economy have led to

undesirable social consequences, such as chronic unemployment, growing uncertainty due to constant downsizing, increasing stress, heavier workloads with declining satisfaction, increasing depression, climbing rates of suicide among youth and more crime and violence. Underlying all this is a decline in social well-being which is increasingly being suggested as an alternative indicator of societal performance (Lane, 2000).

After two decades of neoliberal dominance (particularly in Anglo-American countries) the question of the role of the state in mixed economies has now to be seen as a response to its very excesses – the neglect of the moral and ethical dimension, the very foundation on which capitalism was based (Etzioni, 1985; Hirschman, 1986). By cutting back the state and encouraging the free play of the market, policy-makers, particularly in Anglo-American countries, have allowed speculative capital without a social conscience to dominate. Success is judged by shareholder value and not by its contribution to broader community values. O'Sullivan (2000) provides data which shows that in 1965 CEOs in the United States earned 44 times the average factory worker's wages. This rose to 326 in 1997 and to 419 in 1998 (p. 200). In an assessment of the 'new economy' that promoted the idea of shareholder value, she comments that 'one group that has gone to considerable ends to secure a place in the winners' circle is corporate senior management. So successful have senior corporate executives been in lining their pockets, under the guise of creating value for shareholders, that to a greater extent than has ever been the case since the rise of the corporate economy, they have separated their fate from that of the rest of the working population' (O'Sullivan, 2000, p. 199). Even *The Economist*, eschewing its usually sympathetic view of markets, concluded that no value had been created for shareholders (27 January, 2001, p. 14). In avoiding the excesses of neoliberal thinking in government and business, policy-makers in Western Europe and East Asia have recognized the social inclusiveness of workers. Such social inclusiveness is reflected in the differentials in pay between top executives and ordinary workers in the two groups of economies. That social inclusiveness demands that the state play a more active role in the economy (Henzler, 1995, p. 7).

Conclusion

Recent studies of comparative political and historical analysis of industrial capitalism have generated a variety of questions doubting the magical qualities of markets promoted by neoclassical or/and neolib-

erals. The pro-market anti-state vision of the 1980s and 1990s has led academic researchers to explore the areas where the state and the market could effectively cooperate to promote wealth and welfare. In examining the role of the corporation in harnessing knowledge and technology for mass production through large-scale organization in the first and second industrial revolution (Chapter 4), one observes, with the onset of the third industrial revolution, the emergence of a more diversified trend. Based on modern transport, communications and computer technology, the third industrial revolution demands greater flexibility and adaptability to cope with the dynamic changes constantly occurring in the environment. Size, ownership, competition and semi-skilled workforce once required for large-scale mass production have given way to smaller or medium-sized units, public–private mix, the need for multiple skills and flexible production technology. This has clearly divided industrial capitalism into Anglo-American, strongly identified with competitive markets operating on a transnational basis, and West European and East Asian models based on close cooperation between public and private sectors adopting a variety of strategies to promote the economy.

To conclude, it appears to have been an exciting interlude in the history of industrial capitalism when capital and labour cooperated within the framework of rules and regulations decided by public authorities. Described as bounded capitalism, this led to 'the golden age' of steady growth and stability. Its end opened up a new debate on the merits of state involvement in the economy, resulting in cutting back the state particularly in the Anglo-American group of countries. For purposes of this study, this is seen as marking the growing divergence within industrialized economies largely centred around the relationship between government and business in mixed economies.

Despite continued coverage of the success of the other model by Anglo-American writers (Johnson, 1982; Lodge and Vogel, 1987; Dore, 1987), policy-makers in the Anglo-American countries, supported by international agencies, appear to be moving further towards a laissez faire model, which, while enjoying limited economic success, has actually been accompanied by disastrous social consequences. If one accepts the embeddedness thesis, then one must accept that the different models reflect their own history and social constructive abilities and that adapting to new market models in the absence of social institutions and culture is difficult.

References

Albert, Michael, *Capitalism vs Capitalism* (New York: Four Walls and Eight Windows, 1987).
Amin, Ash (ed.), *Post-Fordism: A Reader* (Oxford: Basil Blackwell, 1994).
Arrighi, Giovanni, *The Long Twentieth Century: Money, Power and the Origins of Our Times* (London: Verso, 1994).
Boyer, Robert, *The Search for Labour Market Flexibility* (Oxford: Clarendon, 1988).
Chandler Jr, Alfred D., 'Government versus Business an American Phenomenon', in John T. Dunlop (ed.), *Business and Public Policy* (Cambridge, Mass.: Harvard University Press, 1980).
Chandler, Jr, Alfred D., *Scale and Scope: The Dynamics of Industrial Capitalism* (Cambridge, Mass.: Belknap Press of Harvard University, 1990).
Chandler Jr, Alfred D. et al., *Big Business and the Wealth of Nations* (Cambridge: Cambridge University Press, 1997).
Cowen, M. M. and R. W. Shenton, *Doctrines of Development* (London: Routledge, 1996).
Crouch, Colin and Wolfgang Streeck, *Political Economy of Modern Capitalism: Mapping Convergence and Diversity* (London: Sage, 1997).
Dahl, Robert A., *On Democracy* (New Haven and London: Yale University Press, 1998).
Delorme, Robert and Kurt Dopfer (eds), *The Political Economy of Diversity: Evolutionary Perspectives on Economic Order and Disorder* (London: Edward Elgar, 1994), 102–25.
Dore, Ronald, 'Goodwill and the Spirit of Market Capitalism', *British Journal of Sociology*, vol. 34 (1983), 459–82.
Dore, Ronald, *Taking Japan Seriously: A Confucian Perspective on Leading Economic Issues* (Stanford: Stanford University Press, 1987).
Etzioni, Amitai, 'The Political Economy of Imperfect Competition', *Journal of Public Policy*, vol. 5 (1985), 69–186.
Fligstein, Neil, *The Architecture of Markets: An Economic Sociology of Twenty-First Century Capitalist Societies* (Princeton: Princeton University Press, 2001).
Galbraith, John Kenneth, *The New Industrial State* (Harmondsworth: Penguin, 1967).
Goldthorpe, John H., 'Problems of Political Economy after the Postwar Period', in Charles Maier (ed.), *Changing Boundaries of the Political: Essays on the Evolving Balance Between State and Society, Public and Private in Europe* (Cambridge: Cambridge University Press, 1987), 363–407.
Gourevitch, Peter, *Politics in Hard Times: Comparative Responses to International Crisis* (Ithaca: Cornell University Press, 1986).
Gourevitch, Peter, 'The Political Sources of Democracy: The Macropolitics of Microeconomic Policy Disputes', in Theda Skocpol (ed.), *Democracy, Revolution, and History* (Ithaca: Cornell University Press, 1998).
Hall, Peter A. and David Soskice, *Varieties of Capitalism: Comparative Institiutional Advantage* (Oxford: Oxford University Press, 2001).
Hart, Jeffrey A., 'The Effects of State-Societal Arrangement on International Competitiveness: Steel, Motor Vehicles and Semiconductors in the United States,

Japan and Western Europe', *British Journal of Political Science*, vol. 22 (1992), 255–300.

Harvey, David, *The Condition of Postmodernity: An Enquiry into the Origins of Cultural Change* (Oxford: Blackwell, 1990).

Heilbroner, Robert L., *The Nature and Logic of Capitalism* (New York: W. W. Norton & Co., 1985).

Henderson, David, 'Comparative Economic Performance of the OECD Countries, 1950–87: A Summary of the Evidence', in Andrew Graham and Anthony Seldon, *Government and Economies in Postwar World: Economic Policies and Comparative Performance:1945–85* (New York: Routledge, 1990), 273–83.

Henzler, Herbert A., 'The New Era of Eurocapitalism', in Kenichi Ohmae (ed.), *The Evolving Global Economy: Making Sense of the New World Order* (Boston: Harvard Business Review Books, 1995).

Herrigel, Gary, *Industrial Constructions: The Sources of German Industrial Power* (Cambridge: Cambridge University Press, 1996).

Hirsch, Fred, *Social Limits of Growth* (Cambridge, Mass.: Harvard University Press, 1976).

Hirschman, Albert O., *Exit, Voice and Loyalty: Response to Decline in Firms, Organizations and States* (New York: Free Press, 1970).

Hirschman, Albert O., *Rival Interpretations of Market Society and Other Essays* (New York: Viking, 1986).

Hollingsworth, Rogers J. and Robert Boyer (eds), *Contemporary Capitalism: The Embeddedness of Institutions* (Cambridge: Cambridge University Press, 1997).

Jessop, Bob, 'Regulation Theories in Retrospect and Prospect', *Economy and Society*, vol. 19 (1990), 153–216.

Jessop, Bob, 'Changing Forms and Functions of the State in an Era of Globalization and Regionalization' in Robert Delorme and Kurt Dopler (eds), *The Political Economy of Deversity: Evolutionary Perspectives on Economic Order and Disorder* (London, Edward Elgar, 1994).

Jessop, Bob *et al.*, *The Politics of Flexibility: Restructuring State and Industry in Britain, Germany and Scandinavia* (London: Edward Elgar, 1991).

Johnson, Chalmers, *MITI and the Japanese Miracle* (Stanford: Stanford University Press, 1982).

Kester, Karl W., 'Industrial Groups as Systems of Contractual Governance', *Oxford Review of Economic Policy*, vol. 8 (1992), 24–43.

Kumar, Krishan, *The Rise of Modern Society: Aspects of the Social and Political Development of the West* (London: Basil Blackwell, 1988).

Lane, Robert E., 'Market Justice, Political Justice', *American Political Science Review*, vol. 80 (1986), 383–402.

Lane, Robert E., *The Loss of Happiness in Market Democracies* (New Haven: Yale University Press, 2000).

Lazonick, William and Mary O'Sullivan, 'Maximizing Shareholder Value: A New Ideology for Corporate Governance', *Economy and Society*, vol. 29 (2000), 13–35.

Lindberg, Leon N. *et al.*, 'Economic Policy Research: Challenges and a New Agenda', in Heinhoff Dierkes *et al.* (eds), *Comparative Policy Research: Learning from Experience* (New York: St Martin's Press, 1987).

Lindblom, Charles E., *Politics and Markets* (New York: The Free Press, 1977).

Lodge, George C. and Ezra F. Vogel (eds), *Ideology and National Competitiveness* (Boston: Harvard Business School Press, 1987).

Maddison, Angus, *Dynamic Forces in Capitalist Development: A Long-Run Comparative View* (Oxford: Oxford University Press, 1991).

Marglin, Stephen A. and Juliet B. Schor, *The Golden Age of Capitalism: Reinterpreting the Postwar Experience* (London: Clarendon, 1991).

Mascarenhas Reginald C., 'State Intervention in the Economy: Why is the United States Different from other Mixed Economies?', *Australian Journal of Public Administration*, vol. 51 (1992), 385–97.

Mascarenhas, Reginald C., *Government and the Economy in Australia and New Zealand: The Politics of Economic Policy Making* (San Francisco: Austin & Winfield, 1996).

Mason, Edward S. (ed.), *The Corporation in Modern Society* (New York: Atheneum, 1973).

Means, Gardiner S., 'The Problems and Prospects of Collective Capitalism', in Warren J. Samuels (ed.), *The Economy as a System of Power, Vol 1, Corporate System* (New Brunswick: Transactions Books, 1979).

O'Sullivan, Mary, *Contests for Corporate Control: Corporate Governance and Economic Performance in the United States and Germany* (New York: Oxford University Press, 2000).

Panitch, Leo, 'Recent Theorizations of Corporatism: Reflections on a Growth Industry', *British Journal of Sociology*, vol. 31 (1980), 159–85.

Piore, Michael J. and Charles F. Sabel, *The Second Industrial Divide: Possibilities for Prosperity* (New York: Basic Books, 1984).

Polanyi, Karl, *The Great Transformation: The Political and Economic Origins of Our Time* (Boston: The Beacon Press, 1944).

Porter, Michael E. and Claas van der Linde, 'Green and Competitive', *Harvard Business Review*, 1995, 120–34.

Ruggie, John Gerard, 'International Regimes, Transactions and Change: Embedded Liberalism in Postwar Economic Order', *International Organization*, vol. 36 (1982), 379–415.

Shapiro, Ian and Grant Reeher (eds), 'Roundtable Discussion: Politics, Economics, and Welfare', in *Power, Equality, and Democratic Politics: Essays in Honour of Robert Dahl* (Boulder: Westview Press, 1988).

Schultz, Charles L., *The Public Use of the Private Interest* (Washington, DC: Brookings Institution, 1977).

Shonfield, Andrew, *Modern Capitalism: The Changing Balance of Public and Private Power* (Oxford: Oxford University Press, 1965).

Streeck, Wolfgang, 'Beneficial Constraints: On the Economic Limits of Rational Voluntarism', in J. Rogers Hollingsworth and Robert Boyer (eds), *Contemporary Capitalism: The Embeddedness of Institutions* (Cambridge: Cambridge University Press, 1997).

Tickell, Adam and Jamie A. Peck, 'Social Regulation after Fordism: Regulation Theory, Neo-liberalism and the Global–Local Nexus', *Economy and Society*, vol. 24 (1995), 357–86.

Vogel, David, *Kindred Strangers: The Uneasy Relationship Between Business and Politics* (Princeton: Princeton University Press, 1996).

Weiss, Linda and John M. Hobson, *States and Economic Development: A Comparative Historical Analysis* (London: Polity Press, 1995).

Williamson, Oliver E., *Economic Organization: Firms, Markets and Policy Control* (New York: Wheatsheaf Books, 1986).

Williamson, Oliver E., 'Transaction Cost Economics and Organization Theory', *Industrial and Organizational Change*, vol. 2 (1993), 107–56.

Zysman, John, *Governments, Markets and Growth* (Ithaca: Cornell University Press, 1983).

5
Globalization and Its Effects on Capitalism

Introduction

While advances in technology and the internationalization of the economy have led to declining costs in transport and communication, liberalization of trade and financial regimes have increased the flow of goods and capital across national borders. Termed 'globalization', such changes have had tremendous impact on societies and governments. To maximize advantage, firms converge in basic structure and strategy and move production in search of cheap labour. Such firms exploit exit options by pressurizing governments to change the regulatory framework to lower labour costs and taxes and deregulate internal markets (Hall and Soskice, 2001).

Such a scenario has been promoted by globalization theorists 'who painted a picture of a world set free for business to serve consumers' (Hirst and Thompson, 1995, p. 421). Hollingsworth and Boyer (1997) challenge globalists' view on the basis that its assumptions of certain conditions presuppose 'a complete globalization of factor markets;... the integration of product markets that can deliver anywhere a single price for the same good once exchange rates and transportation costs are taken into account and finally the high mobility and transferability of modern technologies. Such an interpretation assumes that social systems of production would then converge toward the one best way and deliver equivalent productivity levels and standards of living' (p. 462).

While complete globalization is an unrealistic goal, Hirst and Thompson (1997) seek to distinguish it from the worldwide international economy which involves growing interaction between national economies and nation-states as principal entities, a process assisted by the

relative separation of the domestic and international frameworks of policy-making and management of economic affairs. Further progress towards globalization requires changes in the international economy such as floating exchange rates which have in the past led to the abandoning of exchange controls and the deregulation and liberalization of financial markets.

Observing the increasing interaction between national economies, it must be said that insofar as such interaction relies on political and economic institutions to either promote or restrain them, then the problem is one of governance: that is, the ability to develop public policies which need to be coordinated from international to regional levels. In developing proper systems or mechanisms to cope with internationalization of the economy, a frequent reference point is the role of the nation-state. While states may face problems in managing the economy in the face of 'globalization', so far as they remain political communities with power to influence economic actors, states have important functions to perform (Hirst and Thompson, 1997).

To understand the difference in response between countries to increasing globalization, it is helpful to adopt the distinction between liberal market economies (LMEs) and coordinated market economies (CMEs) (Hall and Soskice, 2001). The pressures toward liberalization and deregulation to respond to international competition is likely to be greater in liberal market economies than in coordinated market economies. The evidence now available from studies of comparative capitalism helps to make subtle distinctions between different countries. In market liberal economies, apart from limited institutional capacity to cope with increasing globalization, there is an underlying tendency for governments to encourage liberalization and deregulation. It is less likely in coordinated market economies where institutional capacity balances states with markets in this trend towards globalization.

In the next section of the chapter, I undertake an analysis of globalization as a product of multiple factors, particularly political or ideological, and also as an outcome of developments in communication and transportation technology. Following that, I examine how such globalization in the context of technological developments has encouraged financial capitalism, a type of capitalism which exposes the domestic economy of weaker or smaller countries to external pressures. The fourth section discusses the implications to state capacity in terms of their autonomy and sovereignty. The fifth section looks into recent neoliberal policies as being responsible for this transformation in the role of the state. The last section offers a brief conclusion.

Focus from national to global economy

In essence, globalization, seen as the liberalization and deregulation of capital flows and of trade in goods and services, is a product of several factors. Precipitated by the energy crisis of the 1970s and encouraged by the end of the cold war, it has gained momentum with the impact of communication technology on international business and financial transactions. Such international movement of capital has become politically acceptable and legitimized by the election of governments in Britain and the United States ideologically favouring free enterprise. Transnational organizations such as the World Bank, IMF, OECD and WTO have promoted policies to bring about a global free market overlooking the underlying diversity of economies around the world. In doing this, their intention is to export a particular type of capitalism identified with Anglo-American free enterprise – essentially a type of laissez faire. In such an economy the market is deregulated with little or no social or political control.

It is apparent that this social experiment of a global free market has been influenced by the ideology of the new right which derives its inspiration from mid-nineteenth-century England. While the new right falls back on Adam Smith and other liberals whose experience was largely confined to England of those days, it fails to realize that the free market was engineered and that it survived for a short period only under special circumstances. Recalling the two periods when free markets were attempted, Gray (1998a) comments:

> It illuminates even more clearly the hubris of seeking to transplant worldwide a social institution that has figured only briefly in the history of one strand of capitalism – once in the nineteenth century, in the English paradigm case, and again in the 1980s of this century, in Britain, the United States, Australia and New Zealand, as a consequence of neoliberal policies. (p. 14)

In promoting a universal model of free enterprise, there is an ideological component – market freedom identified with neoliberalism and its policies. Changes to technology have hastened the movement of capital across countries through unrestrained markets which promote a particular political system encouraging self-initiative, freedom of choice, greater competition, rights of association and free speech. While associating free enterprise with political democracy, such a system is intended to promote democratic capitalism with western values of liberalism.

In the context of this worldwide attempt to promote a global free market devoid of any political or social constraints, Gray (1998a) writes:

> By privileging individual choice over any common good it tends to make relationships revocable and provisional. In a culture in which choice is the only undisputed value and wants are held to be insatiable, what is the difference between initiating a divorce and trading in a used car? (p. 37)

A qualitative difference in the global free market of the 1980s from that of mid-nineteenth-century England is the revolution in communication and transportation technology. Modern technology has made it easier to set up and manage business, with greater ease in the case of financial markets where transactions have gradually changed from investment for producing goods and services to investment of financial capital. In the case of the former, the capital is physical, fixed at a location, generating returns over a period. The time period may vary between a steel plant requiring enormous investment with returns coming over a longer period and one producing microelectronics requiring lesser investment with quicker returns. The situation differs in financial markets as there is greater flexibility with volatile markets and greater volume and speed of transactions.

The above trends have led to both transnational and localized institutional arrangements. In tracing the impact of international economic changes, Simmons (in Kitschelt *et al.*, 1999) sees a distinct difference between trade liberalization and capital liberalization in their impact on institutions of social democracy. The fact that unprecedented growth and stability was achieved during a period of 'relatively closed national capital markets' is a cause for concern for analysts of politics and policy, who find it difficult to plan and implement compensation strategies owing to the fast impact of macroeconomic policies (Simmons, in Kitschelt *et al.*, 1999).

Arrighi (1994) notes the qualitative difference in the 'scale, scope and technical sophistication' of the current financial expansion which is much greater than those in the past. In a way, it has led to a loss of control on the part of powerful capitalist states over the production and regulation of world money (pp. 300–13).

In posing the question 'Can capitalism survive?', Arrighi speculates on the capitalist West having gone so far that its power can only be increased through the formation of a truly global world empire. If that were possible, he wonders about the means the traditional power

centres of the West would use to acquire and retain that control (p. 354).

Advances in technology and communication have encouraged liberalization in trade while financial regimes have increased flows of goods and capital across national borders. Fligstein (2001) suggests that the political-cultural approach to capitalism offers analytical tools to comprehend 'why trade can grow and yet national capitalisms persist' (p. 192). Adoption of the economic 'globalization' indices, he says, can help identify various trends.

Those who adopt the globalist view believe that, as firms are becoming similar in basic structure and strategy, competitiveness rests increasingly on labour costs. They argue that countries that withstand pressure for competitive deregulation will face a situation when firms will move production in search of cheap labour. The view that governments have few policy options assumes that labour costs drive international economic competition. Fligstein takes the position that there is empirical evidence to show that this view is wrong and competitiveness in any industry is a mix of factors, some dealing with costs. A more important factor, however, is the competence of firms in organizing production and creating new technologies (2001, p. 214). In the view of globalists, this case for promoting international competition is based on the private sector's capacity for making efficient use of resources.

In this study, I adopt the view that the role of the state in mixed economies is basic to the functioning of markets. Those who take the position that the private sector is competing for resources that could be put to better use overlook the positive role of states. While this view predominates in Anglo-American countries, there is growing evidence to the contrary in Japan and Germany where the state has contributed to growth. As the political balance has moved towards capital, the latter, in Anglo-American countries, continues to demand reduction in the size of government and workers' rights and promotion of shareholder value. At the same time, the post-Fordist acknowledgement of craft-based industry and its success in Europe contradict the claims of globalists (Fligstein, 2001, pp. 214–17).

However, this anti-state view was primarily an American phenomenon and advocated by the ideologues of globalization. 'An ideology is a set of ideas that reflects a point of view. The ideology of globalization and shareholder value have become united, so that globalization is now not just the Japanese challenge, but now the challenge of a more diffuse "other" and shareholder value means the firms should maximize profits for owners, and governments should stay out of it. This ideol-

ogy is a generalization about the American experience' (Fligstein, 2001, p. 221).

Distinctive or changing nature of globalization

When using the above analysis to evaluate the relative capacity of states to manage globalization, one needs to consider the political or ideological dimension to globalization. Is it market generated or ideologically generated or both? An interesting concomitant to the globalization phenomenon is the isomorphism one observes in the spread of free enterprise economies across the world (Rosenau, 1997, p. 93).

The trend towards a competitive market economy received a boost when governments encouraged international capital through liberalization and deregulation and removed subsidies and tariffs. As a result, individual consumers and producers now possess the capacity to make decisions in the domestic and international markets ignoring boundaries. In this process, financial capital markets more so than other areas of the economy have become more open and competitive. The internationalization of money and financial markets since the 1970s has posed a challenge to the governability of national economies by undermining the credibility of policies of national macroeconomic management (Hirst and Thompson, 1992, p. 366). Fuelled by the ongoing revolution in information technology, the impact of financial capital mobility has increased turbulence and revealed the vulnerability of national economies with the state in eclipse. If the variation in response to globalization is distinctive and determined by the type of financial organization, that response is seen in the way that some countries have been able to cope with the new demands, particularly the impact of international finance capital – that is, short-term capital flow as distinguished from capital investment or even trade. Daily transactions in foreign exchange markets is forty times the daily value of trade across borders. Such capital flows (inward/outward) have reached enormous proportions and are sensitive to interest rate fluctuations and exchange rate expectations. As a result they influence the dynamics of national policy-making. The gravity of the problem becomes clearer when one views the volume of financial capital flows, which have increased from US $3 billion a day in 1973 to US $6 billion in 1989, reaching US $1 trillion a day in 1996 (Cable, 1995, p. 27). This represents a significant shift from the 'bounded capitalism' created after the Second World War where the private sector operated within a system of rules that offered stability to 'an anarchy of sovereign states, rival capitalisms and stateless zones' (Gray, 1998b, p. 32).

The movement of money across countries is unrelated to the movement of commodities, lacking any relationship with their production. Of the $1 trillion a day mentioned above, only 3 per cent constituted payment for internationally traded commodities, the rest being financial transactions. Such increases in largely speculative financial transactions have contributed to balance of payments current account imbalances and volatility in exchange rates, prompting Bryan (1995) to warn individual nation-states of the difficulties in managing or regulating accumulation (p. 123).

Such movement of financial capital has the following implications: (1) it reduces the capacity of governments to pursue independent macroeconomic policies, (2) it encourages more short-term investments in financial markets and discourages longer-term investment in productive enterprises, (3) governments increasingly lose capacity to regulate such transactions for fear of losing investments, and (4) financial markets are more volatile and risky because of the rapidity of financial inflows and outflows.

Goodman and Pauly (1993) believe that capital inflow or outflow is equally threatening to the autonomy of national policy-making (p. 51). Increasingly, globalization is becoming a theme for serious analysis in the comparative political economy of industrialized economies. The reasons for this are:

1. the decrease in policy instruments which enables the state to control activities within and beyond its boundaries
2. the flow of private capital across borders which threatens anti-inflation measures, exchange rates and other government policies
3. the need for states to collaborate in many traditional domains of state activity like economic management, communication and so on
4. the consequent necessity for states to increase the level of political integration with other states
5. the resulting growth of institutions and organizational regimes which have laid the basis for global governance. (Held, 1995, p. 146)

Changing role of the state

Globalization has radically altered the role of state in the economy. While Evans (1997) feels 'it has undermined the power of the state, leaving it marginalized as an economic actor' (p. 63), Weiss (1998) asserts that the powerless state is a myth. Such comments appearing frequently in academic literature reflect the growing convergence to-

wards liberalization and deregulation that one has witnessed since the late 1970s. The adoption of an institutionalist approach in this study suggests that should there be a slide in state capacity, it would not be uniform. In our discussion of the distinctive role played by the state in relation to business in different industrialized economies, one observes an underlying divergence in their capacity for adjustment. Despite globalization, that difference in adjustment remains reflected in institutional variation (Zysman, 1983).

State action is further constrained by transnational economic relations where production for the larger world market has transformed enterprises into transnational corporations (TNC). Strange (1996) views transnational corporations as fearsome, seeing in them the potential to become political institutions. In so doing, she attempts a redefinition of politics to refer to all sources of authority possessing power to allocate values. As they are no longer based in one national location and (unlike MNCs) are not constrained by the policies of particular nation states, TNCs are referred to as stateless corporations (Hirst and Thompson, 1992, p. 362). A case in point is Germany, once known as the ideal capitalist economy with over 666 foreign manufacturing subsidiaries in 1971 and categorized as an exporter of productive capital next only to the USA and UK (Lash and Urry, 1987). Declining disciplinary power has enabled the latter to gain ascendancy, encouraging evasion from domestic laws and earning the description 'disorganized capitalism' (Lash and Urry, 1987; Hirst and Thompson, 1992, p. 363; Schmidt, 1995). The sovereignty of the state in the context of globalization 'is being eroded slowly, and differentially but not eliminated' (Cable, 1995, p. 38). To understand such variable capability in the role of the state, one has to understand the political and economic institutions of capitalism discussed in Chapter 4, and examine to what extent governments have willingly subscribed to the global hegemony of Anglo-American ideology.

A distinctive phenomenon of economic globalization is the shift from primacy of defence and security of the cold war era to protection from or opening of economies to foreign private investment. As markets become global, governments appear more concerned about their performance being judged by financial markets. Their response to such changes, particularly financial capital mobility with corresponding technological changes, has led to market restructuring. 'The price sensitivity of the "paperless world" of the global financial marketplace is increasingly controlling market – and political – decisions elsewhere' (Cerny, 1997a, p. 176). Globalization has transformed the 'nation state' into a

'competition state' as governments adopt a range of strategies to render markets internationally competitive (Cerny, 1997b, pp. 251–74). In adapting to globalization by making the economy more internationally competitive, the state is increasing its vulnerability to outside forces. The declining capacity of state autonomy to decide on macroeconomic policy is a cause of concern for analysts who do not recognise that this is an outcome of the very globalization process initiated by the states themselves.

What is now obvious is that the authority of governments has weakened with globalization. The failure to manage the national economy in terms of growth, balance of payments, interest rates and exchange rates is because states have become victims of the market economy (Strange, 1996, p. 14), unable to provide political and social guidance to markets. Rosenau (1997, p. 341) explains the phenomenon metaphorically:

> Like the shell of the lobster the outer facade of the nation-state retains its general appearance and consistency, even as the societies within are bombarded to the point where they barely resemble the original contents. The lobster in the sea and the lobster on the plate are both lobsters, but the change in their circumstances is certainly qualitative. The same is true of states and their constituent societies amidst the political warming of the last generation. Their borders remain largely intact and their constitutions are in place, but the shells of these sovereign crustaceans have often proved too porous to prevent their contents from being cooked to someone else's taste.
> (Rosenau, 1997, p. 341)

In terms of such a globalized international economy, Evans (1997) asks whether TNCs are the 'most economically empowered citizens' and questions 'the extent to which such private power can (or should) be checked by public authority'. He comments that 'underlying the transnational mobility of capital and the construction of global production networks is a radically globalized financial system, whose operation poses a fundamental challenge to public authority in the economic realm' (pp. 65–7). Using the low stateness and high stateness distinction, Evans (1997) suggests that countries more exposed to trade are likely to have a strong government and consequently possess competitive advantage in a globalized economy. Observing East Asian economic success, Evans is reluctant to accept the notion that the incompatibility of the 'institutional centrality of the state' with globalization 'must be

explained in terms of the ideological face of the current global order' (1997, p. 70).

The developments analysed thus far clearly establish a shift in the role of private enterprise in the economy. Prior to the liberalization and deregulation of the early 1970s, private enterprise operated within a system of rules and regulations that provided both economic and political stability. A kind of 'bounded capitalism' (Gourevitch, 1986, p. 18) has now been transformed through globalization into 'disorganized capitalism' (Held, 1995, p. 134) or 'casino capitalism' (Strange,1996). In such cases, Evans (1997) is willing to concede an increased role for the state. 'Moreover, a look at the nations that have been most economically successful over the last thirty years suggests that high stateness may even be a competitive advantage in a globalized economy.' This is best illustrated by the East Asian 'developmental state' (pp. 67–8). Based on other studies, he states that the configuration of public institutions continues to shape the impact of globalization (p. 68), a view that I attempt to establish in Chapter 4 of this study.

Weiss (1998) counters critics of her claim that the powerless state is a myth and questions some of their assumptions. Based on her analysis of Japan, Germany and Sweden where the state–business relations (referred to as private-sector governance or PSG) function as a coordinating mechanism, she claims that: (1) state power prior to globalization was exaggerated, (2) that such a view ignores variation by assuming a uniform response, and (3) a feeling of helplessness was created by neoliberal governments acceding to the convergence thesis (pp. 190–3; see Mascarenhas, 1998). In clarifying her position, Weiss underscores what I have set out to do in this study – that is, that the post-1970s trend towards neoliberal convergence, a feature of Anglo-American capitalism, has inadvertently prompted an upsurge in comparative political economy studies which highlight the growing divergence that Weiss (1998) predicts. Building her argument on her case studies of 'strong transformative capability supported by robust linkages between government and industry (p. 212), Weiss predicts greater state adaptation rather than decline of functions, the emergence of stronger states as midwives rather than victims of internationalization and the emergence of catalyctic states.

Zysman (1983) categorizes industrialized economies on the basis of their financial structure, capital market or credit based, and uses that distinction to predict the type of adjustment likely to be adopted in an economic crisis. According to him, 'the particular arrangements of national financial systems limit both the marketplace options of firms and

the administrative choices of governments. That is, financial markets in each country are one element that delimits the ways in which business and the state can interact' (p. 16). Broadly, industrialized economies can be grouped into three types of financial systems – capital market (Britain, USA), the credit-based financial system with administered prices (France, Japan), and finally the credit-based system dominated by financial institutions (Germany). Using this typology, Zysman (1983) postulated that state-led adjustment during economic crisis is possible in credit-based systems, while in capital markets under similar conditions, the state maintains an arm's length relationship (pp. 16–18).

Pauly (1994) considers the financial structure as essential to the understanding of capital mobility. To establish his point of view, he uses the Zysman (1983) taxonomy and supplements it with Porter's (1992) distinction between two ideal types. The first of these is the American system, termed the 'fluid capital system' where owners and managers seek to maximize narrowly defined investment returns. The second is the 'dedicated capital' prevalent in Japan and Germany embodying a close relationship between permanent owners and managers and driven principally by the goal of corporate perpetuity (Pauly, 1994, pp. 347–8). What emerges from such analysis is that there are types of capitalism, like the social market democracies in Europe identified as Rhenish capitalism and developmental states in East Asia identified as collective capitalism, that can stand up to the dictatorship of international finance. This however comes at a price (Evans, 1997, p. 67). In the absence of a hegemonic power (a role undertaken by the US after the war until 1973), most countries (with the probable exception of Japan and Germany) have failed in their national monetarist policies. As a result, Hirst and Thompson (1992) believe that 'national macroeconomic management has ceased to provide a viable means of steering national economies in an internationalized system and that the nation state has lost its salience in the face of globalization and supranational economic blocs' (p. 371). However, they acknowledge like Evans the political role of government in 'new forms of economic management'. They also anticipate delinking of fiscal from monetary policy (decisions taken elsewhere) with prospects for innovation and greater independence in fiscal policy (pp. 371–2).

In line with these trends, Lowi (2001) seeks to induct political science into an understanding of institutions of government in an era of globalization, thereby salvaging democracy from 'the tyrant whether the tyrant be repressive rule by malevolent political elites or repressive rule by mechanisms that recognize no law except the law of the market

place' (p. 132). By focusing on globalization as 'borderless trade', Lowi (2001) adopts a three-level scheme to identify the forms that such globalization takes – into macro, meso and micro tracks.

Accordingly, the macro level as the most globalized resembles the pure market and is governed by international institutional structures such as GATT (WTO), IMF and WB. At the meso level, the firm or corporation as the main actor is dependent on state-provided frameworks which provide law and order and protection of private property. This political and institutional framework meets the functional prerequisite of a market economy within which a firm or corporation operates. These functional prerequisites become essential to any business corporation at the micro level on an ongoing basis irrespective of their size or spread of operation (Lowi, 2001, pp. 133–6). By disaggregating globalization into tracks, Lowi is thus asserting that it is 'impossible to deal with any of the levels or tracks without recognizing the deep and systematic involvement of the state' (pp. 136–7).

Bryan (1995) suggests a distinct shift from a theory of international trade based on comparative advantage to one of competitive advantage, where one shifts from adopting endowments of a national economy to specific industries. To make such industries competitive in international global markets, he agrees with Porter (1990) that governments can play an active role and create advantage (Bryan, 1995, p. 174).

Hirst and Thompson (1992) recognize that governments play a role that markets by themselves cannot, aptly described by Lindblom as a limited use institution (1977, p. 89). While accepting the possible implications of globalization for the capacity of states, it is necessary for them to gain support for broad-based economic policies for which they need to construct a distributional coalition. Such a distributional coalition can be constructed only if the state can orchestrate social consensus between industry, labour and itself with the willingness to work within a collaborative political culture. In the changed economic environment there is a need for a shift from techniques to a new mechanism of economic coordination and cooperation which rests on 'specific ensembles of social institutions and these are more difficult to adopt or transfer by deliberate choice' (pp. 373–4).

Was globalization voluntary or involuntary?

What one would now like to ask is whether these developments, contributing to the gradual globalization of the international economy, occurred as nation-states stood by watching? The states did not stand

by helpless. Rather, in a process that was unmistakably political (Andrews and Willet, 1997, p. 482), they actively promoted liberalization and deregulated markets by becoming partners in the process of international financial liberalization. As corporations and financial institutions became increasingly global it became easier for them to adopt strategies of evasion and exit while governments found it difficult to enforce capital controls. 'Countries that sought to control capital inflows faced different incentives from those facing countries that sought to control capital outflows. The reason lies mainly in the asymmetric impact of capital movements on foreign exchange reserves. Current account deficits, capital outflows, weakening exchange rates, and depleting reserves often go together; when they do, governments must either adjust their policies or adopt controls before the loss of reserves is complete' (Goodman and Pauly, 1993, pp. 59–60).

The Anglo-American ideological pressure that supports a pro-market globalized economy raises a new dimension – one that did not exist during the 'bounded capitalism' of the postwar consensus or that of the 'embedded liberalism' of the 1950s or 1960s when citizens were protected from external pressures. The present phenomenon of economic liberalism attempts to promote economic gain independent of sovereignty and across the board (Evans, 1997, p. 71). According to Evans: 'only when viewed through the peculiar prism of our current global ideological order does globalization logically entail movement towards statelessness' (1997, p. 74).

In the current ideological climate and the globalization of financial capital 'the central paradox or dilemma facing states in public policy terms in today's world therefore is not that states simply lose power to other structures, rather, they undermine and legislate away their own power, confronted by the imperatives of international competitiveness' (Cerney, 1994, p. 321). When that develops into a pattern of rapid spread of free enterprise economies, it relates into a kind of isomorphism (Rosenau, 1997, p. 93).

The role of the state in responding to the new global economy has become somewhat constrained with the emergence of credit rating agencies. These have been transformed into 'private makers of public policy, as rating agencies acquire power and authority within a context of a global economy of mobile financial resources' (Sinclair, 1994, p. 448). With specialized knowledge of finance and localized information, rating agencies cause concern for businesses and governments by (1) adopting fundamental analysis of economic and political organizations, (2) stating their views on management and policy, and (3) favouring a

particular model of the economy identified as the 'Anglo-American ideological hegemony' (Evans, 1997). When the economy is judged on the value of the dollar, on debt, balance of payments and interest rates, then credit rating becomes vital. The current influence of credit rating agencies as 'private makers of public policy' indicates a new phase in the development of the global political economy, while the approach they adopt has been described as 'new constitutionalism':

> New constitutionalism is a doctrine and associated set of social forces which seeks to place restraints on the democratic control of public and private economic organization and institutions. It is intended to guarantee freedom of entry and exit of internationally mobile capital with regard to different socio-economic spaces.... The scope of these constraints in an era of substantial mobility of capital means that political leaders will need to be as accountable to international market forces as they are to electorates.
> (Sinclair, 1994, p. 458)

Since the breakdown of the Bretton Woods agreement and increased capital movements, the G7 group of countries has emerged as the only mechanism to 'cool the casino' (Hirst and Thompson, 1992). Footloose capital, globalization, advances in communication and information systems have resulted in disproportion between global financial markets and the economic leverage available to individual states. Countries are now torn between tailoring macroeconomic policies to meet diverse economic conditions and being pressured towards conformity by investors looking for the best rate of return. Under such conditions, is the G7 group of nations the only alternative to the hegemonic role needed to bring about stability in financial markets? In the absence of a lender of last resort in the international market, there is a need for an agency to take on that hegemonic role (Kindleberger, 1989). John Gray advocates a regime of global governance to regulate currencies, capital movements, trade and environmental conservation (1998b, p. 32). Other suggestions include the 'Tobin tax' and a universal currency.

In line with the theme of this study, a significant development in an otherwise turbulent environment is the development of regional forms of regulation of production centring on public/private collaboration in providing key inputs, local cooperation of industry and labour in such areas as training, manpower policy and regional provision of welfare and the development of a confederal welfare state (Crouch and Marquand, 1996, p. 14). Such regional centres are more likely to be found in

countries like Italy, Germany and Japan with politically weak centres, and decentralized power in the regions (discussed in Chapter 6).

Conclusion

The coincidence of the demise of the Bretton Woods agreement with the oil price hikes and the Third World debt crisis created immense opportunities in a worldwide market with equal prospects for a 'wave of creative destruction' (Gray, 1998a, p. 32). A significant development in this trend from bounded to unbounded capitalism is the flexibility and volatility of financial capital influenced largely by changes in markets and in information technology. This transformation has been helped by governments which ideologically favour open markets with limited state intervention. State intervention adopted by the 'strategic state' (Zysman, 1983) and the 'developmental state' (Johnson, 1982) declined with the 'competitive state' (Cerny, 1997b) which advocated limited state intervention to promote competitiveness in the international market.

This chapter has examined the role of the state in an era of globalization. In doing so, one has recognized the concept of relative capability which is governed by several factors like financial structures, structure of the economy and regime characteristics. The point overlooked by analysts is that the state which is the foundation of an effective capitalist system has constantly adapted its role according to changing demands of the economy. We are currently in the midst of yet another phase or transition similar to earlier versions like entrepreneurial capitalism, managerial capitalism and collective capitalism, and appear to be proceeding towards interdependent or transnational capitalism in which the state may have to play a different role similar to that witnessed in Europe and East Asia. That role is likely to emerge as the demands of the transnational economy become clearer. By legislating away the role of governments in order to promote open internationally free markets, there is now no central authority to promote the public good of international economic stability.

References

Andrews, David M. and Thomas Willet, 'Financial Interdependence and the State: International Monetary Relations at Century's End', *International Organization*, vol. 51 (1997), 479–511.

Arrighi, Giovanni, *The Long Twentieth Century: Money, Power and the Origins of Our Times* (London: Verso, 1994).

Bryan, Dick, *The Chase Across the Globe: International Accumulation and the Contradictions for Nation States* (Boulder: Westview, 1995).
Cable, Vincent, 'The Diminished Nation State: A Study in the Loss of Economic Power', *Daedalus*, vol. 124 (1995), 29–53.
Cerny, Phillip G., 'The Dynamics of Financial Globalization: Technology, Market Structure, and Policy Response', *Policy Sciences*, vol. 27 (1994), 319–42.
Cerny, Phillip G., 'International Finance and the Erosion of Capitalist Diversity', in Colin Crouch and Wolfgang Streeck (eds), *The Political Economy of Modern Capitalism* (London: Sage,1997a), 173–81.
Cerny, Phillip G., 'Parodoxes of the Competition State: The Dynamics of Political Globalization', *Government and Opposition*, vol. 32 (1997b), 251–74.
Crouch, Colin and David Marquand (eds), *Reinventing Collective Action: From the Global to the Local* (London: Blackwell Publishers, 1996).
Evans, Peter, 'The Eclipse of the State? Reflections on Stateness in an Era of Globalization', *World Politics*, vol. 50 (1997), 62–87.
Fligstein, Neil, *The Architecture of Markets: An Economic Sociology of Twenty-First Century Capitalist Societies* (Princeton: Princeton University Press, 2001).
Goodman, John B. and Louis B. Pauly, 'The Obsolescence of Capital Controls? Economic Management in an Age of Global Markets', *World Politics*, vol. 46 (1993), 50–82.
Gourevitch, Peter, *Politics in Hard times: Comparative Response to International Crises* (Ithaca: Cornell University Press, 1986).
Gray, John, *False Dawn: The Delusions of Global Capitalism* (London: Granta Books, 1998a).
Gray, John, 'Globalization – the Dark Side', *New Statesman*, 13 March (1998b), 32–4.
Hall, Peter A. and David Soskice (eds), *The Varieties of Capitalism: The Institutional Foundations of Comparative Advantage* (Oxford: Oxford University Press, 2001).
Held, David, *Democracy and the Global Order: From the Modern State to Cosmopolitan Governance* (Stanford: Stanford University Press, 1995).
Hirst, Paul and Graham Thompson, 'The Problem of "Globalization": International Economic Relations, National Economic Management and the Formation of Trading Blocs', *Economy and Society*, vol. 21 (1992), 357–96.
Hirst, Paul and Graham Thompson, 'Globalization and the Future of the Nation State', *Economy and Society*, vol. 24 (1995), 408–42.
Hirst, Paul and Graham Thompson, 'Globalization in Question: International Economic Relations and Forms of Public Governance' in Roger J Hollingsworth and Robert Boyer (eds), *Contemporary Capitalism: The Embeddedness of Institutions* (Cambridge: Cambridge, University Press, 1997).
Hollingsworth, Rogers J. and Robert Boyer, *Contemporary Capitalism: The Embeddedness of Institutions* (Cambridge: Cambridge University Press, 1997).
Johnson, Chalmers, *MITI the Japanese Miracle* (Stanford: Stanford University Press, 1982).
Kindleberger, Charles P., *Manias, Panics, and Crashes: A History of Financial Crises* (New York: Basic Books, 1989).
Kitschelt Herbert *et al.* (eds), *Continuity and Change in Contemporary Capitalism* (Cambridge: Cambridge University Press, 1999), 36–9.
Lash, Scott and John Urry, *The End of Organized Capitalism* (London: Polity Press, 1987).

Lindblom, Charles C., *Politics and Markets* (New York: Free Press, 1977).
Lowi, Theodore, 'Our Millennium: Political Science Confronts the Global Corporate Economy', *International Political Science Review*, vol. 22 (2001), 131–50.
Mascarenhas, Reginald C., 'Managing Globalization: The Role of the State', Paper presented to Australia – New Zealand International Business Association Conference, Melbourne, 13–14 November 1998.
Pauly, Louis, 'National Financial Structures, Capital Mobility, and International Economic Rules: The Normative Consequences of East Asian, European, and American Distinctiveness', *Policy Sciences*, vol. 27 (1994), 343–63.
Porter, Michael, *The Competitive Advantage of Nations* (London: Macmillan, 1990)
Rosenau, James N., *Along the Domestic – Foreign Frontier: Exploring Governance in a Turbulent World* (Cambridge: Cambridge University Press, 1997).
Ruggie, John Gerard, 'International Regimes, Transactions and Change: Embedded Liberalism in Postwar Economic Order', *International Organization*, vol. 36 (1982), 379–415.
Schmidt, Vincent, 'The New World Order: The Rise of Business and the Decline of the Nation State', *Daedalus*, vol. 124 (1995), 75–106.
Sinclair, Timothy, 'Between State and Market: Hegemony and Institutions of Collective Action under Conditions of International Capital Mobility', *Policy Sciences*, vol. 27 (1994), 447–66.
Strange, Susan, *The Retreat of the State: The Diffusion of Power in the World Economy* (Cambridge: Cambridge University Press, 1996).
Weiss, Linda, *The Myth of the Powerless State* (Ithaca: Cornell University Press, 1998).
Williamson, John (ed.), *The Political Economy of Policy Reform* (San Francisco: Institute of International Economics, 1994).
Zysman, John, *Governments, Markets and Growth: Financial Systems and the Politics of Industrial Change* (Ithaca: Cornell University Press, 1983).

6
Alternative Models of Capitalism

Introduction

Advanced capitalist economies that had experienced postwar growth and stability faced an economic crisis in the 1970s. In earlier chapters of this study, I note that in response to this crisis, Anglo-American countries pursued neoliberalism (Kitschelt et al., 1999), while others, because of their distinct social systems of production, avoided it. That distinctive response between countries led to the acknowledging of comparative capitalisms called liberal market economies (LMEs) and coordinated market economies (CMEs). In examining the adjustments to the crisis, some studies focused on Fordist–Keynesian systems of mass production, signifying the dominance of the Anglo-American model while noting its inability to contain inherent contradictions (Harvey, 1990). Piore and Sabel (1984) claim the cause of the economic crisis of the 1970s is deeper – that is, 'it results from the limits of the model of industrial development that is founded on mass production'. The reaction to the Fordist model of mass production identified as post-Fordist or flexible specialization was seen as an alternative accumulation regime in response to saturation of markets.

If the crisis is to be overcome, Piore and Sabel (1984) suggest that technologies and the operating procedures of most modern corporations need to be discarded or modified. Such crises arise when existing institutions can no longer secure a workable match between production and consumption of goods. Or, they may be concerned with the choice of technology (Piore and Sabel, 1984). The first refers 'to the institutional circuits that connect production and consumption as regulatory mechanisms; we call the disruptions of these circuits regulation crises. The two major regulation crises in the epoch of mechanized production

are associated with the rise of the large corporations in the late nineteenth century, and of the Keynesian welfare state in the 1930s' (pp. 4–5). The second crisis relates to the choice of technology. 'The brief moments when the path of technological development itself is at issue we call industrial divides... Industrial divides are therefore the backdrop or frame for subsequent regulation crises' (p. 5).

The emergence of mass production in the nineteenth century in the United Kingdom and United States has been described by Piore and Sabel (1984) as the first industrial divide, occurring when other less rigid manufacturing technologies, which had coexisted until then in Western Europe, were facing restrictions. These less rigid technologies were the craft systems, the more advanced of which produced a range of products for diversified markets using general purpose machines and skilled labour. Overtaken by mass production in the first industrial divide, this type of flexible production technology re-emerged in the second industrial divide to counter the decline of industrial economies in the 1970s, when markets for mass products started to decline (Piore and Sabel, 1984). According to Piore and Sabel (1984) this offered opportunities for small firms to exploit the new technology and specialized markets for diverse products. They predicted that a network of small firms in the form of industrial districts similar to the nineteenth-century industrial districts that existed prior to the first industrial divide were likely to emerge.

The survival of craft or small firms amid the success of mass production can be explained by the theory of dualism and the fact that 'the special purpose machinery required for mass production cannot itself be mass produced' (Piore and Sabel, 1984, p. 27). Such machinery is designed for specific customer needs with a limited market. 'Because the product is a speciality with a limited market, production must be continually reorganized; and workers must have the range of skills and general understanding of the process that are classically attributed to preindustrial artisans. Thus industrialization should, according to the dualism theory, revitalize part of the craft sector reorienting it toward its own ends' (Piore and Sabel, 1984 p. 27).

While this to some extent justifies the perception for the dualists of craft production as a complement to mass production, it does not, according to Piore and Sabel (1984), do justice to the famous industrial districts of the nineteenth century. 'The technological dynamism of both these large and small firms defies the notion that craft production must be either a traditional or subordinate form of economic activity. It suggests instead, that there is a craft alternative to mass production as a model of technologial advance' (p. 28).

Industrial districts are defined by three mutually dependent characteristics. The first is their relation to markets through the production of a range of goods for regional markets at home and abroad which are constantly adapted to changing tastes. Such a relationship has encouraged the next two characteristics: 'their flexible use of increasingly productive, widely applicable technology and their creation of regional institutions that balanced cooperation and competition among firms, so as to encourage permanent innovation' (p. 29).

Despite the inevitable progress of industrialization and the gradual adoption of mass production by industrialized countries, the vitality and survival instincts of industrial districts ensured that they succeeded in staying afloat by adapting to changing consumer demand. In contrast, the downturn of the 1970s showed that, regardless of the efforts at cost reduction, downsizing or government protection, standardized systems of production for mass consumption were incompatible with changing markets (Hollingsworth, 1997). One consequence of this was the rapid spread of flexible production in some mass-scale industries but more so in small-scale industries. Several studies have since raised questions about the viability of large industrial organizations, once seen as the natural evolution of modern capitalism (Herrigel, 1996; Sabel and Zeitlin, 1997).

This chapter explores industrial districts identified here as 'alternative capitalism' by looking into their history in the next section. The third section discusses the significant characteristics of such districts to try to understand why they differ from other types of industrial enterprises. Having differentiated these from the Fordist type, in the fourth section I discuss various types of industrial districts from the perspective of their unique historical and institutional context. I then examine specific cases in terms of industry and country to analyse whether the social embeddedness thesis is applicable. In the final section (as a conclusion) I take a look at alternative capitalism as competing or complementary in nature to the type of industrial capitalism discussed thus far in this study.

Historical evolution

While specialized small production or 'alternative capitalism' has existed since the first industrial revolution, its recognition as a viable force is attributable to Piore and Sabel (1984) (also see Sabel and Zeitlin, 1997). Alfred Marshall (1919) is credited with the initial use of the term 'industrial district', commonly used in the literature to identify

concentrated centres of production. An industrial district is a 'socio-territorial entity which is characterised by the active presence of both a community of people and a population of firms in one naturally and historically bounded area' (Dei Otati, 1994, p. 530). In attempting to explain why specialized products such as pottery or cutlery became identified with certain places like Staffordshire or Sheffield in England, Marshall points to physical causes such as climate or quality of soil or the existence of mines or quarries in the neighbourhood. Another explanation is the existence of patronage where demand from the rich for goods of high quality attracted skilled workpeople to a particular area. In tracing the historical origins of such enterprises, Marshall notes:

> the greater part of England's manufacturing industry before the era of cotton and steam had its course directed by settlements of Flemish and Huguenot artisans; many of which were made under the immediate direction of Plantagenet and Tudor kings. These immigrants taught us how to weave woollen and worsted stuffs, though for a long time we sent our clothes to the Netherlands to be fulled and dyed. They taught us how to cure herrings, how to manufacture silk, how to make lace, glass, and paper, and to provide for many other of our wants.
> (Marshall, 1919, p. 152)

Other factors that are seen to have facilitated the development of industrial districts are underlying social conditions, such as the existence of a religious minority, a common ethnic base, common craft pride or common political affiliation. 'Without some forms of common social bonds, it has historically been difficult to develop the collective institutions which are prerequisites for social systems of flexible production' (Hollingsworth and Boyer, 1997, p. 26).

While Marshall (1919) enumerates the reasons for the association of certain areas with certain specialized products, historical analysis of various industrial districts reveals how contextual factors have influenced the strategic decisions of actors. In areas like Prato in Italy or Lyons in France which specialized in small-scale production, foreign models of mass production were deemed inappropriate for local circumstances. Swiss watchmakers or Soligen cutlers admired the standardization of mass produced goods in America but found it incompatible with the organization of their markets (Sabel and Zeitlin, 1997, p. 12). In Switzerland, where the mountainous terrain had rendered bulk transportation very difficult if not impossible, precision skill emerged to compensate for the lack of mineral resources so abundant in other areas like the Ruhr. In

the late 1960s the Indian government established a watch manufacturing unit in Kashmir for similar reasons (Mascarenhas, 1982).

Footloose capital is a phenomenon of globalization. By contrast, traditional industries identified with a region or a district have deep roots and a distinct history, and are institutionalized within local society. When one refers to context, one is actually speaking about social embeddedness. According to Marshall (1919):

> When an industry has thus chosen a locality for itself, it is likely to stay there long: so great are the advantages which people following the same skilled trade get from near neighbourhood to one another. The mysteries of the trade become no mysteries; but are as it were in the air, and children learn many of them unconsciously. Good work is rightly appreciated; inventions and improvements in machinery, in processes and the general organization of the business have their merits promptly discussed; if one man starts a new idea it is taken up by others and combined with suggestions of their own, and thus becomes the source of further new ideas. (pp. 152–3)

With the literature on modern industrial capitalism focusing on large-scale manufacturing in countries such as the United States, Britain and Germany (Chandler Jr, 1990), the task of rescuing industrial districts or 'alternative capitalism' from virtual oblivion has fallen on scholars whose recent work has enriched our understanding of their role in industrialized economies (Piore and Sabel, 1984; Herrigel, 1996; Sabel and Zeitlin, 1997). One such study (Herrigel, 1996) revises our understanding of industrial districts in Germany where the immersion of industries in their social surroundings has somewhat blurred the boundary between firm and society. In exploring the range of industries covered by industrial districts, Herrigel (1996) disputes the 'organised capitalism' label attributed to Germany by Gershenkron (1962). According to Herrigel (1996), in the decentralized form of industrial order 'production and its governing institutions grew to be embedded in a dense network of relations among and between producers and public and private institutions in particular regional political economies.... To a large extent, local governments and producers in these regions created their own savings and cooperative banks, the latter pooling capital from among the many family owned small-scale industrial establishments in the community' (p. 20).

In the context of the growing power of mass production through large-scale organization, the continued vitality for over two hundred

years in specialist production like silk in Lyons, textiles in Prato and cutlery in Soligen is intriguing and has attracted the attention of researchers like Sabel and Zeitlin (1997) and Herrigel (1996). While large-scale organizations tend to draw boundaries around a factory or a firm and thus isolate or separate themselves generally from the community, the industrial district's sustenance is its community or region. This relationship becomes so important that the enterprise and the community virtually merge. Such close association, described as 'social systems of production' when fully developed, explains why well-known industries such as textiles in Prato are reluctant to move even when local governments try to entice them with a range of incentives (Hollingsworth, 1997, p. 26). As long as these industries remain craft based, their major resource base for skills and raw materials will remain local.

Herrigel's (1996) explanation for their survival as diffuse and decentralized industrial districts despite the onset of factory production is the specialist orientation of producers and the broad distribution of small property holders. 'Specialization demanded flexibility and flexibility made the extension of fixed costs in production always a risk. Consequently expansion and growth in individual firms tended always to be accompanied by decentralization (subcontracting of outworkers and so on). In effect firms grew by spreading their risks onto one another. The growth of the firm was inseparable from the growth of an industry, the growth of an industry inseparable from the growth of a region' (p. 48).

Herrigel uses the concept of 'constructivist political economy' to explain change occurring through the reconstruction of existing institutions rather than their complete replacement. Continuity plays an important role alongside the vitality needed to adapt to changes in fashion, technology and the market. Illustrative of this is the ability of producers to purchase their own materials when the merchants, from whom they once received materials as outworkers, disappeared. An important outcome of this was that their output which until then had been coordinated by merchant capitalists had to be coordinated by the producers themselves. As a result they 'gradually came to deal with one another as independent specialists, each capable of performing a crucial operation in the production of a regional product' where relations had to be negotiated with a common end in purpose (Herrigel, 1996, p. 51).

In the absence of a directing centre, producers reached an understanding built on ties of honour and loyalty. This was followed by the establishment of vocational and technical training institutes and cooperative regional banks to assist with capital, labour and technical knowledge. Such action by a group of independent producers to establish a network

of mutually beneficial institutions illustrates the regional character of industrial districts (Herrigel, 1996). Unlike the neoclassical concept of a business as an independent operation, in industrial districts, 'each producer understood itself as a specialist among specialists, all of whom together were engaged in the production of the output of an industry.... For individual producers, this was a collective, industrial, regional problem, not an individual one' (Herrigel, 1996, p. 52).

The role played by regional government through such change was significant. To the neoliberal concept of the economic human being as a self-interested opportunist, a regional or decentralized economy of individual producers, organizing institutions for research and training, and setting up cooperative banks for credit with the support of local or regional government, seems alien. One is led to understand that such cooperation cannot be sustained by calculating agents seeking to exploit an opportunity:

> What is exceptional in these cases, the argument goes, is precisely that because of some accident of socialization the agents' interests are so synchronized or their sense of solidarity and mutual responsibility so strong that they do not calculate the cost and benefits of exchanges amongst themselves in a normal way. In particular each forbears from exploiting the vulnerability of the other parties to an exchange and knows that this forbearance will be reciprocated. This forbearance is called trust and hence trust is considered a historically given cement of society that makes possible a contractual regime which could not arise spontaneously from an antecedent chain of contracts.
> (Sabel and Zeitlin, 1997, p. 22)

The historical analysis of industrial districts attempted in this chapter provides a background for a discussion of their characteristics so as to distinguish them from other forms of industrial enterprise.

Comparing types of industrial production

The continued survival and vitality of industrial districts despite the dominance of mass production demands a comparative analysis of their respective characteristics. Traditional economic analysis, which relies on responses to price signals as the sole mechanism, ignores the influence of technical and social institutions. One factor not to be overlooked is that the organization of production needs to be tailored to the type of economic conditions. Under stable economic conditions

it is economical for investors to set up large vertically integrated firms, whose production of outputs is fed into the next process as inputs. Thus long-linked technology is based on an interdependent process. The equipment required for such mass production involves a huge investment to achieve economies of scale. Such equipment cannot be turned to any other use when demand for a product declines or changes. Therefore if an economy is more volatile it may be worthwhile for an investor to organize different aspects of production in separate businesses, thus allowing the producer the flexibility to adapt to shifts in demand and reduce the risk of retaining assets to a minimum. Specialized businesses with generalized capacities are likely to contract with one another to produce what the market demands (Sabel and Zeitlin, 1997, pp. 20–1). While the two systems of production represent basic responses to markets, it is apparent that the mass production model flourishes in the United States. Hollingsworth (1997) attributes this to the size of the economy and to the consequent difficulties of bringing together innumerable interested parties into a social system of collective coordination. Unlike smaller economies the United States economy is complex with uneven levels of development, and much racial, ethnic and religious diversity. 'When these societywide collective forms of coordination are either absent or weak, markets and hierarchies are more prominent as forms of coordination, and as a result Fordist systems of production are more likely to occur' (p. 29). While the model was successful under the postwar consensus, its limitations became obvious during the 1970s crisis when such firms, accustomed to stability, suddenly found themselves struggling in an even less certain world (Piore and Sabel, 1984, p. 16).

As domestic demand for mass produced consumer durables became increasingly saturated, industrialized economies were left with the option of expanding trade or becoming globalized. This response reflects the low level of technological innovation associated with mass production where new product development requires extensive retooling. While producers are able to anticipate the precise cost of retooling, they are, however, unable to anticipate its likely benefits. In such a situation Piore and Sabel (1984) believe that investors become cautious and prefer to reduce costs through downsizing rather than reduce wages or seek government protection.

While large-scale manufacturers desperately sought ways to weather the crisis of the 1970s, regional economies in the 'Third Italy' and Baden Wurttemberg in West Germany developed new products such as speciality steel, precision machine tools, luxury shoes, motor bikes, furniture

and ceramics (pp. 205–6). The differing response to the industrial crisis from the craft industries highlights the importance of flexible technology that can adapt to a more volatile market and to social systems of production. A significant outcome was that small-scale operators, who had merely survived as sub-contractors, quite suddenly entered a period of prosperity. Observing the phenomenal growth of regional economies and the adoption of the craft model as a reaction to the crisis of the 1970s, Piore and Sabel offer an explanation for the adoption of mass production in some countries. They suggest that craft production was conserved to a greater extent in some countries than in others.

In later sections of the chapter I examine how such industrial districts operate and the characteristics that set them apart from other forms of industrial enterprise. While Europe and Japan adopted some large-scale production, they also retained some craft type characteristics, making it easier to respond to the crisis of the 1970s. Another explanation offered is the influence of cultural diversity on the type of consumer demands between Europe and the United States. That such districts are more likely to emerge in Europe rather than the United States is due to the persistence of some remnants of flexible specialization, albeit subordinate to mass production. If the 'feudal blessings' and 'feudal shackles' theses suggests the absence of ideological diversity in the United States and its presence in Europe (Hirschman, 1986), the theory of cultural diversity may be used to explain the homogeneity of tastes in the United States and their diversity in Europe. This last point is demonstrated by American acceptance and European rejection of machine-made cutlery. 'Conversely, one reason for the persistence of the specialized industrial district in Europe was the diversity of continental taste. This diversity of taste was perpetuated by producers' and retailers' education of consumers to appreciate the fine distinction among products' (Piore and Sabel, p. 190).

Another interesting comparison is the linkage between development of railroads and the distribution of mass produced consumer goods through departmental stores such as Sears Roebuck and Montgomery Ward in the United States and Bon Marche in France: 'unlike its American analogue, the French department store drew on highly flexible industrial districts to produce its wares, often to its own specifications; and the Bon Marche and other *grands magasins* provided their clients with the opportunity to customize these goods still further with extensive in-store alterations. Such stores used the railroad network to make the flexible production capacities of the scattered districts more accessible to the country as a whole, rather than to homogenize the market' (Piore and Sabel, 1984, p. 329).

Characteristics of industrial districts

In the context of the dominance of mass production, any study of industrial districts is necessarily an attempt to distinguish this form of production from other types of enterprise. Piore (1992) reiterates two distinguishing characteristics of industrial districts identified in most studies: their technological dynamism and their peculiar combination of cooperation and competition (p. 308).

Underlying these common characteristics one observes a special setting in which they thrive. In the absence of a clear directing centre, the working of industrial districts is monitored by ties of honour and loyalty. That they thrive in some regions and not in others is attributable to the social structure or community in which they are embedded. It has already been noted that the existence of raw materials or skills specific to an industry in a particular area contributes to the origin of industrial districts. A cooperative environment derived from the social structure comprised of family, religion and political parties is also instrumental in ensuring their development and survival. As I intend to discuss the success of industrial districts in certain countries in a separate section of this chapter, I will at this stage confine my analysis to their general characteristics.

Industrial districts enjoy a common discourse about the productive process and are often likened to a language community (Piore, 1992). Their existence over long periods while giving the impression of stability does not reveal their constant state of flux, as they try several products, some of which succeed while others fail. The risk of failure engineers a combination of cooperation and competition with pressure to enter into subcontracting arrangements. Although bankruptcies are a frequent occurrence, they tend not to affect an enterprise's future (Piore, 1992, p. 309).

The close association between different producers sharing common interests and values and interacting frequently within a community or a territorial region is described as a network. Within such a network, producers visit each other's premises and discuss problems without the fear of commercially sensitive information being divulged. Such networks are characterized by a high level of trust and, in effect, are the foundation for cooperation. Termed 'social capital' by Coleman (1988), such trust is typified in the transactions between diamond merchants in Brooklyn where the wholesale market in diamonds is dominated by the close-knit Jewish community. Just as one dealer can trust another with his bag of diamonds, small producers in industrial districts treat each

other with openness, holding no trade secrets from each other (Piore, 1992). Again this resembles the mutual obligations that characterize relations between manufacturers and suppliers in the textile industry in Japan (Dore, 1983). Thus trust is central to the functioning of industrial districts. 'Trust as a collective capital is largely a by-product of the common culture. And it is this culture that ensures the reproduction of this capital, at least in so far as decentralised social control remains effective' (Dei Otati, 1994, p. 532).

When one acknowledges that social structure or community is the foundation of successful industrial districts, then one must accept that prior socialization, be it ethnic, religious or political, is the logical explanation for the underlying cooperation between producers in industrial districts. While that explanation is supported by the success of some regions where religion and political parties have influenced their functioning, a more plausible explanation is the need for continuous adaptation and change to achieve product differentiation. The interrelationship between social structure and the successful functioning of industrial districts questions the basic assumption of classical political economists that the economy is separate from society (Piore and Sabel, 1984, p. 275; Weiss, 1988, p. 203).

To understand the changed work environment in industrial districts in which workers take greater initiative in the absence of direct supervision, Piore (1992) uses Arendt's three modes of productive activity – labour, work and action. The distinction is based on the durability of the product. Labour has to do with meeting one's basic needs, that is, survival. Work is identified with producing a durable product that outlives the producer or creator, such as a work of art. Action involves a relationship among human beings, an activity in which individuals reveal themselves to others and through which they achieve meaning as persons. Action involves a community of people who are assumed to be equal and among whom discourse can take place – that is, a context for their actions (pp. 312–13). While mass production turned work into labour, the revival of craft in industrial districts indicates that 'labour is now being transformed into action' (Piore, 1992, p. 314). 'Certain characteristics of districts, which otherwise appear irrelevant or even contradictory, become self-evident once production is conceived as the arena of action. The openness of the production process and of the innovations in the instruments of production become almost a prerequisite for their existence' (p. 314). Thus by looking at industrial districts as arenas of action, 'the paradox of competition and cooperation, which is so central in every characterization of these districts, also dissolves' (p. 314).

The socially embedded nature of industrial districts is constantly highlighted in numerous studies. In the face of a constantly changing market, producers have had to make flexible use of productive machinery, create cooperative institutions that balanced cooperation with competition, and experiment with new products (Piore and Sabel, 1984). Gradually these districts have emerged as centres of specialized products identified with particular regions. The institutional framework supporting the ability of industries to constantly innovate are municipalism, welfare capitalism and familialism (Piore and Sabel, 1984).

Municipalism refers to territorially dispersed centres of production comprised of a confederation of small shops each specializing in a phase of production. To guarantee mobility of resources, the municipality protected firms from market changes, provided access to skills, policed competition by ensuring quality under a local trademark, and oversaw a system of wage-stabilization, wage cutting and price wars (Piore and Sabel, 1984). In some areas where social democratic ideals influenced workers, municipalities controlled the length of the working day, supplied power, and played an active role in improving health and working conditions (Piore and Sabel, 1984). In areas where a large number of producers worked collectively in large factory-like premises producing a range of products, a type of welfarism operated, including initiatives such as maternity care, worker housing, public baths, old-age homes and savings societies. 'The purpose was to make the company town into a community in which artisan skills, scientific knowledge, and artistic imagination were continually regenerated and advanced' (Piore and Sabel, 1984, p. 34).

That small-scale specialized producers survived the onslaught of mass production through such large-scale organization is a tribute to their vitality, a vitality attributed to the supply of specialized markets of consumers worldwide instead of the large-scale sector (the dualist argument). In order to compete and survive in a hostile world, producers cooperated by spreading the risks and sharing common facilities. Such sharing led to the description of producers as 'cooperative enterprises'. A critical concept in understanding industrial districts is the notion of a community of equals. 'Only within such a community can one differentiate one's self: if the other members of the community are not like one, they cannot appreciate one's differences.... Such a community must be relatively small, small enough so that its members can see and know each other as persons...and explains why we are looking at relatively limited and contained geographical areas' (Piore, 1992, p. 315).

The functioning of industrial districts

Any industrial or economic enterprise involves relationships between people who engage in producing, buying, selling or working. These relationships are governed by historical and cultural influences particular to a region or community. Barring exceptions, one can categorize business-type relations of the Anglo-American type as being more adversarial and more opportunistic in terms of promoting one's self-interest, while interactions are likely to be formal or contractual and in Adam Smith's oft-quoted words 'not from the benevolence of the butcher, brewer or baker' (Dore, 1983, p. 459). An alternative mode of business relationship practised in Japanese business (and in some industrial districts) is based on cooperation and mutual obligation of trust in which 'goodwill and give and take is likely to temper the pursuit of self-interest'. Goodwill includes 'sentiments of friendship and the sense of diffuse personal obligation which accrue between individuals engaged in recurring contractual economic exchange' (Dore, 1983, pp. 459–60). Speaking of Europe, Sabel refers to the experience of the civil wars of the 1920s and 1930s, concluding 'Yet all today enjoy, reasonably, in the light of their economic performance, a reputation of putting to productive use a national culture of cooperation which is itself a source of national pride and identity' (1997, p. 341).

Mass production and flexible production co-existed until the 'first industrial divide' when mass production technology became dominant and limited the growth of industrial districts that had existed in Europe in the nineteenth century. Their revival in the 1970s when mass production experienced a setback with the energy crisis has been termed the 'second industrial divide' (Piore and Sabel, 1984), which saw the revival of industrial districts involving networks of small enterprises. Using a range of machinery, the industrial districts promote skill and cater to a diverse market. Such flexible quality production involves changes in shop-floor processes and in industrial relations so as to encourage greater involvement of the workforce in a system regarded as continuously innovative. Such institutional change and innovation are possible because of the social environment of industrial districts characterized as:

1. a common culture identified with people living in a historically bounded area
2. frequent face-to-face interactions of residents of an area with a common culture

3. a society governed by norms of reciprocity accompanied by social sanctions; and
4. the practice of self-help, which is important for economic dynamism. (Dei Otati, 1994, pp. 530–1)

A significant characteristic of such socio-economic organizations is the reciprocal cooperation that governs relationships between firms in the district. If such cooperation generates a high enough level of trust in transactions, it can reduce the need for monitoring and reduce costs. According to Dei Otati, 'Even if limited, trust based on the custom of co-operation constitutes a collective capital, available to all members of the district, and is of considerable economic importance' (1994, p. 532). However, social sanctions, which may be effective in a small homogeneous community, are insufficient to guarantee conformity in a large industrial district. These then need to be complemented by a set of local institutions, such as political parties, local government, trade unions and local entrepreneurial associations to ensure cooperation in support of the collective capital of trust (Dei Otati, 1994, p. 532).

When business is conducted on a face-to-face basis or where contracts are incomplete, reputation plays an important part in establishing and maintaining relationships. For example, a reliable reputation may facilitate the process of obtaining credit to set up a new business. 'There are many transactions which can only be carried out if trust between contracting parties is not limited to respect of the custom of reciprocal co-operation, but it is also based on a knowledge of the personal, moral and professional characteristics of the other party' (Dei Otati, 1994, p. 533). Like other forms of capital, including social capital (Coleman, 1988), 'Trust based on reputation, as distinct from trust based on custom, to which it is eventually added, is therefore personal capital with its own particular characteristic' (Dei Otati, 1994, p. 533). In Dore's terminology this is characterized as 'moralized trading relationships of mutual goodwill' (1983, p. 463).

That industrial districts operate on a different set of assumptions such as cooperation, trust and reputation as against the neoclassical assumptions of competition, self-interest, opportunism and contractualism, raises questions about the distinct social environment of business in the two systems. One is implicit, informal and long-term, while the other is explicit, formal and short-term. Stability of relationships to provide certainty in industrial districts is different from the language of risk taking and uncertainty in the neoclassical competitive firm. While one focuses on flexible specialization and produces a wide array

of products using skilled labour, the other produces standardized products using special purpose machines and unskilled labour.

The underlying assumptions on which the industrial district functions makes it 'incompatible with the neoliberal regime of unregulated markets and cut-throat competition.... In each of its institutional forms, flexible specialization depends for its long-term success on an irreducible minimum of trust and co-operation among economic actors, both between managers and workers within the firm and between firms and their external sub-contractors' (Hirst and Zeitlin, 1991, p. 7). Alternative capitalism, as I have described it, is an attempt to counter the neoliberal vision of the economy where individuals are autonomous actors in a competitive market in which the local community is gradually losing control as a result of globalization. 'The most striking point of conflict between the liberal vision and the new reality is the network organization and the way in which they depend, not upon autonomous economic actors, but upon the interaction of individual actors embedded in a social network' (Piore, 1995, p. 85).

Industrial districts: unique or universal?

The fact that industrial districts predominate in Europe, particularly in Italy and Germany, has prompted questions about the scope for replication elsewhere. One can identify the characteristics of their functioning as I have attempted in this chapter. Is it possible, however, for them to be adopted in a different historical and institutional context ? As industrial districts seem to thrive in specific political, social and institutional contexts, one doubts their capacity to adapt elsewhere, especially in the absence of such conditions. Learning and transferability of knowledge and skills rests on whether they are codified or tacit. The latter is less easily transferable from localized to other settings where the cultural and institutional context differs. 'What is not ubiquified, however, is the non-tradable/non-codified result of knowledge creation – the embedded tacit knowledge – that at a given time can only be produced in practice. The fundamental exchange inability of this type of knowledge increases its importance as the internationalization of markets proceeds' (Maskell and Malmberg, 1999, p. 172). Tacit knowledge is a product of a region's history, culture, religion, political traditions and other basic values. Together they combine to form 'institutional endowment', 'embracing all the rules, practices, routines, habits, traditions, customs and conventions associated with the regional supply of capital, land, labour and the regional market for goods and services' (Maskell and Malmberg, 1999, p. 173).

The research undertaken thus far attempts to synthesize various elements of the model, drawing largely from the Italian experience. However in attempting to replicate a model, apart from the issues already noted, there are certain other weaknesses in studies that must be taken into consideration. These are: (1) their observations are valid only at a given point of time, (2) the nature of the research tends to be prescriptive, (3) ignorance of factors outside the control of managers responsible for an enterprise, and (4) ignorance of the institutional support received by such enterprises (Humphry, 1995, pp. 151–2). The other aspect that one notes from the recent literature on industrial districts is their dominance in specific parts of countries, such as Third Italy, and their predominance in some industries like textiles, watch-making, cutlery, shoes and machine tools. Two issues that need explanation are: one, whether small enterprise or micro-capitalism is specific to some industries, and two, the reasons for their survival in some countries and not in others. Both questions while interrelated are open to different explanations.

Considering the first issue of the existence of any relationship between types of industries and size, the three important characteristics of specialization, flexibility and sub-contracting associated with industrial districts seem appropriate to small rather than large enterprises. In the case of large enterprises demands of transaction costs encourage direct control of operations while production of mass standardized products reduces the scope for flexibility and specialization. Flexibility is achieved through adaptation of the labour force to changing demands and specialization through breaking up production into phases using home workers. Increasing specialization and flexibility within a particular district leads to cooperation between producers and a need to off-load or sub-contract. Such cooperation between producers becomes a valued commodity in a community as actual benefits in the form of trust, reputation and stability emerge.

Factors such as the small-scale nature of operations such as cutlery, shoes, textiles, and watch-making explain why micro-capitalism has survived and indeed thrives in countries like Italy or Germany when compared with the United States. Other factors strongly associated with small-scale enterprises are the role of the family and the local social structure. Here we are focusing on the particular context, the institutional endowments that favour this type of enterprise. Weiss (1988) identifies two other influences for this preference for micro-capitalism in Italy – these are, the Christian Democratic Party and the role of the labour movement (p. 105). Christian Democrats strive to bring capital and labour together, in such a way that capital is not seen as an op-

pressor and labour not as a rebel. 'To be a collaborator rather than an agitator required a sense of dignity and responsibility; and for Christian Democracy there could be no productive form more respondent to the dignity of individuals and more suited to develop in them a sense of responsibility than the small-scale business' (Weiss, 1988, p. 108). Following the war in Italy, the state promoted small-scale enterprises through special credit and tax schemes. Compared with other forms of enterprise, small-scale units of production are better at achieving efficiency and promoting personal development for its workers. By working alongside their employees, the distinction between owners and workers erodes as they relate to each other at a personal level. Working conditions are humane, dignity is protected and a sense of responsibility is encouraged (Weiss, 1988, pp. 110–11).

If the cohesive characteristic of small firms offered a political rationale for adopting such a policy in Italy, Weiss (1988) asks why France did not, under similar political conditions, adopt a small firm policy. The answer lies in their respective objectives. While France saw industrial organization as a means to further its political power as a nation, in Italy it was seen as a means to promote the political framework and the power of Christian Democracy. 'To this end, small business and – as we shall see – the public enterprise sector became the two key pillars, the former providing its social and moral force, the latter its power base' (p. 138).

While Weiss (1988) attributes the success of industrial districts in Italy and their economic progress to the Christian Democrats' philosophy of cooperation between capital and labour, Putnam attributes economic cooperation and prosperity to civic engagement – that is, social capital. Putnam notes the difference in the level of civic engagement in regions of north and south Italy, where mutual aid societies ranging from neighbourhood associations to choral groups have existed over the years. Observing the difference between regions, Putnam notes how the industrial districts are concentrated in the northern region. In Putnam's words:

> Typically singled out as essential for the success of industrial districts, in Italy and beyond, are norms of reciprocity and networks of civic engagement. Networks facilitate flows of information about technological developments, about the credit-worthiness of would be entrepreneurs, about the reliability of individual workers, and so on. Innovation depends on 'continual informal interaction in cafes and bars and in the street'. Social norms that forestall opportunism are so deeply internalized that the issue of opportunism at the expense of

community obligation is said to arise less often here than in areas characterized by vertical and clientelistic networks. What is crucial about these small-firm industrial districts, conclude most observers, is mutual trust, social cooperation, and well-developed sense of civic duty – in short, the hallmarks of the civic community.

(Putnam, 1992, p. 161)

While extensive studies of industrial districts have focused on Italy and Germany, there is, however, growing evidence of similar clusters in France, Switzerland, Denmark and India specializing in industries such as textiles and watch-making. Silicon Valley and Route 128 in the United States merit inclusion, incorporating as they do some of the characteristics associated with industrial districts. As in Italy, political parties and organized interest associations played an important role in creating a balanced system of rules and service-providing institutions. For example, in Denmark the success of the economy in the late nineteenth century and early twentieth was attributed to 'joint control of vocational training by labour and capital; agrarian reform in favour of small holders; a shift in tax burden from landed, particularly agricultural property to intangible capital; and in the crisis of the 1930s a series of elaborate horse-trades and compromises by the various political parties to respect the rights of groups represented by the others to maintain their way of life' (Sabel and Zeitlin, 1997, pp. 25–6). 'If there was any country where the historical alternative to mass production was successful enough to be treated as a matter of fact, Denmark was' (Kristensen and Sabel, 1997, p. 346).

Conclusion

This discussion of alternative capitalism may appear strange when the past two decades (1979–99) have witnessed the ascendancy of neoliberalism and market capitalism of the Anglo-American variant. The alternative that I discuss is small-scale and medium-sized enterprise based on craft and flexible technology, successfully adopted in Denmark, Italy, Sweden, Switzerland and Germany. Industries such as watch-making, silk, textiles, pottery, cutlery and machine tools appear to adopt a distinctive organizational culture in which relations between owners and workers, enterprises and suppliers, operate on the basis of trust and cooperation. Identified with 'industrial districts', this culture has gained recognition with Piore and Sabel's *Second Industrial Divide* (1984).

In recognizing the survival of industrial districts as an alternative and not as an appendage to large corporations, one has to note the involvement of the state and other institutions, like local banks, municipalities, political parties and educational institutions. These small firms which until recently were close to extinction due to the dominance of large-scale mass production have been resurrected through a variety of combinations, prompting Sabel and Zeitlin (1997) to comment that 'it is as though the prehistoric and imaginary creatures in the industrial bestiary had suddenly come to life' (p. 3). Having noted their unique characteristics, I explore the reasons for their success in Italy, and conclude with Weiss (1988) that it is a product of Christian Democracy which discourages excesses of capital and labour. From this analysis one has to acknowledge the significance of historical and social context to understand why a certain type of institution can thrive in a certain area. To transplant an institution outside a specific context is difficult, if not impossible.

References

Chandler Jr, Alfred, *Scale and Scope: The Dynamics of Industrial Capitalism* (Cambridge: Belknap Press, 1990).
Coleman, James S., 'Social Capital in the Creation of Human Capital', *American Journal of Sociology*, vol. 94 (Supplement) (1988), S95–S120.
Dei Otati, Gabi, 'Trust, Interlinking Transactions and Credit in the Industrial District', *Cambridge Journal of Economics*, vol. 18 (1994), 529–46.
Dore, Ronald, 'Goodwill and the Spirit of Market Capitalism', *British Journal of Sociology*, vol. 34 (1983), 459–82.
Gershenkron, Alexander, *Economic Backwardness in Historical Perspective* (Cambridge: Harvard University Press, 1962).
Hall, Peter and David Soskice (eds), *Varieties of Capitalism: Comparative Advantage of Institutions* (Oxford: Oxford University Press, 2001).
Harvey, David, *The Conditions of Postmodernity: An Enquiry into the Origins of Cultural Change* (Oxford: Blackwell, 1990).
Herrigel, Gary, *Industrial Constructions: The Sources of German Industrial Power* (Cambridge: Cambridge University Press, 1996).
Hirschman, Albert, *Rival Interpretations of Market and Other Essays* (New York: Viking, 1986).
Hirst, Paul and Jonathan Zeitlin, 'Flexible Specialization versus Post-Fordism: Theory, Evidence and Policy Implications', *Economy and Society*, vol. 20 (1991), 1–55.
Hollingsworth, Rogers J., 'Variation among Nations in the Logic of Manufacturing Sectors and International Competitiveness', in Dominique Foray and Christopher Freeman (eds), *Technology and the Wealth of Nations: The Dynamics of Constructed Advantage* (London: Pinter Publishers, 1997).
Hollingsworth, Rogers J. and Robert Boyer, *Contemporary Capitalism: The Embeddedness of Institutions* (Cambridge: Cambridge University Press, 1997).

Humphry, John, 'Industrial Organization in Developing Countries: From Model to Trajectories', *World Development*, vol. 23 (1995), 149–62.

Kitschelt, Herbert *et al.* (eds), *Continuity and Change in Contemporary Capitalism* (Cambridge: Cambridge University Press, 1999).

Kristensen, Peer Hull and Charles Sabel, 'The Small-holder Economy in Denmark', in Charles F. Sabel and Jonathan Zeitlin (eds), *World of Possibilities: Flexibility and Mass Production in Western Industrialization* (Cambridge: Cambridge University Press, 1997), 344–78.

Marshall, Alfred, *Elements of Economics of Industry* (London: Macmillan, 1919).

Mascarenhas, Reginald C., *Technology Transfer and Development: India's Hindustan Machine Tool Company* (Boulder: Westview Press, 1982).

Maskell, Peter and Anders Malmberg, 'Localised Learning and Industrial Competitiveness', *Cambridge Journal of Economics*, vol. 23 (1999), 167–85.

Piore, Michael J., 'Work, Labor, and Action: Work Experience in a System of Flexible Production', in Thomas A. Kochan and Michael Useem (eds), *Transforming Organizations* (Oxford: Oxford University Press, 1992), 307–19.

Piore, Michael J., 'Local Development on the Progressive Political Agenda', in Colin Crouch and David Marquand (eds), *Re-Inventing Collective Action: From the Global to the Local* (Oxford: Blackwell, 1995), 79–87.

Piore, Michael J. and Charles F. Sabel, *The Second Industrial Divide: Possibilities for Prosperity* (New York: Basic Books, 1984).

Putnam, Robert, *Making Democracy Work* (Princeton: Princeton University Press, 1992).

Sabel, Charles F., 'Studied Trust: Building New Forms of Cooperation in a Volatile Economy', in Dominique Foray and Christopher Freeman (eds), *Technology and the Wealth of Nations: The Dynamics of Constructed Advantage* (London: Pinter Publishers, 1997), 333–52.

Sabel, Charles F. and Jonathan Zeitlin, *World of Possibilities: Flexibility and Mass Production in Western Industrialization* (Cambridge: Cambridge University Press, 1997).

Weiss, Linda, *Creating Capitalism: The State and Small Business since 1945–1985* (Oxford: Blackwell, 1988).

Part III
Comparative Studies of Modern Capitalism

7
Types of Capitalism: Anglo-American

Introduction

The relationship between the state and the market varies in mixed economies and changes constantly to cope with situations. Over a period of time, circumstances determine the dominance of one or the other in most democracies. While markets and authority play distinctive roles, their effectiveness, however, varies. Markets are proficient in making choices from innumerable options where price and incentives are involved, while authority is important in situations where, incentives being ineffective, compulsion may be necessary (Lindblom, 1977). With the upsurge of neoliberal ideas in the 1970s, markets have been presented as an alternative in place of the state in Anglo-American countries. However, countries like Germany and Japan have been as successful, if not more so, than Britain or the United States by adopting a pragmatic mix of state and market (Hollingsworth and Boyer, 1997).

In the 1970s and 1980s, both Japan and Germany were regarded as serious competitors to the United States. This threat led to serious soul-searching within the latter, causing considerable uncertainty. Such uncertainty was partly attributable to globalization as it effectively lowered restrictions on cross-border transactions and increased competition for capital. This pressure for capital and the growing influence of neoliberal ideology brought about a change in corporate orientation. Thus we witness a dramatic transformation in Anglo-American corporate culture from entrenched managerial capitalism or managerial control to greater emphasis on shareholder control (Fligstein, 2001). Having discussed in Chapters 5 and 6 the contradictory trends of globalization and flexible quality production (industrial districts), one notes that the shift in emphasis in Anglo-American corporations towards shareholder value

has brought pressure on the institutional foundations of the German 'social market' (Chapter 8) and the Japanese 'developmental state' (Chapter 9).

In this comparative study of industrial capitalism, my focus is on analysing the role of the state in the economy. In Chapter 3, I have clarified the state's distinct roles as political authority and economic agent. The state, characterized by political authority, is basic to any civilized society in which the rights of the citizen to freedom of choice, the fundamental right to property and so on are ensured through the exercise of coercive mechanisms over which the state has a monopoly. To ensure that such power is exercised with restraint and in the public interest, societies have developed appropriate political institutions in the form of representative democracy. By contrast, the role of the state as economic agent is contingent upon a variety of factors and the response to such factors is a product of several influences. That role emerged during the postwar consensus which accepted the Keynesian welfare state and legitimized its implications when the private sector indicated its willingness to work within the framework of rules and regulations developed by the state.

In earlier chapters, I have dealt with five broad themes. While the first dealt with the importance of adopting a political economy approach to the study of industrial capitalism, the second traced the underlying philosophical foundations governing the functioning of capitalism. The third discussed the role of the state in mixed economies and raised the issue of divergent or national types of capitalism, while the fourth traced the changing nature of capitalism from entrepreneurial to managerial capitalism with a specific analysis of large-scale mass production. Chapter 5 explored the emergence of globalization while Chapter 6 studied the survival and vitality of industrial districts or alternative capitalism. Having developed these broad themes in preceding chapters, I proceed, in the next part of this study, to analyse the three types of capitalism briefly touched upon in earlier chapters. Beginning with the Anglo-American model, which is examined in this chapter, the other two, the Rhenish or German 'social market' and the Japanese 'developmental state' are discussed in the next two chapters.

In analysing the Anglo-American model of capitalism I will, in the next section, offer a historical background by tracing its development and focusing on its association with freedom and democracy. The third section traces significant developments of the Anglo-American model of capitalism – the Fordist corporate device – and examines reasons for its decline in the 1970s. Following that, I discuss the evolution of the

mixed economy in which the state gradually emerged to play an active role in regulating and promoting business. The fifth section examines the post-Second World War performance of Anglo-American economies and how their decline in the 1970s was met with flexible specialization on the one hand and liberalization and privatization on the other. These responses are then discussed. In the final section, I conclude.

The historical background

The term 'Anglo-American' in this study is essentially a socio-economic, political and cultural category which incorporates the economic and political systems prevalent in English-speaking or Anglo-American western democracies. Accordingly, modern industrial capitalism that has prevailed in this group of countries (Australia, Britain, Canada, New Zealand and the United States) has been influenced by liberal philosophy wherein a free enterprise economy and individual freedom are closely related. This underlying relationship has, in turn, had implications for the functioning of their respective political systems (democratic) and economies, and it is this philosophical foundation based on the thinking of Adam Smith, J. S. Mill and others (see Chapter 2) that still influences the current debate on the role of the state in the economy. Individualism, which is the foundation of Anglo-American capitalism, advocates individual initiative and its promotion involves a restriction of state intervention. Expressed as a form of anti-state and pro-private enterprise, this view was particularly pronounced in the early history of the United States (Glassman, 1987; Ketcham, 1987).

While the philosophy of individualism is at the very basis of modern capitalism in Anglo-American countries, its development in Britain has differed from that of the United States (Moore Jr, 1966), with variations in Australia, Canada and New Zealand influenced by their unique history, indigenous resources and their values and culture. Despite subtle variations within their respective political and economic systems, one observes a common set of institutions governing business across such countries, warranting their inclusion in the Anglo-American category and distinguishing them from the Rhenish and Developmental States. While included as a group, our focus will primarily be on the United States, and, to some extent, on Britain.

Chandler Jr (1990) asserts that in any comparative historical study of modern industrial enterprise one must begin with the story of the United States, keeping in mind that country's role as the world's leading industrial nation (p. 47). This rapid advancement of modern industrial

enterprise in the United States, when compared with Britain and Germany, was due, in great measure, to the size of its domestic market. Having beaten the pioneer of the industrial revolution to second place early in the twentieth century, the United States was taken over by a culture of technocratic efficiency, attracting consumers of mass-produced standardized products. Enumerating certain social norms which he associates with a material culture of merchants, Hollingsworth (1997b) feels that the absence of an aristocracy explains the American acceptance of standardized mass production (p. 134).

The American system of manufacturing had emerged by the 1850s with the production of machinery. Landes (1998) explains its emergence as a creative response to two related factors: (1) a market free of the local and regional preferences and the class and status distinctions that prevailed in Europe, hence the readiness to accept standardized articles; and (2) the scarcity of labour relative to materials. In a labour-scarce economy, standardization was a way of dividing tasks, thereby simplifying and making them repetitive and substantially enhancing productivity (p. 301). Chandler Jr (1990) states that 'the interrelated investments in manufacturing, marketing and management made by these machinery producers, which were generally larger than those of the producers of branded, packaged products, brought such powerful advantages to the American first movers that they dominated world markets for decades' (p. 66). Thus individualism, combined with a consumer-oriented society, led to a type of capitalism that focused on:

- a short-term horizon on decisions catering to the share-market;
- continuous need to develop new products without the capacity for producing high-quality products;
- weak commitment to collective governance in the private sector but with a reliance on regulation by the state;
- a strong commitment to continuous economic change; and ,
- a weak commitment to economic equality. (Hollingsworth, 1997b, p. 133)

While the domestic market was instrumental in the advancement of industries in the United States, that very market later became an obstruction, constraining it from adaptation and innovation in its battle with Japan and Germany in the latter part of the twentieth century (Thurow, 1992). O'Sullivan (2000) questions the utility of neo-classical theory as a foundation with which to understand the governance of corporations. Neo-classical economics, she writes, 'was never designed

to deal with the innovation process, let alone the role of corporate resource allocation in that process' (p. 1). In questioning market control over allocation of resources advocated by economists of the neo-classical persuasion, O'Sullivan offers instead an organizational approach to corporate governance that can provide a framework for the analysis of institutional conditions which support the innovation process (2000, p. 4).

Managerial capitalism in the United States had taken root in industries essential to the health of the American economy by the time of the First World War. The expansion of modern industrial enterprise was encouraged by (a) an extensive domestic market, (b) the development of capital-intensive technologies for production, and (c) laws that prevented price and output arrangements between firms. These developments differed from the personal and family capitalism practised in Britain (Chandler Jr, 1990, p. 89) wherein entrepreneurs failed to make the three-pronged investment in manufacturing, marketing and management that characterized the development of capital-intensive industries in the United States. The management of British enterprises continued to be dominated by their founders, which proved detrimental in the long term.

Chandler Jr (1990) identifies three types of governance adopted by enterprises: (1) those administered without an extensive managerial hierarchy, termed personal enterprise, (2) the entrepreneurial or family-controlled enterprise where the founders hired professional managers but continued to be influential stockholders, and (3) the managerial enterprise where executives had no connection with the founders and little or no equity in the company. The term 'personally managed' is a description of British capitalism referring, first, to the system of governance, and second, to its culture or management style. That culture is described as the concentration of authority in a group located at a head office exercising close supervision and control over lower levels, the absence of a clear organizational structure, selection to top positions dependent on personal ties rather than competence and the retention of control over top-level decisions by the founders (Chandler Jr, 1990). Chandler Jr (1990) notes that the contrast in managerial styles was noticeable in the first half of the twentieth century. 'In the United States, salaried managers with little or no equity in the enterprise, who administered it through extensive managerial hierarchies, were making the critical coordinating and allocating decisions. In Britain those decisions were still being made by the major stockholders, who had inherited their positions and continued personally to manage their enterprises' (p. 249).

In attempting to explain this, Chandler Jr (1990) cites two important factors: first, the smaller size of the British domestic market when compared with that of the United States, causing business to rely on exports for expansion; and, second, Britain's continued reliance on the technology of the first industrial revolution for manufacturing and transportation while the United States and Germany were already using the telecommunication and transportation technology of the second industrial revolution (Chandler Jr, 1990). 'Precisely because Britain was the first urban industrialized nation, it became the world's first consumer society.... The small geographical size of the domestic market, its concentrated richness, and the excellent transportation system had as much impact as did legal, educational, and cultural factors on the continuing of personal management and personal capitalism in British industry' (Chandler Jr, 1990, pp. 251–2). The entrenched class distinctions into gentlemen (sons of owners) and players, the salaried or practically-oriented, were reflected in institutions of learning. Their response to the needs of modern industrial enterprise was slow when compared with both the United States and Germany. Apart from the late appearance of the educational infrastructure required for modern industry, it was clear that the industrial output of the United States and Germany was fast outpacing that of Britain (Chandler Jr, 1990, pp. 293–4). The lack or slowness of response in new processes in manufacturing and management in Britain is explained thus by Jones (1997): 'British managerial decision making drew on a personal value system which favoured financial, entrepreneurial, and trading business activities (such as many services), and was unfavourable to the kind of skills and mental outlook needed to succeed in activities involving complex tasks and long-term horizons (such as the new capital intensive industries)' (p. 112). This links up with Adam Smith's depiction of classical political economy based on the invisible hand which sought to promote what existed in Britain as a universal model of free enterprise. As Mann (1988) notes:

> From Adam Smith to Mrs Thatcher the connection has been made between national greatness and free competition, and it is correct – or at least it *was* correct. That is how Great Britain rose up. Unfortunately, however, these conditions of success were then institutionalized to become the core of British ruling class. When global economic realities changed, the British ruling class tightened up the institutions which had made them Great, leaving Britain trapped into a downward spiral of inappropriate institutional response to change. (p. 217)

Another plausible explanation for the decline of British economy is Mancur Olson's (1982) theory of distributional coalitions whereby the enjoyment by several associations of freedom with stability contributes to the low rate of growth. As a result, Britain suffers from institutional sclerosis that slows its adaptation to changing circumstances and technologies (p. 78). Failure by Britain to respond to technological and organizational changes in the early twentieth century as in the United States and Germany is attributable to 'its institutional legacy associated with atomistic, nineteenth century economic organization. Entrenched institutional structures – in industrial relations, enterprise and market organization, education, finance, international trade, and state–enterprise relations – constrained the transformation of Britain's productive system' (Elbaum and Lazonick, 1986, p. 2). In refuting the cultural conservatism argument for Britain's economic decline in the late nineteenth century, Elbaum and Lazonick (1986) offer instead the competitive capitalism of numerous firms with small market shares as the real problem. While Britain was consolidating the institutions of competitive capitalism, we note the emergence of corporate capitalism in Japan, Germany and the United States (pp. 3–4).

The emergence of corporate capitalism, a product of the second industrial revolution, was a response to technological and market challenges through vertical integration of production and distribution through managerial hierarchies. To meet this challenge, British 'industries required transformation of their structures of industrial relations, industrial organization, and enterprise management' (Elbaum and Lazonick, 1986, p. 5). The success of capitalism in Germany, Japan and the United States in the twentieth century demonstrates, according to Elbaum and Lazonick (1986), 'the ubiquitous importance of the visible hand of corporate bureaucratic management' (p. 5). By persisting with the invisible hand of self-regulating markets, Britain overlooked the need for a 'visible hand of co-ordinated control' (Elbaum and Lazonick, 1986, p. 10). While Britain continued to rely on competitive capitalism and its entrenched investment in the technology of the first industrial revolution, the latecomers enjoyed the advantage of the latest technology, particularly transportation.

Analysts of British decline in the late nineteenth century and early twentieth tend to overlook the fact that the type of industry that developed was linked to Britain's colonies. Raw materials from the colonies were processed, branded and packaged and re-exported as finished products. In such a process, economies of scale had little to do with efficiency. 'We shall argue that the slowness to organise at the top is

attributable to the existence of a *Makler* (middleman) economy in organised capitalist Britain, whose main characteristics were an over development of markets; a sectoral balance in which the weight of liberal-capitalist, or service industries such as brewing, food, textile, tobacco, and the "City" were over preponderant and both heavy industry and the "new industries" weak; and a very high profile for commercial firms, financial firms and overseas investment' (Lash and Urry, 1987, p. 42).

Following the Second World War and the emergence of the United States as a leader, financial power shifted from London to Washington. Arrighi (1994) points to Britain's highly extroverted, decentralized and differentiated structure as a major obstacle in a corporate reorganization on the lines of Germany or the US (p. 283). However, the very same decentralized and differentiated structure of British business has been recognized as an advantage in the recent emphasis on flexible productive systems (p. 283). The landed aristocracy, prevalent even today in Britain, was unwilling to change, adhering to a culture quite unlike the frontier culture one observes in the United States. While there are differences in the historical development of capitalism within the Anglo-American model, there is still a certain underlying uniformity as a form of capitalism which is distinct from both Germany and Japan.

Origins of the corporate device

While manufacturing of a product is located within a factory, the operation of the business must, for the protection of investors, be recognized as a legal entity backed by the machinery of state. The government thus determines and enforces the *legal matrix* within which the market operates, and this involves the definition of the nature and uses of property rights, the extent and limits of enforceable contracts and the rules governing firms and associations (Spulber, 1995, p. 48). The publicly held corporation emerged to meet the needs of commercial groups engaging in such economic activity. At a later stage, the vertical integration of mass production and mass distribution led to the modern industrial corporation, which has taken various forms in various countries, influenced by respective historical and political developments. The power and influence of the corporation is a phenomenon of American business and society where it overshadows all other institutions. Its impact and influence is such that all problems of the economy and, to some extent, those of society, fall at its doorstep (Mason, 1973). While its emergence as an institutional form was in response to the need for capital, it offered, in addition, a form of organization for the manage-

ment of large-scale business enterprises. The influence it enjoys in the United States is greater when compared with Britain, Germany, or Japan because big business preceded the public service in the United States while the reverse was the case in other countries. Business corporations inevitably led to managerial hierarchies whose personnel were drawn from universities. While the universities have provided manpower, they also relied heavily on business corporations for support through endowments that are unmatched elsewhere in the world. Likewise, political parties and candidates for public office, lobby groups and media rely on business for both funds and survival.

The power and influence enjoyed by the private corporation in American society is legitimized owing to the general preference for private enterprise over the state. Unlike in other countries, individualism is deep-seated in American values and culture and is, in fact, the very basis on which American private enterprise has thrived. However that situation cannot last with the current changes taking place. As professional managers have taken over, accountability to shareholders has declined to the point where their voice is rarely heard. The growing influence of the 'organization man' working for large corporations with plant locations outside traditional communities for purely business reasons has gradually alienated them from society. 'All over the country, the paternalistic company town with mill-supported public service is giving way to a new philosophy that shuns the responsibility and the doubtful glory of conspicuous community dominance' (Mason, 1973, p. 206). Corporation–community relations have also been affected by the territorial base of modern corporations which extends beyond local, national and sometimes international markets. Modern technology allows for mobility of capital, which being 'footloose', moves in search of favourable business conditions in the form of incentives, low wages and so on. To some extent, the community and the shareholder regained that lost power in the 1990s when shareholders sought company realignment that would reflect the interest of shareholders (Useem, 1993).

Being a product of managerial capitalism and because of its access to critical information, American top management, when compared with its European counterpart, has an advantage over shareholders, employees, customers, the community and government. This extraordinary power over information in a society where private enterprise is highly regarded adds further clout to its dealings. In terms of social systems of production, the American corporation enjoys greater autonomy in its functioning. Unlike Germany and Japan which are identified with the

community model, the United States corporation is modelled on the company law model where, owing to insider trading laws, shareholders are disallowed from interacting with managers. Prevailing ideology subscribes to the view that occurrences within a firm are its internal business. Other differences in the governance of firms in the United States date back to pre-New Deal legislation and include the Interstate Commerce Act which regulated transportation, the Sherman Antitrust Act which broke up cartels and monopolies, the McCarren Act which prohibited inter-state banking and the Glass–Steagal Act which severed the link between banking and industry. Together this range of regulations created a setting for the adversarial model of government–business relations, which differs greatly from the Japanese and German model (Spulber, 1995: Gourevitch, 1998).

Gourevitch (1998) attributes the gradual divergence between industrialized economies such as the United States, Japan and Germany, which adopted the organized capitalist model between 1870 and 1910, to their political makeup. A major role was played by lobby groups in the United States which organized the attacks on the great trusts, railroads and monopoly power in general. While such voices against business did exist in other countries, in the United States they enjoyed greater power because 'the structure of interests, of society, and of property gave forth a different balance of preferences and numbers'. America had the family farm, countless small independent proprietors and an economy so diverse that it spawned different clusters of interests with competing views. Most importantly, the institutional arrangements of federalism, universal suffrage and competitive parties provided voice for these groups. Such political differences led the structure of American industry down a path which differed from its Japanese and continental European counterparts (Gourevitch, 1998, p. 224).

In earlier chapters of this study I have had occasion to comment on the distinctiveness of the United States and its choice of market-based solutions in preference to the state – that is, 'the tenacious hold of market capitalism on the public mind.... The market is thought to be "fair and wise", but not the government' (Lane, 1986, pp. 384–5). In identifying this uniqueness, it is appropriate to return to Hirschman's (1986) 'feudal blessings' thesis which, according to Louis Hartz (1955), was more a curse than a blessing. Lack of a history of conflict or a revolution has for Hartz resulted in a lack of diversity, in the absence of which Americans have shown a preference for the status quo rather than change (Mascarenhas, 1992). This lack of ideological diversity has led to reluctance on the part of governments in the United States to

adopt public ownership to promote the public interest. In the United States, regulation of private enterprise appears to be the preferred choice in promoting the public interest. Notwithstanding this preference for the market and dislike for the state, there still remains an underlying mistrust arising from an adversarial model of government–business relations (Vogel, 1996). However, increasing social regulation in the area of health and safety and environmental and consumer protection in recent years has resulted in increased government intervention and growing conflict between business executives and government officials (Vogel, 1996, p. 131).

The lack of ideological diversity in the United States was demonstrated when pragmatism overtook ideology during the time of the New Deal, thereby bringing the United States closer to other industrialized economies. Such active involvement by the state under business influence was once again witnessed during restructuring of railroads, the energy crisis and selective industry support in the 1970s. However, even while adopting such policies, it was apparent that the United States had a weaker corporatist system of regulation than Japan or Germany. With the collapse of the New Deal consensus in the 1970s and 1980s, governments reverted to neoliberal policies which, while giving shareholder value greater importance in corporate governance, increased divergence.

This shift in power from professional managers to shareholders, a phenomenon of the 1980s, can be traced to the gradual decline in the performance of giant corporations caused by investing revenues generated in the 1950s and 1960s in mergers and acquisitions. As companies grew in size, they became difficult to manage, and this resulted in poor performance which was exacerbated by the unstable macroeconomic environment and global competition particularly from Japan and Germany. Observing the increasing debate on America's manufacturing decline, Lazonick and O'Sullivan (2000) note the growing influence of 'agency theory' that advocates the concept of shareholders as principals and managers as agents. It questions the judgement of managerial control over allocation of resources and views the market as superior in the efficient allocation of resources. According to agency theory, poor performance can be overcome by the threat of takeover of companies which fail to meet the rate of return as per shareholder value (p. 16).

The concept of shareholder value was supported by institutional investors like mutual and pension funds which initiated takeovers, giving shareholders collective value. This trend was facilitated by a series of government decisions that encouraged the deregulation of the financial

sector. With this gradual shift in the market towards corporate control, the enhanced market capitalization of the company after takeover became the sole measure of corporate performance. That this trend survived for over two decades despite the 1987 crash is an indication of the shift in allocation of resources from 'retain and invest' to 'downsize and distribute'. By adopting this approach, corporations increased returns on equity.

While acknowledging the role of institutional investors in promoting this shift to shareholder value, two other explanations are offered by Fligstein (2001): first, the Reagan administration's suspension of antitrust laws and the tax policies of the 1980s which provided incentives to institutional investors and finance-oriented managers; and second, the opportunity for large corporations to alter the balance following the 1970s which left them asset-rich and stock price-poor (p. 168). As a result of the shift towards a shareholder value conception, large firms are now evaluated primarily on their effect on share price. Those instrumental in promoting this view happen to control some of the largest firms in the US (p. 168). Despite considerable pressure from neoliberals, both Germany and Japan have avoided adopting the shareholder value approach (Lazonick and O'Sullivan, 2000).

While shareholder value became a creed in the 1980s, it resulted in a sharp decline in job security as companies adopted policies to rationalize, restructure and downsize. 'In 1969, fifty largest United States industrial corporations by sector directly employed 6.4 million people, equivalent to 7.5 per cent of the civilian labor force. In 1991, these companies directly employed 5.2 million people, equivalent to 4.2 per cent of the labor force' (Lazonick and O'Sullivan, 2000, p. 19). Explaining this shift from 'retain and invest' to 'downsize and distribute', Lazonick and O'Sullivan (2000) state that, until the 1970s, top management was integrated into the organization by separating share ownership and management control. In the absence of shareholders or owners, top management worked its way up with compensation being determined by pay structures within the managerial organization (p. 24). When stock option became a component of salaries and increased throughout the 1980s and 1990s, it created an enormous gap in wages, with the average pay of CEOs being 44 times that of ordinary workers. Thus corporate managers developed a personal interest in boosting the market value of their company stock, leading them to overlook other stakeholders like employees, suppliers and customers who had earlier benefited from the 'retain and invest' regime (Lazonick and O'Sullivan, 2000).

In defence of shareholder value, its proponents believe that 'downsize and distribute' benefits the economy by (1) making businesses efficient through restructuring, (2) releasing capital and labour for new ventures, and (3) by enabling both capital and labour markets to reallocate resources. Comparing this with Japan and Germany where such dynamism is lacking, they use such arguments to promote the Anglo-American style of restructuring in other industrialized economies (Lazonick and O'Sullivan, 2000).

There is no doubt that the shift to shareholder value in the American economy since 1990 has coincided with a booming stock market and low rates of unemployment. However, critics attribute the present boom to historical factors such as the military-industry complex and government-supported research and development in critical areas. They also point to the increasing insecurity of employment, declining job tenure, increasing income inequities and the creation of an economy based on low wage rates for most of the working population. While one per cent owns 37 per cent of all outstanding corporate equities, 80 per cent of all households own less than 2 per cent. High returns have served only to exacerbate income inequality. When United States corporations favoured retain and invest strategies between the Second World War and 1970, workers were well paid and enjoyed stable employment which ensured their cooperation on the shop-floor. The subsequent decline of shop-floor skills, has, according to Lazonick and O'Sullivan (2000), emerged as a serious drawback of the shareholder value approach. They conclude:

> the experience of the United States suggests that the pursuit of shareholder value may be an appropriate strategy for running down a company and an economy. The pursuit of some other kind of value is needed to build up a company and an economy. (p. 33)

Government and business in Anglo-American capitalism

If Adam Smith's *The Wealth of Nations* (1776) is regarded as an observation of industrial capitalism that existed in Britain under the first industrial revolution, it also reflects a situation that became identified with laissez faire. Even in that era of economic enterprise largely confined to private entrepreneurship, there were certain functions expected of the state. Those functions, identified broadly as general supportive functions for successful performance of markets, led to a limited role for the state. As already elaborated in earlier chapters, that role varied in different countries according to historical evolvement. 'National

economies have distinct institutional arrangements that outline the relations among investment, ownership control and economic growth. While they are interested in world trade, national systems are set up to preserve their national systems of property rights and governance structures' (Fligstein, 2001, p. 187).

In exercising that role, the United States government has had to create a complex machinery to intervene. While exploring such complex machinery, Fligstein (1991) examines the contexts within which organizations operate. Known as institutional spheres, they comprise the existing strategy and structure of the organization, the set of organizations comprising the organizational field, and the state (p. 312). As all business enterprises operate within an organizational field, the context then becomes a constraint which can sometimes be altered. This depends on how certain actors interpret the environment of the firm; an interpretation, which, according to Fligstein (1991), differs from accounts of action based on rationality and bounded rationality. Any changes from a stable field are caused by shocks like the depression and the anti-trust legislation of the federal government. To understand the response, Fligstein (1991) focuses on the functional background of the president of the organization in his historical analysis of diversification. According to him, a production, marketing or finance person perceives the problem of an organization from a functional perspective.

Unlike earlier commentators on the business corporation, Fligstein (1991) lays emphasis on the state and its policies as being instrumental in shaping the competitiveness of business:

> The state has been the central arbiter of legal and illegal market behaviour on the part of firms.... The practices that emerged in the largest firms were a response to the state's perception of the need to control markets. These practices reflect only one way of responding to the situation and, as such, are not provided by an a priori reading of the logic of markets. Rather, they are best viewed as a result of the strategic interaction between actors in the state and actors in firms. In this sense, markets in the abstract do not suggest anything about how to organize production. The organization is an outcome of social processes whereby firms interact with one another and the state to produce what can be called a market.
> (Fligstein, 1990, pp. 19–20)

By viewing an organization's strategy as an attempt to control competition within a stable organizational field, Fligstein (1990) analyses three

dominant phases – manufacturing, sales and marketing, and the finance phases in the diversification of the American corporation. All three were, to some extent, responses to the legal environment of business in the United States where the Clayton and Sherman Acts had rendered competition increasingly difficult. 'The only stable solution to the problem of competition was the manufacturing conception, which emerged when all the more direct strategies of control were made illegal. The manufacturing conception of control developed in fields of single products or industries and those tended to be highly capital-intensive industries, that is, steel, oil, and electrical machinery. The key managers in this endeavour were those engaged in manufacturing the product, since they had most knowledge of the production process' (Fligstein, 1990, pp. 25–6). Such industries were able to achieve stability because of their large size and price leaders and by utilizing a unitary and functional organizational structure. Adopting vertical integration and price controls, this form of organization was considered legal and increased in numbers in the 1920s (Fligstein, 1990, p. 26). As a defensive strategy, however, the vertically integrated firm was limited in terms of its capacity for growth, being particularly vulnerable during economic downturns.

The answer to the limitations of the vertically integrated firm was the sales and marketing conception when firms began to produce related products and set up multi-divisional forms of organization for large corporations. This form of organization flourished between 1920 and 1970 in the consumer area, producing food, drugs, chemicals, automobiles and so on. Intent on applying anti-trust laws with the objective of promoting competition in the American economy and reducing monopoly in related products, the federal government passed the Cellar–Kefauver Act. 'The dominant theory of anti-trust at the time was that concentration within product lines restricted competition. The unintended consequence of the Cellar–Kefauver Act was that it set up the preconditions for the third largest merger movement. But the mergers of the late 1950s and 1960s did not produce monopolies or oligopolies. Instead they produced conglomerates and the large modern diversified multinational firm' (Fligstein, 1990, p. 29).

The third phase of diversification, identified as the finance conception, developed because firms needed to diversify and investment decisions were made on a financial basis irrespective of whether a product made money. More attention was paid to short-term objectives, making it easier to buy an existing company than to build a new plant. The other impetus for the financial conception was the anti-trust

environment which was hostile towards large firms and particularly towards horizontal and vertical mergers. 'The large firms quickly responded and stopped merging for market share. Instead they turned their attention to product related and unrelated mergers as a strategy for growth' (Fligstein, 1990, p. 30).The above analysis of the response of American large business corporations to the regulatory environment dispels the popular notion relating to the hands-off approach of the United States government.

The relative role of the state in industrial capitalist economies became crucial in the 1980s in the context of the economic decline of the Anglo-American group in comparison with the West European and East Asian countries. Analysts adopting comparisons note the distinctive pattern of government–business relations in Western Europe and East Asia and advocate a more active role for government in the economy in the Anglo-American political system (Lodge and Vogel, 1987). 'The modern economy demands a corrective agency with strategic, think-tank, coordinating functions to make extensive reorganization possible. And in many countries where technological and organizational shifts are under way, this is precisely the enabling role the state has come to play, in combination with organized industry and industrial finance' (Weiss and Hobson, 1995, p. 202). Just as there are advocates for an active role, there are those who argue against such a role for the state in the economy. The neoliberal school using agency theory seeks to enhance shareholder value in which takeovers and mergers become important sources for dislodging inefficient management if it fails to meet a stipulated rate of return on investment. The success of the model in the 1990s in the United States and the growing globalization of markets is being used to pressure Japan and Germany to reform their institutions of capitalism (Williams, 2000). Irrespective of the competing views on the role of the state in the economy, the position I adopt in this study is that the state has a distinctive impact on industrialized economies and the differences between economies have engaged us in this comparative study of industrial capitalism. It is appropriate at this stage to analyse the economic performance of Anglo-American economies so that one can evaluate the true extent of their decline between 1973 and 1995.

Performance of Anglo-American economies

Britain and the United States lost the dominance achieved by them in the first and second industrial revolutions to other countries in Western Europe and to East Asia in the third industrial revolution. The search for

explanations for this decline has brought up various likely reasons: the work ethic of American labour which seeks high wages with low productivity, inadequate technological innovation, excessive regulation and high taxes and the current trend for short-term profits at the cost of long-term goals. These are seen as diametrically opposite to German and Japanese business enterprises whose work ethic, technological innovation and long-term goals encourage growth (Thurow, 1992). The overall outcome for the United States and Britain and their allies, Australia, Canada and New Zealand, during the 1980s, therefore, was a decline in their industrial base.

Economic growth in Britain in the 20 years preceding 1979 averaged 2.75 per cent but declined to 2 per cent in the 20 years preceding 1994. Decline in international trading position and competitiveness followed, with the saga of decline becoming a familiar theme. Compared with its competitors, Britain experienced lower economic growth, declining profitability, sluggish innovation and chronically low investment levels. While its share of world manufacturing production slipped from 8.6 per cent in 1953 to 4 per cent in 1980, its share of world trade in manufactured exports fell from around 30 per cent in 1900 to 16.5 per cent in 1960 and to a mere 8 per cent over the next 20 years (Weiss and Hobson, 1995, p. 203).

Similarly the United States industrial base also declined from the mid-1970s. Between 1945 and 1980, the US share of world manufacturing fell from 50 per cent to 31.5 per cent. Its share of manufactured exports fell from 30 per cent in 1945 to 13 per cent in 1986. Its world share of income also dropped from 40 per cent in 1950 to 21.5 per cent in 1980. 'Even allowing for some inflation for war production, the cumulative picture is one of a giant in distress. Translated into social terms, the deterioration in America's industrial capacity means that real wages have been steadily declining and income inequality steadily growing since 1980' (Weiss and Hobson, 1995, p. 206). Since the early 1970s the United States has had to cope with recessions, unemployment, stagnation and inflation and make costly adjustments to meet increasing military expenditure and growing competition from both Japan and Germany. The worst occurred with the oil price hikes of the 1970s. Together this accounted for decline in GNP growth rate to 1.6 per cent. Unemployment rose 7 per cent, annual inflation reached 9 per cent and the federal budget deficit as a percentage of GNP increased to 6.3. The tax cuts of the 1980s Reagan administration 'evoked barely a response in regard to personal saving, investment and productivity growth' (Spulber, 1995, p. 46), similar to the experience of Britain, Australia and New Zealand.

While Anglo-American economic performance was on the decline, American dominance in mass production of cars, television, audio and video equipment and computers was challenged in the 1970s and 1980s by Japan, whose share of the United States market for consumer electronics rose from 6 per cent in 1960 to 50 per cent in 1979. It was estimated that a plant in the United States spent on average 26.5 hours on the production of a vehicle compared with 19.1 hours at a Japanese plant. Once a pioneer and then a leader in automobile manufacture, the United States increased automobile imports from 13 per cent in 1965, to 38 per cent in 1970, climbing to 55 per cent in 1979. Between 1964 and 1979 the import of cars increased from 20,000 to 2.5 million. As pressure on imports increased, Japan shifted its investment to the United States, setting up nine manufacturing plants totalling $9 billion. As American competitiveness slowed further, Japan set up 275 plants in the United States employing 300,000 directly in the manufacture of steel, computers, industrial machinery, rubber and plastics, automobiles and consumer electronics (O'Sullivan, 2000, p. 149).

The emergence of Japan and Germany as genuine competitors and the overall decline in US economic performance generated serious debate within the United States on the need to develop an industrial policy, with commentators advocating an active role for the government. In the course of that debate, a major ideological shift occurred resulting in the election in 1979 of Margaret Thatcher in Britain and Ronald Reagan in 1980 in the United States. Their governments implemented neoliberal policies of economic liberalization, deregulation, privatization, tax reform and public sector, and labour market reform. These were not measures tailored to confront the disease of industrial decline; rather they were intended to favour unfettered markets as the solution to the ills of industrialized economies. In placing blind faith in markets, no attempt was made to examine reasons for the success of the Japanese and German political economies.

Weiss and Hobson (1995) 'seek to show that any account of Anglo-American decline that ignores the state is seriously inadequate. This is because the state stands at the intersection of the ensemble of priorities, policies, and institutions that has seriously jeopardized industrial recovery in Britain, and compromised its renewal in the United States. In short, we argue that it is not simply a problem of commission – what the state has done – that matters; it is also the problem of omission – what the state has not done – that explains Anglo-American decline' (p. 207). To add to the difficulties, the Anglo-American countries were faced with the energy crisis of the 1970s, resulting in inflation, unemployment, balance of

payments problems and ultimately low growth which threatened long-term economic and political stability. While business normally regards state intervention as a hindrance, in times of economic decline it tends to look towards the state and its policies not only as a target of blame, but also as a source for rectification. 'But these limits on government do not lead to exculpation of the government for any injustices perceived in the market; in the end, the responsibility for rectifying any injustices of the economic system lies not with the market, but with the government' (Lane, 1986, p. 395). Liberal market economies (LMEs) which lack the high concentration of informal coordination facilitated by banks, industry associations and unions in coordinated market economies (CMEs), have no option but to rely on government intervention to bolster their competitiveness (Kitschelt et al., 1999, pp. 374–5). In the absence of favourable institutional arrangements that exist in Western Europe and East Asia linking business with government, the presence of a strong anti-state public attitude in the Anglo-American countries places the state in a difficult situation in any remedial role when the economy is in decline. In an environment where incapacity of political institutions is held as a reason against state intervention, seeking recourse to state machinery when in crisis and as a mender of last resort only reinforces that view because any attempt to intervene in a crisis without that institutional capacity is likely to be unsuccessful (Mascarenhas, 1992).

Returning to specifics, the underlying cause of declining economic performance is the loss of American competitiveness in skills required to effectively utilize the technology of the third industrial revolution. Essentially this amounts to a decline in manufacturing. Irrespective of the level of technology or superiority of designs, ultimately it is effective manufacturing that proves decisive for competition. O'Sullivan (2000) notes the inability of the market to allocate resources efficiently and traces the underlying cause of US decline in manufacturing to organizational segmentation between managers and shop-floor workers that originated with the second industrial revolution. Managers were treated as insiders and workers as outsiders in the organizational learning process. Such a division rendered it difficult to respond to international competitors who were producing higher-quality, lower-cost products through the integration of managerial and shop-floor employees into the process of organizational learning (p. 107). Two other factors that contributed to this decline between 1965 and 1980 were the declining productivity and the falling wages when compared with Japan and Germany. By the 1970s, the rebuilt economies of Japan and Germany posed a threat to the industrial primacy of the United States.

The US decline had been predicted well before the postwar boom which led to the golden age of capitalism and ended with the energy crisis. In the 1930s Schumpeter identified the major forces destroying capitalism as (1) the stifling of entrepreneurship by bureacratization of management in large firms, (2) disincentives of taxation and power of trade unions, (3) growing power of socialist ideas, and (4) the unpopularity of capitalism (Maddison, 1991, p. 104).

Studies during the 1970s reveal a higher rate of decline in manufacturing employment in the United States (29 per cent) when compared with Britain (35 per cent), Germany (43 per cent) and Japan (35 per cent). Apart from other macroeconomic factors like inflation, such factors as high wages, increased cost of imports and high prices rendered competition with other countries increasingly difficult. The distinctive role played by interest groups in Anglo-American countries (Olson, 1982) and the decline in the hegemonic role of the United States as the leading military power (see Marquand, 1992) further complicated the situation.

Response to the crisis of Fordism

The central issue nevertheless is declining productivity. 'The writing was already on the wall for the Fordist system of production in the 1970s.... "Having in the most deliberate manner possible committed themselves to standardization, managers usually believed they had no alternative to sticking with it to the bitter end. As events have shown the end has been bitter indeed"' (Marglin and Schor, 1991, p. 88). As a leader in standardized mass production, the United States catered to universal culture through mass marketing. This period of industrial dominance through large-scale organization became an impediment as markets became more customized and fragmented while attempting to cater to unique tastes. As we have already noted in Chapter 6, the emergence of diversified quality production has posed problems for American industry. Observers of twentieth-century capitalism proclaimed the fading of 'Fordism' together with its various associated regulation regimes contrasting the rigidities of large-scale production with the virtues of flexible specialization (Whitley, 1999, p. 4). The US model of mass production based on Fordist principles faced pressure from Germany and Japan in the 1960s and 70s stemming from their inability to respond to changing technology and markets. The latter's combination of large with small-scale enterprises, their emphasis on job training plus multiple skilling, and the supervisory and monitoring role of banks placed them at an

advantage over the Anglo-American group. The United States, owing to its protected market, mass production, hierarchical organization and reliance on equity markets, was unable to adjust to such change. Their response was to take the low road by reducing costs, cutting wages or moving to low-cost countries. This neo-Fordist response of the United States of reducing labour costs by adopting automation (Aglietta, 1979) was contrary to requirements of post-Fordist flexible specialization where workers with multiple skills analagous to craft production are necessary.

Flexible systems of production require workers with broad levels of skills, employees who have learned to learn about new technologies and can easily shift from one task to another and who can work closely and cooperatively with other employees and management (Hollingsworth, 1997a, p. 307).

Interestingly, this transition from the Fordist–Keynesianism of the postwar era was seen as a regime of accumulation and its associated mode of social and political regulation (Aglietta, 1979; Jessop, 1990). This new regime of accumulation is termed flexible specialization (Piore and Sabel, 1984). Arrighi (1994) equates this transition of the 1970s and 1980s to previous eras of capitalism when financial expansions signalled the transition from one regime of accumulation on a world scale to another (p. x).

Regulation theory as a critique of advanced capitalism gained in stature in the late 1970s and the 1980s, adding to the growing literature on control and coordination of economic activities with the emphasis on the socially embedded, socially regulated character of economic activities (Jessop, 1995, p. 327). The French regulationists emerged as critics to neoclassical economists' obsession with the market-driven tendency towards general equilibrium. When American business operates on a short-term basis, it overlooks not only history but also 'its inability to express the social content of economic relations and consequently to interpret the forces and conflicts at work in the economic process' (Aglietta, 1979, p. 9). In other words, the regulationists appeared to be placing emphasis on the role of institutions in promoting overall efficiency of the economy, a view that is not subscribed to by their American counterpart, the Social Structure of Accumulation (SSA) school, which argues that sustained periods of accumulation require specific social and political conditions to support and reinforce the economic factors for growth (Jessop, 1990).

By focusing on relative stability as essential to rapid and sustained accumulation, the SSA school recognizes the importance of introducing

socio-political relations. Like other regulationists, they distinguish periodic business cycles from economic crisis which is 'a period of instability whose resolution depends on reconstruction of a social structure of accumulation' (Jessop, 1990, p. 182). In some other areas, the SSA school adopts a different perspective from the French regulationists who attribute the 1970s crisis to the exhaustion of Fordism as a regime of accumulation. SSA theorists view accumulation as having undermined the power of US capital against workers, foreign capital and citizens.

Jessop (1995) believes that the emergence of regulation theory is related to the crisis in Atlantic Fordism and the search for a new social mode of economic regulation 'through which to make sense of the continuing economic crisis and to frame possible solutions to the crisis' (p. 311). While closely identified with classical Marxism, the regulationists differ from the former in their ability to distinguish between types of capitalism in different countries and between late-nineteenth-century capitalism and the capitalism of today (Painter and Goodwin, 1995, p. 338).

A criticism made against the regulationists is their failure to come up with a theory of the state and the lack of a clear definition (Jessop, 1990). Bowles and Gintis (1982), in seeking to balance the liberal democratic state with capitalist production, see an underlying conflict between rights in persons and rights in property. The interpenetration of person and property rights is thus central to an understanding of the contemporary crisis of US capitalism (1982, pp. 63–4). They feel that this internal contradiction of the liberal democratic capitalist state and the capitalist production sysem attributed to the crisis of the 1970s can be overcome with a less interventionist state. Further, they contend that 'all have recognized the potential disruptiveness of liberal-democratic state intervention in the accumulation process and advocated market-based cost effectiveness criteria for all state programs and regulatory activities in order to impose the "rationality" of the commodity form as the sole allocational role outside the state and relying upon monetary rather than fiscal macromanagement policies' (p. 91).

Marx had argued in *Capital* that the conditions for a capitalist system of production were inconsistent and contradictory and thus the dynamics of capitalism were crisis-prone (Harvey, 1990). Competitive capitalism encourages the introduction of new technology so as to increase productivity, reduce costs and increase profits. Such incentives for improving productive technology in the longer term sow the seeds of its own destruction. 'The stagnation of American capitalism of the 1970s and early 1980s may thus be largely due to one of the fundamental

contradictions of the system' (Wolf, 1987). Further, Wolf contends that the existence of individual capitals that are forced to compete creates the realization problem, which Marx calls the 'anarchy of the marketplace' (Wolf, p. 174). In this trend towards diversion of resources for unproductive use by American capital, West German and Japanese companies have moved towards improving and advancing their technology so as to gain advantage over others.

Two outstanding efforts towards flexibility in the US are Silicon Valley and Route 128. Efforts in the United States to adopt Japanese manufacturing practices remained at most in appearance only, a conclusion based on Jaikumar's (1986) analysis of American adoption of flexible manufacturing systems (FMS). 'With few exceptions, the flexible manufacturing systems installed in the United States show an astonishing lack of flexibility. In many cases, their performance is worse than the conventional technology they wish to replace' (p. 69). The study highlights that American businesses were using FMS for high-volume standardized production 'which is precisely what it is not. Captive to old-fashioned Taylorism and its principle of scientific management, these executives separated the establishment of procedures from their execution, replaced skilled blue-collar machinists with trained operators and emphasized machine uptime and productivity' (p. 71). Operators assigned to each shift were given routine tasks and advised not to change procedures, while similar systems adopted by Japanese operators on the shop-floor made continual programming changes (Jaikumar, 1986). The Japanese success in competing against America is attributed to their resolution of the classical conflict between gains in efficiency and losses in flexibility arising from specialization of resources by the participation of shop-floor workers in the continuous adjustment of the firm to changing circumstances (Sabel and Zeitlin, 1997, p. 7).

If there was worker discontent with the separation of conception from execution as entrenched in Taylorism, the alternative lay in Japanese systems of industrial production which combined flexibility and rigidity as well as quality and price competitiveness within mass production. That new system of production, identified with the Japanese, is sometimes called 'Toyotaism' (Grahl and Teague, 2000, p. 164).

Coriat (1997) identified globalization and the ongoing technological and organizational revolution as the two important determinants that contributed to post-Fordist regime(s) of accumulation (pp. 240–1). While a variety of possibilities through flexible specialization were available, the Anglo-American group sought flexibilization of products through an intensification of competition in labour markets without

major reform within enterprise. This approach to labour market flexibility is described by the regulation school as defensive flexibility as opposed to offensive flexibility with more involvement of workers (Grahl and Teague, 2000, p. 164). Employers took advantage of weakening union power to adopt flexible work regimes and labour contracts, thus increasing flexible workers in Anglo-American countries in the 1980s. Union power was also undermined with the increase in sweatshops (Harvey, 1990).

Business organized on traditional Fordist lines has been unable to adjust to 'flexible systems of production with its emphasis upon problem-solving, rapid and often highly specialized responses, and adoption of skills to special purposes'. Typical examples of such failures are the Penn Central bankruptcy of 1976 and the Chrysler bail-out of 1981 (Harvey, 1990, p. 155).

Referred to as the 'new economy', the financial growth regime identified with shareholder value resulted in a sharemarket boom. However, it was also accompanied by a spate of takeovers and mergers in the US economy, attracting a fair share of criticism and support. In fact, a French regulationist saw in the finance-led accumulation of the second half of the 1990s a 'totally novel regulation mode, currently labelled the "new economy" this regime would combine labour market flexibility, price stability, developing high technology sectors, booming stock market and credit to sustain the rapid growth of consumption and permanent optimism of expectations in firms' (Boyer, 2000, p. 116). 'Post-Fordism was always a more problematic condition inaugurated by the "crisis of Fordism" as mass markets broke up and institutional stabilizers broke down. It was never entirely clear whether and how coherence could be restored to create another couple of decades of prosperity' (Williams, 2000, p. 7).

Such comments support the view held by a leading regulationist that regulation theory suffers from 'the floating eclecticisms and the lack of consistency arising from research conducted under the heading of regulation' (Delorme, 2001, p. 4).

If Toyotaism was touted as a new flexible production system, that developmental potential is now being re-evaluated. 'Where before what was detected was perhaps the embryo of a new productive system, it is now diagnosed as a full-scale crisis of the Japanese regulatory mode.... Likewise the German social market, once regarded as unique, is now seen as an impediment to rapid innovation' (Grahl and Teague, 2000, p. 167). That uncertainties of the post-Fordist regime of accumulation seem evident is 'because such a system has yet to be comprehen-

sively identified' (Tickell and Peck, 1995, p. 358). According to Tickell and Peck, 'many of the prevailing conceptions of post-Fordism are straightforwardly inconsistent with the central tenets of the regulationists *method*. Critical emphasis in regulation theory is placed on the "structural coupling" between the system of accumulation in (a macroeconomically coherent production–distribution–consumption relationship) and the ensemble of state norms, political practices and institutional networks which regulationists term the "mode of social regulation (MSR)"' (1995, p. 358).

What has been claimed as post-Fordist or flexible regime of accumulation is based on generalizations from developments in production systems. This has led to calls for a more restrained and critical approach to post-Fordism (Tickell and Peck, 1995, p. 363).

Response: deregulation, liberalization and privatization

The election of Margaret Thatcher in Britain (1979) and Ronald Reagan in the United States (1980) marked the start of a conservative revolution which invigorated business into political activism to counteract the power of unions, particularly in Britain. As seen by Useem (1984):

> the challenges of the 1970s and 1980s came from two fundamentally different directions. One was economic, the other political. The economic challenge was the decline in company profitability, a problem endemic to most business sectors. While the economic threat was common to both countries, the political challenge could not have been more different. In Britain, it was the rise of labor socialism; in America, the spread of government interventionism. Trade union and Labour party threats became the rallying call for British business, while consumer activism and federal regulation became the hostile forces around which the ranks of American business closed. (p. 151)

The conservative view is that markets are efficient mechanisms for coordinating the economy while government intervention through public bureaucracy is inefficient. Critics of state intervention point to a limitation arising out of globalization which is that markets can compete only through deregulation and liberalization of the economy. Arguments offered in support of markets as efficient coordinating mechanisms include the traditional invisible hand of anonymous decisionmakers, efficient dissemination of information, rational behaviour of actors, known expectations of people, encouragement of technological

innovation and selection of appropriate organizations for managing an enterprise.

The initial impact of the anti-big-government and market endorsement thrust came across as an aggressive conservative form of capitalism. Accompanying this form of capitalism was an ideology that advocated monetarism – that is, reduction of public expenditure and budget deficits, tax cuts to encourage savings and investment, liberalization and deregulation of the economy, privatization of public enterprise and labour market reform. The outcome of such policies in the early 1980s was declining growth, low inflation and high unemployment. This however was short-lived. Of the Anglo-American countries, Britain and New Zealand, lacking constitutional constraints, more keenly sought to engineer the free market model. While the United States, Australia and Canada were no less enthusiastic, their failure in promoting it was due to their complex political and institutional structures which acted as a constraint. In rejecting state intervention as incompatible with a market economy, Britain and New Zealand did however acknowledge the strong arm of the state in maintaining law and order and defence and in promoting national values.

The reaction to the economic crisis of the 1970s was a fundamental redefinition of the objectives and concern of government within the economic sphere labelled 'new laissez faire' (Goldthorpe, 1987). 'Exponents of new laissez-faire share with their nineteenth-century predecessors a basic conception of the capitalist market economy as a quasi-natural system.... From such a conception, a distinctive view of economic policy derives. Governments should be concerned primarily with sustaining an institutional context within which the economy may freely operate according to its own inherent logic and should modify their claims to be "in control" or even "in charge" of the economy itself' (p. 367).

While this resurgence of the neoliberal view of markets in the 1980s is a reaction to the excesses of state intervention, or, more appropriately, to ineffective state intervention, what is needed now is a sense of moderation to stop the pendulum swinging from one extreme to the other. Based on the sociological view of markets as socially embedded (Granovetter, 1985), this has resulted in varying interpretations coming from institutional theory. 'Instead a plurality of social relations have been observed that structure markets within and across societies. These observations have challenged the neoclassical economists' view that markets select efficient forms which, over time, converge to a single form' (Fligstein, 1996, p. 657). Acknowledging the broader view of social

systems of production, Hollingsworth and Boyer (1997) suggest that 'an elegant solution of the dilemma between inefficient bureaucrats on the one hand and unstable or unfair markets on the other is to recognize the existence of a quasicontinuum of coordinating mechanisms. They can be selected at a micro level – given the structural and institutional external conditions – but may be combined at the economy wide level' (p. 60). As a realistic alternative to both market failure and government failure, this lesson has not been heeded in Anglo-American countries which in the last 20 years have sought to promote markets or market-like arrangements to correct government failure. Governed more by ideological justification based on neoliberal political rationality, their response has not been pragmatic. 'This new political language may be seen as an ephemeral phenomenon, as ideology, or as merely a reprise on the atomistic individualist characteristic of capitalism' (Miller and Rose, 1990, p. 24).

The underlying argument for neoliberal policies is the need for international competitiveness in a globalized economy. In pursuit of this, governments in the Anglo-American group of countries have in recent years adopted economic liberalization, deregulation and privatization. State intervention has been reduced by liberalizing the banking and industrial structure, removing tariffs, eliminating subsidies, encouraging more competition by strengthening agencies which regulate anti-competitive behaviour, encouraging foreign private investment by liberalizing investment regimes and reducing state ownership through privatization. Reform has been directed at reducing public and social welfare expenditure, adopting 'user pays' in education and health, deregulating the labour market, introducing private sector practices within the public service through contracts and performance-based incentives and evaluating public service performance through performance measurement.

The new laissez faire policies adopted in Anglo-American countries are thus summed up by Will Hutton (1995) with reference to Britain:

> The country is increasingly divided against itself, with an arrogant officer class apparently indifferent to the other ranks it commands. The privileged class is favoured with education, jobs, housing and pensions. At the other end of the scale more and more people discover they are the new working poor, or live off the state in semi-poverty... In between there are growing numbers of people who are insecure, fearful for their jobs in an age of permanent 'down-sizing',

'cost-cutting' and 'casualization' and ever more worried about their ability to maintain a decent standard of living. (p. 3)

Attempts in the United States at restructuring and downsizing in the 1980s and 1990s which accounted for the boom of the 1990s have also resulted in economic insecurity and income inequality and been described as 'plenty of nothing' (Palley, 1998).

Conclusion

The Anglo-American model of capitalism has undergone a phenomenal transformation. That model of capitalism, in which individual producers adopted specialization based on Adam Smith's pin factory helped by the invisible hand, dramatically changed with advancement of technology and growing markets for both producer and consumer goods. Britain, the leader of the first industrial revolution, enjoyed dominance until the late nineteenth century, continuing to adopt the ideas of classical political economy. The second industrial revolution in communication and transportation led to the emergence of the United States as a leading industrial power, and with it emerged the corporate device or managerial capitalism. The United States became the model of mass standardised production for consumers using modern managerial skills supported by graduates coming from business and engineering schools. However, both Britain and the United States faced growing competition from postwar Germany and Japan and both lagged behind their competitors in their ability to exploit the third industrial revolution in computers and communication technology and in adapting to market changes.

The emergence of Germany and Japan as industrial rivals exposed the differences within the so-called mixed economies in the changing balance in relations between government and business. The Anglo–American, more particularly the American, adopted the adversarial model of government–business relations based on anti-trust legislation to promote competition and restrain monopolies. Although it did allow business a special role, there was a certain amount of antagonism between the two although some commentators feel that this has been exaggerated (Vogel, 1996). Characterized by strong individualism and a belief in the value of freedom of choice, American business has always questioned the role of the state in the economy. Recognition of the state's distinctive role in the postwar consensus or 'bounded capitalism' era and its role in the success of industrialized economies described as the

'golden age of capitalism' was an insufficient bulwark against the anti-state sentiments which arose following the economic downturn of the 1970s. This led to the laissez faire policy of unfettered markets and cutting down the state reminiscent of the nineteenth century. Unlike the first, however, this free enterprise model was engineered to reflect the nineteenth-century version which itself survived in Britain for only a generation. That model was faithfully adopted across Anglo-American countries on the assumption that, being disembedded from its social environment, it could be adopted across the world. However, that assumption has been disproved as the success of other forms of capitalism has demonstrated the importance of social systems of production. Commenting on the present regime of limited state intervention in corporate affairs, *Time Magazine* (7 December, 1998) concluded:

> Finally, we must recognize that markets are messy – frequently overshooting or undershooting desired targets – and that it is ordinary working people, not investors, bankers and business leaders, who suffer most when they do. When that happens, as may be the case in the final years of this century, it is worth remembering that there is a role for government in protecting society's weakest members from the markets' excesses while encouraging the animal spirits that free markets unleash. Getting that balance right will be a challenge for business and government in the century ahead. (p. 35)

References

Aglietta, Michel, *A Theory of Capitalist Regulation: The US Experience* (London: NLB, 1979).

Arrighi, Giovanni, *The Long Twentieth Century: Money, Power and the Origins of our Times* (London: Verso, 1994).

Bowles, Samuel and Herbert Gintis, 'The Crisis of Liberal Democratic Capitalism: the Case of the United States', *Politics and Society*, vol. 11, (1982), 51–93.

Boyer, Robert, 'Is a Finance-Led Growth Regime a Viable Alternative to Fordism: A Preliminary Analysis', *Economy and Society*, vol. 29 (2000), 111–45.

Chandler Jr, Alfred D., *Scale and Scope: The Dynamics of Industrial Capitalism* (Cambridge, Mass.: Harvard University Press, 1990).

Coriat, Benjamin, 'Globalization, Variety and Mass Production in the New Competitive Age', in Rogers Hollingsworth and Robert Boyer (eds), *Contemporary Capitalism: The Embeddedness of Institutions* (Cambridge: Cambridge University Press, 1997), 240–64.

Delorme, Robert, 'Regulation as an Analytical Perspective: The French Approach', in Atle Midttun and Eirich Svindland (eds), *Approaches and Dilemmas in Economic Regulation: Politics, Economics and Dynamics* (Basingstoke: Palgrave Macmillan, 2001).

Elbaum, Bernard and William Lazonick, *The Decline of the British Economy* (Oxford: Clarendon Press, 1986).

Fligstein, Neil, *The Transformation of Corporate Control* (Cambridge, Mass.: Harvard University Press, 1990).

Fligstein, Neil, 'The Structural Transformation of American Industry: An Institutional Account of the Causes of Diversification in the Largest Firms, 1919-1979', in Walter D. Powell and Paul J. DiMaggio (eds), *The New Institutionalism in Organizational Analysis* (Chicago: University of Chicago Press, 1991), 311–36.

Fligstein, Neil, 'Markets as Politics: A Political-Cultural Approach to Market Institutions', *American Sociological Review*, vol. 61 (1996), 656–73.

Fligstein, Neil, *The Architecture of Markets: An Economic Sociology of Twenty-First Century Capitalist Society* (Princeton: Princeton University Press, 2001).

Glassman, Ronald M., 'The United States: The Anti-Statist Society', in Metin Heper (ed.), *The State and Public Bureaucracies: A Comparative Perspective* (Connecticut: Greenwood Press, 1987).

Goldthorpe, John H., 'Problems of Political Economy after the Postwar Period', in Charles S. Maier (ed.), *Changing Boundaries of the Political: Essays on the Evolving Balance between the State and Society, Public and Private in Europe* (Cambridge: Cambridge University Press, 1987).

Gourevitch, Peter, *Politics in Hard Times: Comparative Responses to International Crisis*, (Ithaca: Cornell University Press, 1986).

Gourevitch, Peter, 'The Political Sources of Democracy: The Macropolitics of Microeconomic Policy Disputes', in Theda Skocpol (ed.), *Democracy, Revolution and History* (Ithaca: Cornell University Press, 1998).

Grahl, John and Paul Teague, 'The Regulation School, the Employment Relations and Financialization', *Economy and Society*, vol.29 (2000), 160–78.

Granovetter, Mark, 'Economic Action, Social Structure, and Embeddedness', *American Journal of Sociology*, vol. 91 (1985), 481–510.

Hartz, Louis, *The Liberal Tradition in America* (New York: Harcourt Brace, 1955).

Harvey, David, *The Condition of Modernity: An Enquiry into the Origins of Cultural Change* (Oxford: Blackwell, 1990).

Hirschman, Albert O. *Rival Views of Market Society and other Recent Essays* (New York: Viking, 1986).

Hollingsworth, Rogers J., 'Varieties among Nations in the Logic of Manufacturing Sectors and International Competitiveness', in Dominique Foray and Christopher Freeman (eds), *Technology and the Wealth of Nations* (London: Pinter Publishers, 1997a).

Hollingsworth, Rogers J., 'The Institutional Embeddedness of American Capitalism', in Colin Crouch and Wolfgang Streeck (eds), *Political Economy of Modern Capitalism: Mapping Convergence and Diversity* (London: Sage, 1997b), 133–47.

Hollingsworth, Rogers J. and Robert Boyer, *Contemporary Capitalism: The Embeddedness of Institutions* (Cambridge: Cambridge University Press, 1997).

Hutton, Will, *The State We're In* (London: Jonathan Cape, 1995).

Jaikumar, Ramachandran, 'Post-Industrial Manufacturing', *Harvard Business Review*, Nov-Dec (1986), 69–76.

Jessop, Bob, 'Regulation Theories in Retrospect and Prospect', *Economy and Society*, vol. 19, (1990), 153–216.

Jessop, Bob, 'The Regulation Approach, Governance and Post-Fordism: Alternative Perspectives on Economic and Political Change', *Economy and Society*, vol. 24 (1995), 307–33.

Jones, Geoffrey, 'Great Britain: Big Business, Management, and Competitiveness in Twentieth Century Britain', in Alfred D. Chandler Jr *et al*. (eds), *Big Business and the Wealth of Nations* (Cambridge: Cambridge University Press, 1997), 102–38.

Katzenstein, Peter, *Policy and Politics in West Germany: The Growth of Semi-Sovereign State* (Philadelphia: Temple University Press,1987).

Ketcham, Ralph, *Individualism and Public Life: A Modern Dilemma* (New York: Blackwell, 1987).

Kitschelt, Herbert *et al*. (eds), *Continuity and Change in Contemporary Capitalism* (Cambridge: Cambridge University Press, 1999).

Landes, David S., *The Wealth and Poverty of Nations: Why Some are so Rich and Some so Poor* (New York: W. W. Norton & Company, 1998).

Lane, Robert E., 'Market Justice, Political Justice', *American Political Science Review*, vol. 80 (1986), 383–402.

Lash, Scot and John Urry, *The End of Organized Capitalism* (London: Polity Press, 1987).

Lazonick, William, *Business Organization and the Myth of the Market Economy* (Cambridge: Cambridge University Press, 1991).

Lazonick William and Margaret O'Sullivan, 'Maximizing Shareholder Value: A New Ideology for Corporate Governance', *Economy and Society*, vol. 29 (2000), 13–35.

Lindblom, Charles E., *Politics and Markets* (New York: Free Press, 1977).

Lodge, George and Ezra Vogel, *Ideology and National Competitiveness: An Analysis of Nine Countries* (Boston: Harvard Business School,1987).

Maddison, Angus, *Dynamic Forces in Capitalist Development: A Long-Run Comparative View* (Oxford: Oxford University Press,1991).

Mann, Michael, *States, War and Capitalism: Studies in Political Sociology* (Oxford: Basil Blackwell, 1988).

Marglin, Stephen and Juliet B. Schor (eds), *The Golden Age of Capitalism: Reinterpreting the Postwar Experience* (Oxford: Clarendon Press, 1991).

Marquand, David, 'Political Institutions and Economic Performance', in Andrew Graham and Anthony Sheldon (eds), *Government and Economies in the PostWar World: Economic Policies and Comparative Performance, 1945–1985* (New York: Routledge, 1992), 315–23.

Mascarenhas, Reginald C., 'State Intervention in the Economy: Why is the United States Different from Other Mixed-Economies?', *Australian Journal of Public Administration*, vol. 51 (1992), 387–97.

Mascarenhas, Reginald C., 'From the Politics of Equality to the Politics of Inequality', Paper presented at the Institute of Governmental Affairs, University of California, Berkeley, 1993.

Mascarenhas, Reginald C., *Government and the Economy in Australia and New Zealand: The Politics of Economic Policy Making* (San Francisco: Austin & Winfield, 1996).

Mason, Edward S., *The Corporation in Modern Society* (New York: Athenaeum, 1973).

Miller, Peter and Nikolas Rose, 'Governing Economic Life', *Economy and Society*, vol. 19 (1990), 1–31.

Moore Jr, Barrington, *Social Origins of Dictatorship and Democracy: Lord and Peasant in the Making of the Modern World* (London: Penguin, 1966).

Olson, Mancur, *The Rise and Decline of Nations: Economic Growth, Stagflation, and Social Rigidities* (New Haven: Yale University Press, 1982).

O'Sullivan, Margaret, *Corporate Control: Corporate Governance and Economic Performance in the Contests for Control in the United States and Germany* (New York: Oxford University Press, 2000).

Painter, Joe and Mark Goodwin, 'Local Governance and Concrete Research: Investigating the Uneven Development of Regulation', *Economy and Society*, vol. 24 (1995), 334–56.

Palley, Thomas I., *Plenty of Nothing: The Downsizing of the American Dream and the Case for Structural Keynesianism* (Princeton: Princeton University Press, 1998).

Piore, Michael J. and Charles F. Sabel, *The Second Industrial Divide: Possibilities for Prosperity* (New York: Basic Books, 1984).

Rose, Nikolas and Peter Miller, 'Political Power Beyond the State: Problematics of Government', *British Journal of Sociology*, vol. 42 (1992), 173–205.

Ruggie, John Gerard, 'International Regimes, Transactions and Change: Embedded Liberalism in Postwar Economy', *International Organization*, vol. 36 (1982), 379–415.

Sabel, Charles F. and Jonathan Zeitlin, *World of Possibilities: Flexibility and Mass Production in Western Industrialization* (Cambridge: Cambridge University Press, 1997).

Spulber, Nicolas, *United States: The Struggle for Supremacy in the 21st Century* (New York: Cambridge University Press, 1995).

Thurow, Lester, *Head to Head: The Coming Economic Battle Among Japan, Europe and America* (New York: William Morrow & Company, 1992).

Tickell, Adam and Jamie A. Peck, 'Social Regulation after Fordism: Regulation Theory, Neo-Liberalism and Global – Local Nexus', *Economy and Society*, vol.24 (1995), 357–86.

Useem, Michael, *The Inner Circle: Large Corporations and the Rise of Business Political Activity in the US and the UK* (New York: Oxford University Press, 1984).

Useem, Michael, *Executive Defence: Shareholder Power and Corporate Reorganization* (Cambridge, Mass.: Harvard University Press, 1993).

Vogel, David, *Kindred Strangers: The Uneasy Relationship Between Politics and Business in America* (Princeton: Princeton University Press, 1996).

Weiss, Linda and John M. Hobson, *States and Economic Development: A Comparative Historical Analysis* (London: Polity Press, 1995).

Whitley, Richard, *Divergent Capitalism: The Social Structuring and Change of Business Systems* (Oxford: Oxford University Press, 1999).

Williams, Karen, 'From Shareholder Value to Present day Capitalism', *Economy and Society*, vol. 29 (2000), 1–12.

Wolf, Edward N., *Growth, Accumulation and Unproductive Activity: An Analysis of the Postwar US Economy* (Cambridge: Cambridge University Press, 1987).

8
German Capitalism: The Social Market Model

Introduction

In this study I compare types of industrial capitalism with a view to identifying both convergence and divergence between countries. Having taken the position in earlier chapters of this study that a country's economy relies on the relationship between business and state, I establish that private enterprise, the basis of industrial capitalism, varies depending on how such businesses respond to government policies. The debate on the role of the state in the economy has, in recent times, led to distinctive divisions or patterns. The Anglo-American approach, generally identified with the neoliberal position, views markets as efficient and advocates a minimal role for the state in the economy, while the German or Japanese approach advocates a balanced approach where state and market work in cooperation. Both sets of countries are essentially capitalist with a democratic political system within which the market remains the basis for economic exchange. The difference however lies in their view of the state in the economy. While the former envisages a minimal role for the state encouraging competition as the only way for economic survival of individual enterprises, the latter favours an active role for the state encouraging greater cooperation between state and economy.

Having discussed the competitive Anglo-American model in Chapter 7, I intend in this chapter to focus on the German model of capitalism which has been variously described as social market, Rhine or Rhenish, or cooperative capitalism (Katzenstein, 1987; Chandler Jr, 1990; Albert, 1993; Herrigel, 1996). As a latecomer to the industrial scene after Britain and the United States, Germany, when faced with the pressure to catch up, adopted economic policies influenced by Friedrich List who advocated an element of state protectionism for the promotion of industrial

development (Cowen and Shenton, 1996; Greenfeld, 2001). In such a context, the role of the state in the development of industrial capitalism became historically acceptable and remained so before, during and after the world wars. A distinctive element that has become evident in recent studies of German industrialism is the existence of small-scale regional or decentralized industries which has been overlooked by commentators interested primarily in large-scale organized capitalism (Herrigel, 1996). The 'competition abroad and cooperation at home' policy of German industrial development was 'developed along liberal capitalist principles with the important qualification of a powerful protectionism resting on two pillars of tariffs and cartels, both of which were manifestations of a deliberate government policy to curtail competition and to engineer a socially peaceful and stable transition to an industrial society dominated by old elites' (Wengenroth, 1997, p. 139).

Academic interest in German industrial capitalism is attributable in part to the Gershenkron latecomer thesis and in part to the existence of certain unique institutions. Notable among these are the representation of banks as stakeholders on governing boards, co-determination with employee representation on workers' councils and a unique system of apprenticeship training that acts as a regular source of technical manpower. Of special interest to academics is the extraordinary postwar economic recovery identified with a brand of economic liberalism known as 'social market' or 'organized capitalism', 'coordinated managerial capitalism' or a 'coordinated market economy' (Herrigel, 1996).

In looking at the distinctiveness of German industrial capitalism in this chapter, I begin with an analysis of its historical development in the next section. The third section explores the institutional framework of German firms to see how external institutions like the state and banks cooperate in the functioning of business. The fourth section analyses the performance of the German economy and evaluates the role played by the social market model in Germany's 'economic miracle'. The fifth section looks at how German business has been able to resist the neoliberal transformation that has overtaken the Anglo-American group of countries. To understand this we then take a look at policies that were adopted to handle economic downturn arising out of German unification. The final section concludes the chapter with a summary.

Historical background

Herrigel's (1996) preference for the term industrial *orders* rather than industrial structure, or industrial organization, suggests that industrial

capitalism in Germany is a heterogenous system centred around two regional industrial systems. The first is a decentralized industrial order comprised of highly specialized small and medium-sized producers and a host of extra firm-supporting institutions whose origin dates back to the seventeenth and eighteenth centuries when regions had property relations, and political structures favoured small property holders who simultaneously engaged in agriculture and minor industrial pursuits. The second and more recent is the autarkic industrial order (nineteenth century) dominated by large-scale vertically integrated enterprises with ties to universal banks. Producers in the autarkic industrial order, like producers in the decentralized industrial order, 'attempted to maximize flexibility in production and favoured the production of relatively specialized products'. However, the autarkic industrial order 'relied upon the firm and large-scale enterprise to govern the strategy, whereas the producers in the decentralized industrial order did not' (p. 2). Herrigel's thesis is that 'the heterogeneity of governance that exists at the regions and industrial levels also exists at the national level in the form of a non-integrated composite architecture of national industrial-governance structure' (Herrigel, 1996, p. 2).

In offering a different interpretation to the otherwise unified organized capitalism version, Herrigel (1996) adopts a 'constructivist political economy' approach to emphasize the embedded and constructed character of these regional industrial systems (p. 3). He views 'both the social realm of the economy and the organizations and institutions that populate and govern it as the outcome of historically specific struggles among social actors over the constitution of the social division of labor' (p. 23). This approach resulted in his reinterpretation of German capitalism as Industrial Constructions (Herrigel, 1996) thus questioning the postwar political economy version of German industrialization as comprised of advanced technologies, large plants, concentrated markets and universal banks linked closely with enterprises and a helpful state (Herrigel, 1996, p. 4). The organized capitalism interpretation of German industrialization was, according to Herrigel (1996), an extension of the corporate capitalism model centred around (1) a unified concept of industrialization, (2) the firm as the centre of economic activity, and (3) clear separation of the roles of state and business (pp. 10–14). The thriving decentralized regional economy that existed was seen as anti-modern and as an appendage to the large-scale enterprise economy. Although research on the regional economy offered evidence of such a vibrant decentralized sector, academics steeped in mainstream thinking appeared reluctant to use the evidence to offer an alternative thesis

(Herrigel, 1996). The organized capitalism model associated with the Gershenkron catch-up thesis fits in with Herrigel's (1996) autarkic form of industrial order. Essentially, this was a regional specific form of industrialization in poor agricultural regions devoid of pre-industrial handicraft infrastructure. In the absence of infrastructure, production of all aspects took place under one roof leading to large-scale manufacture as late industrializers borrowed technology and aligned with banks for capital. This model of industrialization was regional in character and developed independent of the decentralized industrial order which was embedded in a dense network of relations between producers and public and private institutions involved in specialty production in small and medium-scale operations. Both types of industrial orders however were governed within a single national political economy where in some cases a parallel system of national governance was constructed for each of the forms of industrial order.

Two regional industrial orders exist in Germany. The first, known as autarkic industrial order, is consistent with the classical view of industrialization where production is confined to the boundaries of the firm as the logical outcome of specialization and the division of labour culminates in the sort of organized capitalism discussed in Chapter 4. The other, known as decentralized industrial order, operates on the principles of mutual dependence, trust and cooperation as depicted in Chapter 6 as 'Alternative Capitalism'. Both types have continued to operate within a national political economy in Germany (Herrigel, 1996).

The institutional features unique to German capitalism are, one, the law passed in 1884 requiring joint-stock companies to have a two-tier management – a management board and a supervisory board, and two, the universities which have made a major contribution to the development of industrial enterprise. Chandler Jr (1990) believes that financial and educational institutions played a more important part than government in the development of organizational capabilities. 'The organizational capabilities developed by the German first movers in the industries of the second industrial revolution – the industries so central to the growth of the modern economy – were more responsible for the rise of Germany's industrial power than those developed by American firms were for the industrial growth of the United States' (p. 499). These developments and the crucial role of education, banks and other organizational capabilities in the development of industrial enterprise will be discussed in greater detail elsewhere in this chapter.

The analysis above seeks to explain the development of industrial enterprise identified with the autarkic industrial order and is less applic-

able to the decentralized industrial order which worked in a different institutional environment. While the national political economy during the nineteenth century accommodated both industrial orders through a system of local autonomy, it was not uniform. The institutional arrangements for the two industrial orders were distinct, one relying on local institutions and the other expecting national level institutions to protect firms through a favourable legal, economic and political environment (Herrigel, 1996, p. 120).

While my focus in this study is confined to post-Second World War developments of industrial capitalism, my analysis of Germany as a distinctive model of 'the social market economy' cannot be understood unless one sees it in the context of its experience in the early twentieth century when agriculture, industry and the state aligned in promoting National Socialism which probably had its origins in the 'marriage of iron and rye' in the Weimar coalition (Gourevitch, 1986, pp. 21–2).

Such widespread national support for Fascism in the early twentieth century regarded even now by the Germans as a bleak period in their history has, according to Moore Jr (1966), to be viewed as the persistence of conservatism arising from development of industrial capitalism without a change in the traditional agrarian social structure (p. 438). The rise of Nazi power between 1933 and 1945, according to Wengenroth (1997), caused the institution of managerial capitalism to become politicized with decisions being dictated by governments (Wengenroth, 1997, p. 159).

The revival of the German economy, despite heavy loss and destruction during two world wars, is attributable to its reorganization on the lines of Ordoliberalism, a set of ideas generated by the Freiburg school. According to this philosophy, the state provided the framework for the promotion of a competitive economy allowing the economic and social aspects to meld into the 'social market economy'. Like regulation theory which acknowledges plurality of institutions, Ordoliberalism, according to Eucken's *Foundations of Economics*, emphasized interdependence between organizational forms of societies, that is, between economic, legal and social orders. Fundamental to the principle of constitutional law is the striving for competitive prices where the state plays an active role. 'Two groups of principles for action by the state stand out: the constituent principles, which relate to the creation of rules for a competitive order, and the regulating principles, concerned with keeping the competitive order working. Eucken lists six constituent principles of a well-functioning market economy: free and competitive markets, monetary stability, private ownership of the means of production, freedom of

contract responsibility for economic decisions and stability of economic policy' (Delorme, 2001, pp. 19–20).

In taking responsibility for the constituent principles, the state is not expected to interfere in the day-to-day process of the functioning of the economy. According to the 'Freiburg School', the state's role lies in providing a framework of rules to be monitored with respect to its effects on the competitive process under changing circumstances. However it is only one part of the active role of the state in the social market economy (Delorme, 2001, p. 20).

This combination of a market economy with social principles has gained consensus from the major parties and contributed to both long-term stability and flexibility in adjusting to external economic pressures (Katzenstein,1987). 'More fundamentally, "Ordoliberalism" was deeply rooted in a particular perception of Germany's economic and political history that offered an answer to the question of how Nazi totalitarianism could have risen in a country of Kant, Goethe and Beethoven' (Giersch et al., 1992, pp. 26–7).

Postwar reconstruction was carried out by a generation which had experienced that period of Nazi dictatorship. This ensured a system that would avoid any reversal to that period in history. Constitutionality, democracy, the welfare state and federalism, the four principles of the Basic Law of 1949, became the foundation for the new social economy. These fundamentals of the West German constitution 'testify to the memory of the perversion of justice and the constitution under Nazi rule'. 'Correlating to this "faith in the state" is the high regard paid to *legality* in Germany. In accordance with the principle of constitutionality, any state action will be judged by its conformity to the constitution.... Constitutionality and the idea of the welfare state are seen equally as the expression of moral virtues, such as social justice' (Kaufmann, 1998, p. 90). In this process of reconstruction assisted by the Marshall Plan, the allied occupation forces played a crucial role in breaking down the vestiges of centralized nation-centred approach to economic organization, encouraging the openness and interdependence critical to market liberalism.

The institutional framework

Defeated but not destroyed, Germany in the 1940s was faced with the task of rebuilding its economy as well as extinguishing what appeared to be an extensive and dominant role of the state in industry. The second task was the transformation of its militaristic economy into a civilian

economy. Both tasks were undertaken under a new economic constitution which adopted a middle way between the excesses of capitalism and that of socialist planning. 'The middle course, the "third way", could be presented as both expedient and desirable, thus the concept of the "social market economy" was elevated to a central position in the official doctrine of the Christian democrats and their allies' (Leaman, 1988, pp. 48–9). While Germany's economic recovery has been generally credited to the social market economy, Ordoliberalism contributed a fair share. 'While "Ordoliberalism" is the commonly used expression for the underlying set of ideas, the term "social market economy" became the brand name both for the blueprint of a desirable economic order which the Ordoliberals advocated and for the actual economic system of West Germany since 1948' (Giersch *et al.*, 1992, p. 31). The social market economy was not intended to distance itself from external models, American or Soviet; rather, its selection was guided by the desire to avoid the negative experience of a history of monopolies and price fixing by cartels which had undermined the self-regulatory mechanism of the market. While emphasizing individual freedom as a Christian belief in the equality of all human beings, the Ordoliberals were concerned about safeguarding it from intrusions by private agents, especially monopolies, cartels and organizations of vested interests (Giersch *et al.*, 1992, p. 28). 'Hence, the German Ordoliberals demanded more than the minimal state (Nachtwachterstaat) of laissez-faire liberalism. They explicitly advocated a strong state. Broadly speaking, government was to gain this strength vis-à-vis sectional interests and to preserve its status as the impartial and incorruptible arbiter of the economic process against short-term interventionist temptations by limiting its own scope to a few essential tasks' (Giersch *et al.*, 1992, pp. 28–9).

In this process of economic transformation, the political system where the *Landers* were to be the focus of industrial activity, industry was intended to be small, divided and competitive. This however did not occur. As industry had already been organized on a large scale, the natural outcome was increased concentration. In the 1960s a shift from coal-based industry towards automobile manufacture led to a shift in the culture of German managers from a particular emphasis on technical aspects of industry to a more consumer and market oriented focus. Despite this shift towards the American model, the continued influence of traditional institutions like banks, workers' councils and two-tier boards of engineers and scientists has led to it being dubbed the 'Rhenish model'. Albert (1993) comments:

With the collapse of communism, it is as if a veil has been suddenly lifted from our eyes. Capitalism, we can now see, has two faces, two personalities. The neo-American model is based on individual success and short-term financial gain; the Rhine model, of German pedigree but with strong Japanese connections, emphasizes collective success, consensus and long-term concerns. In the last decade or so, it is this Rhine model – unheralded, unsung and lacking even nominal identity papers – that has shown itself to be the more efficient of the two, as well as more equitable. (p. 18)

In establishing such a unique model after a long period of dislocation involving the world wars, one must not overlook the continued influence of industry associations, the banks, two-tier boards and higher education combined with support from the state. In addition, other institutions such as corporate bodies, foundations and institutes organized under public law also carry out important policy functions. 'The untranslatable German term "subsidiary right" (Subsidiratat's prinzip) expresses the political interest of marshalling the expertise and initiative of the main social sectors under the auspices of state administration. Put briefly, West Germany's parapublic institutions merge public and private bureaucracies and are described as the semi-sovereign state' (Katzenstein, 1987, p. 58).

Unlike other industrialized economies, Germany is, according to Crouch (1993), characterized by two features, 'the organized nature of its business, and its obsession with the creation of industrial skill'. Both features and their relationship to the state 'feed on the legacy of medieval guild society' (p. 84). In summing up the unique institutional basis and its historical links to medieval guilds, Crouch asserts that 'the central import of these institutions was that they embodied the idea of political authority over economic questions being shared between the state as such and representative bodies of the various trades and crafts' (p. 84). These institutions contributed to the unique framework of modern German industrial capitalism discussed below.

(a) Industry associations

Historically German industry has had sector-based industry associations which have constantly lobbied for industry interests with both regional and central governments. A major role was played in postwar reconstruction by the Federation of German Industry established in 1949, an organizational structure comprised of 39 industrial federations with a hierarchy of smaller industrial associations. Such associations are

accorded consultative status in government by the German constitution. A hierarchical arrangement of consultation was initially established in 1926 under the Weimar Republic and that hierarchy was reinforced during the Nazi period (Shonfield, 1965, pp. 242–3). Such industry-based associations, while useful in planning for an industry, also encouraged cooperation in research and development. In the long-term interests of the industry, such cooperation has encouraged consultation of proposed legislation affecting industry, indicating that French-type planning reminiscent of the horse and rider alliances of the Bismarck era are no longer favoured (Shonfield, 1965, p. 246).

That consultative process extends to other areas such as capital and labour, particularly wage bargaining. Albert (1993) comments that German society prefers to avoid contentious issues which are likely to disrupt social consensus (p. 110). By being assigned sole representation for some interests by the state, industry associations foster stable relationships among their members, forsaking the pluralist view of distancing them from the state. Such close association with the state does not prevent them from advancing the interests of their members and obtaining concessions from the state. In exchange for such support there is the expectation that interest associations will contribute to public policy functions by disseminating information to their members and ensuring that such members act responsibly. 'Systems of government in which important public policy functions are carried out by an established structure of organised group interests have been labelled "corporatist"' (Streeck, 1983, p. 266). Weiss (1998) describes public and private sector relations as 'private interest governance' (PSG) by which the state delegates activities avoiding the need for regulation seen in Anglo-American capitalism (1998).

The corporatist model of business associations and the state that has gradually emerged in the process of resolving individual problems is described as 'corporatism by default'. The reality is that German business associations are closer to the state than to the market. 'Compared to an American lobbying firm, business associations in Germany look almost like state bureaucracies: their internal hierarchical and division structure, the career pattern of their staff and their salary scales resemble those of state agencies; their proportion of staff drawn from the civil service clearly exceeds that coming from member firms; and leading officials have no difficulties comparing themselves in terms of status and prestige to corresponding ranks in the civil service' (Streeck, 1983, p. 281). The extensive use of associations assigned with quasi-public functions makes Germany 'the most densely organized civil society

among the larger countries' (Streeck, 1996, p. 39). This relationship between industry associations and the state operates on the principle of 'social partnership' between the state, banks, business and labour. Within the partnership of Ordoliberal philosophy 'which underlines the German social market economy', there is a place for anti-trust anti-cartel legislation to prevent free markets turning into cartels and mergers with monopolistic power (Giersch *et al.*, 1992). In comparative terms, this network of industry associations in Germany plays an intermediary role between state and business, akin to a real community relationship. Acceptance of such a role of mutual obligation and responsibility is seen by Crouch (1993) as a possible substitute to the 'depletion of moral legacy' lamented by Hirsch (1976, pp. 86–7).

(b) Banks

Social partnership or industrial collaboration was extended to banks which played a crucial role in allocation of resources. As initiators of industrial activity, banks screened such policy from politics. They also influenced the functioning of business through equity holdings which allowed them membership of supervisory boards (Kenworthy, 1997). The role of German banks in industrial development evolved from the combined experience of French industrial banks, the Credit Mobiliere, which offered long-term credit, and commercial banks in Britain which offered short-term credit. By comparison they were sounder financial institutions because of the close relations maintained with industrial enterprise, enhanced by their membership of supervisory boards (Gershenkron, 1988). 'A German bank, as the saying went, accompanied an industrial enterprise from the cradle to the grave, from establishment to liquidation throughout all the vicissitudes of its existence' (Gershenkron, 1988, p. 117). This particular role of banks in industrial investment is to be viewed in terms of specific instruments of industrialization in a backward country. Another contributing factor is the stipulation under a law passed in 1896 that prohibits dealings on the stock exchange in the shares and bonds of any company until a year has elapsed after registration. This renders companies dependent on banks for funds during this period. Such farsightedness in German policy elicited the following comment: 'Here one catches a clear glimpse of the underlying vision of the lawmakers who shaped the institutional structure of the German economy – the banks as prefects who will keep a watchful eye on a new company for a test period (one year), who will restrain speculative excesses of undisciplined investors, and who have the authority ultimately, through their control of shareholders' proxy votes, to tell the

managers of German industry where they get off' (Shonfield, 1965, p. 249). That relationship between banks and industry has changed gradually as industry has developed and become independent.

As one of the pillars of corporate governance, banks play a dominant role in company financing and as members of supervisory boards. Their influence in the functioning of banks rests on 13 per cent voting rights from shareholdings, 10 per cent from subsidiary investments, and 61 per cent of proxy voting rights cast for other shareholders. With significant ownership the bank usually has a representative on the supervisory board which controls company management to prevent misuse of power. Their position is further enhanced by their role in company financing of both short-term and long-term credits which account for 25 per cent of corporate funding requirement. Finally banks in their role as independent external monitors contribute to an efficient system of corporate governance. By holding seats on boards of important corporations, they can pool information on the basis of which they steer investment throughout the country. This according to Spulber endows Germany with a kind of unofficial 'collective economic policy' through a system of coordination between private and public banks (1995, p. 98). With the current pressure in certain sectors for promoting shareholder value, Jurgens *et al.*, (2000) suggest that large German banks 'are sheltered from outside pressure by dense networks of cross-holding proxy votes, and undeveloped disclosure obligations. Therefore bank managers are not forced to pursue value-maximizing investment and monitoring policy' (p. 62).

By giving banks a vital role in financing industry, the state indirectly plays a significant role in promoting industry and achieving a level of economic and political stability. However, the role of banks in the development of German industrial capitalism cannot be isolated from other institutional structures like the two-tier boards or codetermination in which the state plays a vital role.

(c) Codetermination

The involvement of banks in the long-term funding of industrial enterprise is closely linked with their operations as members of supervisory boards. Introduced in Germany in the late nineteenth century with the intention of avoiding the centralization of power which had created conditions leading to the unsavoury alliances between economic interests and the Nationalist Socialist state, this practice assumed a different dimension after the Second World War. 'Thus for the advocates of economic democracy, the most important issue in the reform of the

German autarkic industrial order was to make it more self-governing and internally democratic and thereby independent of state power' (Herrigel, 1996, p. 208). The tradition of industrial democracy in Germany through participation of workers in management dates back to 1848. The passage of the Codetermination Law in Coal and Steel Industry ensured that industry would provide for the demands of the general population. This was extended to plant-level codetermination through works councils in all West German enterprises by the passage of the 1952 Works Constitution Act (Herrigel, 1996, p. 208).

The development of codetermination in Germany has to be seen in a historical context. As an institutionalized form of conflict resolution, codetermination developed as an 'expression of a relatively weak position of German entrepreneurs between the still dominant feudal powers on the one hand and the growing workers' movement on the other hand' (Nutzinger and Backhaus, 1988, p. 165). Gradually it has established itself as an effective system of interest articulation within the German system of industrial relations. It is not, as is commonly interpreted, a system of worker participation but one of common responsibility for both employers and employees (Nutzinger and Backhaus, 1988, p. 174). While there are various interpretations and misconceptions on what codetermination sets out to do, Nutzinger 'perceives codetermination as an attempt to increase the area of purposeful co-operation between employer and employees, based on partly uniform interests, e.g., in the economic success of the enterprise, by means of institutional participation of employees and their representatives within the conflict relationship between "capital" and "labor"' (Nutzinger and Backhaus, 1988, p. 177).

The participation of workers through workers' councils is the third dimension of the two-tier boards – the board of directors, responsible for company management and the supervisory board elected by shareholders at the Annual General Meeting (AGM) whose role is to oversee the activities of the board of directors (Albert, 1993, p. 110). Workers' representatives are elected to the supervisory boards and all issues relating to workers are negotiated at this level. Under the co-responsibility arrangement, workers and their unions enjoy considerable influence in the running of business. 'The creators of the institutions of codetermination presupposed a particular conceptualization of the economy in which the firm as the basic organizational unit was completely taken for granted' (Herrigel, 1996, p. 208). The social arrangements between state and society have an influence over the degree of centralization and the level of competitiveness. According to Hart (1992), business is

centralized in Germany because of the role played by the three universal banks and as a counterweight to centralized labour. 'The centralization of German business also stems from a legal environment that creates national forums for tripartite bargaining among government, business and labour for wages and other labour market issues' (p. 283). Unlike other industrialized countries, labour plays an important role in German industrial capitalism. It is built on the high skill level of German workers and is linked to the German educational system and its system of apprenticeship training. Under the tripartite system of participation and consultation, the growing power of labour allows it a voice in policy forums (Hart, 1992, p. 284).

In the type of governance adopted in Germany there is greater involvement of various groups in the community – a factor that can be understood as a reaction to industry–state cooperation during the wars and as a product of the financial structure whereby banks rather than the stockmarket influence the fortunes of business. A clear strategy of postwar German recovery was to keep the militaristic elites, identified with the Nazi state, at a distance. 'The postwar order, therefore, combined a desire for a competitive market with a highly weakened and federalized state to guarantee that the excesses of the recent past would not be repeated' (Hart, 1992, p. 297). Albert (1993) considers the German system of power sharing as rewarding to companies and immensely beneficial to workers. Institutionalized in a legal regime, the important role played by labour in the working of business combined with their skills resulted in consistent growth and support for technological improvements. However the desire to maintain jobs resulted in less enthusiasm among labour unions to the adoption of new technologies such as microelectronics (Hart, 1992, p. 285).

The democratization of industry centred around the functioning of works councils had its impact on the entire functioning of industrial enterprises. While providing a source for generating information on daily operations, such works councils 'created a productive culture of reciprocity, conflictual solidarity, and flexibility between labor and management that encouraged them to resolve conflicts resulting from changing competitive conditions through internal negotiation within the firm' (Herrigel, 1996, p. 209). Employees in German companies have a strong voice through representation and corporatist bargaining. The system that has been institutionalized allows selected works councils the right to negotiate key issues with management, including the hiring of new employees, and the introduction of new technology; and in the case of redundancies to negotiate social plans, covering redeployment,

severance payments and early retirement (Vitols, 2001, p. 343). When compared with the rest of Europe, German industrial relations are relatively peaceful. In Helmut Schmidt's view, 'while the other advanced economies are endowed with the conventional three factors of production, the Modell Deutschland economy is blessed with a fourth, namely "social peace"' (Offe, 2000, p. 16). In seeking to explain this, Olson (1982) attributes the weakness of distributional coalitions in West Germany to defeat in war and foreign occupation. This view is disputed by Giersch *et al.*, (1992). 'In summary, the image of the organizationally weak unions is hardly borne out by facts, except in the first two years after the currency reform, when strike funds were still insufficient. If at all, the "weakness" of the unions must have been of a more indirect sort'. One explanation offered is that unions were so focused on promoting legislation governing codetermination that other issues for practical reasons received less attention (p. 75). The social organization of the industrial order based on codetermination was strengthened by the success of the German economy and this again strengthened the roots of German democracy in the 1950s (Giersch *et al.*, 1992; Herrigel, 1996).

The history of postwar industrial relations in Germany is characterized by harmony between labour and management based on legislation which regulates a strong federation of 17 unions. The sound legal framework of industrial relations lays down working conditions, rules for job security, welfare and fringe benefits, collective wage bargaining and so on. Closed shop and political strikes are illegal. While spared the type of industrial conflict faced by other industrialized countries, Germany views labour as a 'precious commodity', encouraging management to introduce efficiency-enhancing technical innovations, invest in training, and cultivate labour–management relations (Offe, 2000, p. 17).

What makes the German system unique is the underlying cooperation in the labour–management partnership. While the system has been successful during periods of growth and low unemployment, declining growth and increasing unemployment in recent years have strained industrial relations. However the legal framework, historical factors and strong loyalty from both sides have worked together to sustain that harmony even during economic downturns.

A setback to such harmony took place when unions went on strike in the 1970s over the introduction of the 35-hour work week and contemplated changes to rules dealing with strikes and lockouts. The changes were seen as an attempt by a new government to weaken the labour movement. According to Katzenstein (1987), the strike sent a warning

to business to desist from underestimating union power and reiterated the importance of industrial harmony.

Interestingly this episode coincided with the use of coercive power by the Conservative government in Britain to break a strike by coalminers and printing workers against the introduction of new technology. In 1992, Germany experienced a major strike by public service and transport unions seeking higher wages. The Kohl government acceded to these in order to avoid widespread disruption. Unlike labour unions in other industrialized countries (except Sweden), German unions have withstood attempts by right-wing parties and large corporations to dominate politics following the economic downturn of the 1970s. Swenson (1989) commented:

> Comparative evidence from advanced industrial democracies confirms that centralized, politically unified, and 'encompassing' unions score greater social and economic policy successes through the democratic process than their more fragmented counterparts in other countries. It also suggests that the economies they operate in perform comparatively well, if not consistently better than others, because of social and political mechanisms foreign to conventional economic theory. (p. 2)

German industrial relations based on centralized wage bargaining came under pressure from neoliberals who advocated deregulation to overcome the rigidities of the system. Despite the pressure, employers favoured greater flexibility while remaining within the industry-wide bargaining structure. Employers, according to Thelen and Kume, still prefer to negotiate collectively with unions rather than face them alone. In adopting this position, the employers' associations are not united in their stand on deregulation of industrial relations. The study by Thelen and Kume establishes that the survival of the German model of industrial relations hinges not merely on the strength of the ability of the unions to beat back the neoliberal offensive. The more pressing task for unions is to combat the flagging solidarity of the employers and to shore up their embattled organizations (1999, p. 498).

Codetermination, the institutional basis of German industrial relations which has undoubtedly contributed to the extraordinary postwar economic performance, is explicable by the adoption of ideas such as social capital (Coleman, 1988). Whether the cooperation witnessed in the working of German industrial relations or the apprentice scheme based on the type of trust attributed by Putnam (1993) to the high rate

of social engagement in certain regions of Italy can be acknowledged as social capital is debatable. Kenworthy (1997) equates Putnam's social capital with trust and doubts if this is vital in cooperative economic behaviour. Certain institutional arrangements, he writes, generate cooperative behaviour without relying on trust and this is a helpful but not necessary condition for economically beneficial cooperative behaviour (pp. 647–9).

Thelen (2001) sees contemporary changes in industrial relations adopting the varieties of capitalism approach that distinguishes different types of political-economic systems. From that perspective, she sees increasing divergence between the 'coordinated' and 'liberal' market economies. Such divergence between the two types of economies at the macro-level impacts on the micro-level strategies pursued by employers as they respond to the new terms of competition. In liberal market economies, employers search for flexibility at the plant level which brings them into conflict with unions on whom they bring pressure to gain managerial freedom. While coordinated market economies also seek flexibility at the plant level, sectoral bargaining institutions have proved more resilient.

Being embedded institutional arrangements, labour markets encourage employers to adopt competitive strategies around quality which require greater stability and cooperation with labour. While greater deregulation has been predicted with globalization, this applies to Anglo-American economies faced with the decline of unions and collective bargaining. When firms compete on the basis of quality and reliability, their capacity to adjust depends on stable cooperative relations at plant level. That explains, according to Thelen, the reluctance of employers to move towards total decentralization (p. 76).

Attributing the working of industrial relations in Germany to trust, Kern (1998) feels that the gradual decline arising out of changes in the global economy has affected employer–employee relations. Further, Kern believes that this decline in trust has implications for innovation in German industry, if one perceives plant level relations are reciprocal in terms of community and therefore instrumental to German prosperity. That prosperity is now threatened by declining trust as employer groups question the continued relevance of the 'old patterned reciprocal commitment'. Kern argues his case in the context of its effect on innovation by identifying types of employees each influenced by a different nexus of relationship ranging between motivation, risk-taking, creativity and trust. Underlying such analysis is the increasing scepticism of critics who consider German social market institutions as being more

suited to stability than to rapid change. To sum up, 'the consensual, centripetal and cooperative nature of German politics is nowhere more clearly evident than in the field of politics of social policy and economic policy in the 1960s. After all, this decade saw the consensual adoption of basic and comprehensive economic policy, labour market and vocational training legislation' (Offe, 2000, p. 18).

Anglo-American critics who promote shareholder value claim that codetermination has a negative effect on shareholder wealth. In Germany shareholders play a limited role when compared with Anglo-American economies and the roles of capital and labour representatives on supervisory boards are determined by law. Summing up the research on codetermination, Jurgens *et al.* (2000) feel there is no support for such a claim. Unlike Anglo-American boards which represent shareholder interests only, codetermination gives workers' representatives rights of information and consultation, and rights of veto. Offering a balanced assessment to ward off sustained pressure towards shareholder value, Jurgens *et al.* (2000) conclude 'while the financial system is changing very rapidly, as new actors, motivations and behaviours assert themselves, it is much more difficult to find signs of erosion within the system of co-determination. Indeed the system of co-determination is seldom attacked openly by company management' (p. 72). That 'financial mobility as a route to optimal outcomes is gaining ground among influential German corporate managers, bankers and academics' is more than a little ironic for O'Sullivan (2000, p. 232).

In comparing the different types of industrial economies, it is important to note that liberal market economies (LMEs) rely exclusively on share markets for monitoring. In Gemany, information about the reputation and operation of a company is freely available to investors through (a) the close relationship that companies establish with major suppliers and clients, (b) knowledge gained from extensive cross-shareholding, and (c) joint membership in industry associations that gather information about companies in the course of coordinating technology transfer and vocational training (Hall and Soskice, 2001, p. 2). Such intensive networks offer multiple sources for the exercise of voice unlike the liberal market economies which rely on exit. In the context of the recent debacle of Enron in the United States, one wonders if such a situation could eventuate in a coordinated market economy.

(d) Education

In this section of the chapter I have examined industry associations, banks, two-tier governance structures and workers' councils that

combine to promote codetermination. Within that contribution to German capitalism one has to consider the technological rationality of German business in contrast to the pecuniary rationality of British business. While British business has tended to treat technology as a mere means to maximize returns, German business has tended to make the means the end (Landes, 1969, p. 354), placing great importance on higher technical education. In tracing the development of technical education in Germany, Lazonick and O'Sullivan (1997) show how the system gradually developed to cater to scientific needs and practical engineering by setting up higher institutes of technical education as well as trade schools. Disputes between academics and practitioners over their professional status at the turn of the century led to concentration of power in the engineering profession. A third group, the managerial and entrepreneurial engineers, in seeking to integrate both theory and practice, cemented links between German industry and technical education. While developing an education system that focused on industry, the state also played a crucial role by promoting a unified market and a unified Germany. This in turn created a demand for technical knowledge by hiring engineers from the higher institutes of technology and promoting skills in functional design and precision manufacturing. Such technical graduates took over managerial functions as industry became scientifically oriented (pp. 505–7).

The gradual shift from chemical to electrical and heavy machinery sectors required shop-level skills which German employers promoted, and as 'the century unfolded the Germans developed a unique process of shop-floor skill formation at the national level' (Lazonick and O'Sullivan, 1997, p. 508). Rooted in the guild system of craft apprenticeship of the middle ages, the German apprentice system was now transformed into a formal education structure supported by public and private funds. This vocational educational system is managed by industry, labour and local government officials, who determine the curriculum based on national standards as well as the needs of local companies (Wever and Allen, 1992, p. 37). Trainees attend courses, dividing their week at a state vocational training centre and at various positions at work according to their skills. The annual cost to West German industry is estimated at DM 35 billion (Smyser, 1992, pp. 78–9).

Each year over 70 per cent of people between the ages of 15 and 19 undertake two- to three-year apprenticeship schemes in over 40 different occupations. Such extensive skill training assures employment with good salaries and working conditions (Clark *et al.*, 1994). The success of this apprentice training scheme is seen in Germany's youth unemployment

rate – the lowest in any industrialized state. Unlike other industrialized societies, entry into such a programme is not seen as an inferior achievement in comparison with other professional careers. While trainees are assisted in making a gradual transition from school to work, the system of on-the-job training combined with time at a vocational training centre is beneficial for youth as well as the German economy.

There has been discussion on whether companies would invest in the German system of apprentice training for fear of such trainees being poached following completion of the training. Its success however proves that it is possible to sustain the scheme through employer coordination. While the scheme has gained international attention, there is still the issue of how to encourage employees to adopt it in the absence of institutions of the coordinating market economies. 'Existing theories in political economy suggest at least two alternative means of encouraging companies to invest in high skill training practices; private interest governance or the state. Employer led private interest governance is the most widely accepted model for understanding the functioning of high skill equilibrium in Western Germany' (Culpepper, 2001, p. 279).

As industry became both knowledge and capital intensive, the value placed on skills gained through the apprenticeship system declined. Some variations existed, however, across industrial sectors, with machinery production skills being rated higher than those in steel production. The survival of this scheme then became dependent on the medium-sized industries, the Mittelstand (Lazonick and O'Sullivan, 1997, p. 509). Skilled workers trained under the apprentice scheme were also affected by changes in the organization of mass production through dedication and automation particularly in the automobile industry.

Once regarded as having outlived its usefulness, the apprenticeship system has, according to Streeck (1997a, p. 211), emerged as an important social institution making a significant contribution to German economic performance.

Evaluating economic performance

The institutional framework of German industrial capitalism that I have discussed thus far is generally referred to as 'cooperative capitalism' in comparison with 'competitive capitalism' of the Anglo-American type. The major features of the former are: first, the interplay of contradictory principles of economic policy, such as social market economy, with the institutional framework to allow government to enforce rules while

allowing private actors freedom to operate; second, giving banks rather than the state the major role in allocating and reallocating resources between sectors; and finally, the continuing growth of that social partnership initiated in the 1960s intended to develop economic policy through consensus with major economic interests – the state, banks, firms and labour (Kenworthy, 1990, p. 251).

That historical circumstances shape the response of countries helps to explain the diversity within what is referred to as the institutions of capitalism. For example, while Germany and Japan encouraged cartels, the United States displayed a certain amount of reluctance towards them. The differing perceptions of 'large' by different cultures is a contributing factor in addition to the cultural assumptions associated with the freedom to associate and compete. While the state intervened through regulation in Anglo-American countries to promote competition, the German state refrained from doing so, believing that 'only fanatics of individualism would prohibit cartels'. Such differences in perception explain the variation in the development of industry structure in different countries (Fear, 1997, pp. 552–4; Whitley, 1999).

The performance of the German economy since the Second World War belies the generally accepted notion that cartels lead to disastrous economic performance (Fear, 1997, p. 553). Albert (1993) notes the importance attached to both Germany and Japan when the US Federal Reserve consulted the Bank of Japan and the Bundesbank prior to adopting measures to counter the 1987 crash. 'Few observers paused, in the midst of global panic, to savour an irony of this extraordinary reversal of fortunes' (pp. 127–8).

Prior to unification in 1990, West Germany was the most successful of the major economies, enjoying healthy trade and current account balances, low inequality of incomes and living standards, and higher wages than Japan and the United States. The combination of external competitiveness and high wage employment, according to Streeck (1997b), reflected 'the operation of a distinctive set of socio-economic institutions' (1997b, p. 34). An institutional framework, which had since the war accommodated the decentralized industrial order, was required with reunification to refocus the power of central government vis-à-vis regional and local autonomy bearing in mind the need to stabilize an increasingly integrated political economy. To do this, the Bund created a panel of macroeconomists representing five major institutes to undertake independent economic analysis of the German economy, and followed it up with the Stability and Growth Act 1967 to provide macroeconomic 'global guidance'. 'The law enjoined all of the relevant actors

to pursue policies that would keep the German economy within the "magic quadrangle" of full employment, steady growth, price stability, and stable value of the mark' (Herrigel, 1996, p. 270). In line with the cooperative and consultative institutional framework of policy-making, a group called the Konjunkturrat (or business-cycle council) comprising federal, regional and municipal levels of government, the Bundesbank, the industry associations and labour representatives, met on a regular basis to confer on issues generated by the integration of the two industrial orders. Despite efforts to preserve regional identities, what emerged, according to Herrigel (1996), were 'large mass-producing firms, close to large universal banks, engaged in cooperative relations with both the state and the trade unions over the best way to manage the West German economy' (p. 274).

Such emphasis on economic policy-making between 1961 and 1979 resulted in the lowest inflation rate, the lowest unemployment rates and respectable growth rates (Katzenstein, 1987, p. 104). Other factors that contributed to the success of the competitive economy were German consumers' preference for quality and the high savings rate that helped to generate capital. A committed labour force with avenues for exercising voice, rather than exit, enabled management to take a longer-term view. 'Above all, the success of the "German model" as long as it lasted, derived from the way in which it utilized social pressures for an egalitarian distribution of economic outcomes to generate an egalitarian distribution of productive capabilities, with the latter in turn enabling the economy to underwrite the former' (Streeck, 1997b, p. 42). According to O'Sullivan (2000), the system of organizational control influenced not just the patterns of generating wealth but also the manner in which it was generated. And by participating in the fruits of industrial success, employees contributed to relatively low income inequality (p. 252).

Germany emerged relatively unscathed through two oil shocks, declining economic growth, high inflation, adverse balance of payments and increasing unemployment through a period identified as the end of the 'golden age of capitalism'. Inflation fell from 7.1 per cent to 4.0 per cent in 1979. Further control of inflation led to stability in exchange rates and a decline in unemployment, which, having peaked to 3.7 per cent in 1976, fell to 3.2 in 1979. The national debt as a percentage of GNP rose from 20 per cent in 1972 to 28.8 per cent in 1978, well below the OECD average of 40 per cent. Just when it appeared that Germany might rescue the rest of the industrialized world from a depression, a second oil shock occurred resulting in adverse balance of payments deficit between 1979 and 1981, a fall in the rate of economic growth

of 0.7 in 1982 and a rise in inflation of 4.8 in 1980. Recovery, however, was quick. While the current account remained in surplus, inflation fell to 1.6 per cent in 1985 and to zero in 1986. Although economic growth rose to 2.7 in 1984, unemployment remained as high as 7.2 in 1985 (Hallett, 1990, pp. 93–4).

The efficacy of the German economic model which combines competitive economic efficiency with high economic equality and social cohesion is best understood from a historical and cultural context. 'German business was permeated according to Wengenroth by a vision of an organic economy' (Fear, 1997, p. 551). But the postwar economy that emerged – an almost impossible socio-economic mix in the opinion of most business and economic analysts – was, in effect, a reaction to the Third Reich. Dyson (1982) attributes the shaping of West German policy to two factors: (1) determined leadership in the face of crisis, and (2) power-sharing to restrain government in reaction to the leadership principle of the Third Reich (pp. 22–4). Streeck feels that historical and cultural explanations are insufficient and cites other conditions: (1) the existence of large world-wide markets for quality-competitive goods, (2) speedy innovation on the part of manufacturing to sustain edge in quality-competitive markets, and (3) a regular supply of labour to cope with the volume and character of demand in quality markets (1997b, pp. 42–3).

Despite the election of a conservative coalition in 1983, Germany has avoided taking new policy initiatives. An explanation for this lies in the structure of its political and economic institutions, among which the autonomous Bundesbank remains highly influential. 'Government by coalition, a system of cooperative federalism, and parapublic institutions are the three institutional nodes around which the politics of economic policy has unfolded in the Federal Republic... The secret of Germany's success evidently lay in the concentration of economic power in the hands of banks, trusts, and very large firms; the existence of a large number of highly competitive, small and medium sized firms; and the government's unwillingness to impose the trappings of state power over all of economic life' (Katzenstein, 1987, pp. 84–5). Apart from the institutional structure of the German political system, the two other factors that account for the gradualness or incremental nature of economic policy-making are: a distinctive neoliberal economic policy in which the state distances itself, demonstrating that it is not government's task to cope with structural change, and the consensus approach to policy-making which discourages abrupt shifts in policy. Despite the advocacy of alternative programmes by both sides of the political spectrum 'the politics of West German economic policy has constrained the

radical experimentation with either a strong dose of Keynesianism (as in France between 1981–83) or a strong dose of supply-side economics (as in Britain since 1979). Overall West German economic policy-makers have continued to display cautious, step-by-step orthodoxy in their search to defend stability through incremental policy change in a rapidly changing global economy' (Katzenstein, 1987, pp. 93–4). This approach is encouraged within a political system where government depends on the cooperation of other political actors in formulating and implementing economic policy.

While it adopts consultation for concerted action, the government is capable of enlisting the cooperation of business and unions and acting decisively to promote industry adjustment by incorporating other political actors. Examples that come to mind are the conversion from coal to oil in the energy sector and the crisis faced by the steel industry. According to Katzenstein (1987), the German approach to industrial adjustment is less intimate than Japan and France but deviates substantially from the arm's length approach of Britain and the US (p. 101). Commentators attribute Germany's economic stability to the distinctive institutional arrangements of coalition governments, cooperative federalism and its parapublic institutions. Terming this the semi-sovereign state, Katzenstein (1987) believes that its operation as such is the reason for its success (also see Giersch *et al.*, 1992). The semi-sovereign state works on

> three institutional nodes – coalition government, intergovernmental relations and parapublic institutions – that instil political caution and a preference for incremental policy change... The three nodes of West Germany's policy network open the state to the influence of parties, subordinate levels of government, and interest groups. But in fusing state and society, these nodes are also conduits in the formulation and implementation of policy. Since it links tightly most of the major organized political actors, thus multiplying potential sources of veto, West Germany's semi-sovereign state is not well equipped to initiate bold policy change.
>
> (Katzenstein, 1987, pp. 371, 385)

Such a consensus-based adjustment process provided a basis for weathering economic downturns like the persistently high levels of unemployment experienced by West Germany in the 1980s. For example, between 1978 and 1983, the annual rate of unemployment increased from 4.1 per cent to 9.1 per cent, leaving 2.3 million jobless. A

range of options was presented to employers and government by the unions. Thus the short-term-crisis approach which is normally adopted by Anglo-American capitalist markets was avoided and a longer-term beneficial arrangement, a product of the social systems of production, was adopted (Streeck, 1997b, p. 44). The natural responsibility of society in Western Europe to govern 'its' economy, and restrain individual preferences is described by Streeck as 'beneficial constraint'. 'In other words, the notion of beneficial constraint implies that there is no such thing as a self-sufficiently "rational" efficient economy apart from and outside society, into which the latter may or may not decide to intervene, and that how "rational" an economy is depends on the social institutions within which it is enclosed' (Streeck, 1997a, p. 198). That assessment is confirmed by Gray (1998) who emphatically claims that 'none of the countries of continental Europe has ever had an age of laissez faire; market institutions have not achieved the independence from constraint by other social institutions that characterizes the Anglo-Saxon free market. No European society has the long and deep experience of individualist forms of family life and property ownership that distinguishes England, the United States and other Anglo-Saxon societies' (pp. 73–4).

The strong institutional foundations of German capitalism explain why the liberals were unable to extend the neoliberal policies of deregulation and privatization which elsewhere were accepted as automatic solutions to restrain the role of the state in the economy. With unification, the issue of privatizing East German state enterprises came to the forefront. The solution, perceived within a broader framework, was to rescue them with state help (Esser, 1994, pp. 105–6). Once again the explanation lies in the dense network of economic, political and social interests responsible for infrastructure, transport, training, social and industrial policy. The demarcation between public and private that one observes in other industrialized economies is less pronounced in the decentralized industrial order prevalent in Germany where interdependence is the governing principle of relationships. As mutual contribution to the economy of the region is vital, privatization is less of an issue. The social market economy clearly designates a role for the state within a liberal market framework, and certain public monopolies such as the federal railway system, post and telecommunications and inland navigation are protected from denationalization by requiring the passage of a two-thirds majority in both houses of parliament. One explanation offered for limited privatization is the less than successful attempt to privatize VEBA and Volkswagen in the 1960s. Apparently popular

capitalism does not appeal to Germans, who, being reluctant to invest in shares, prefer other forms of investment. Attempts at privatization in the mid-1980s were hesitant, as public ownership, seen as limited in comparison with other European countries, is regarded as essential to national interests (Esser, 1994, pp. 108–17).

The economic miracle: could it last?

German capitalism best known as 'social market economy' has its foundation in its historical past and includes the strength of Bismarck's welfare system, while avoiding the dangers of concentration of power in business and the state (Offe, 2000). This reflects the importance attached by the Ordoliberals to safeguarding individual freedom against intrusions by private agents, especially monopolies, cartels and organizations of vested interests (Giersch *et al.*, 1992, p. 28).

The underlying arrangement between capital and labour, the foundation of the German social market which, for several decades, had ensured international competition, high level of wages and welfare with low levels of social inequality was, in the 1980s, threatened by the occurrence of persistent structural unemployment. More difficulties emerged with a new generation of leaders within the unions and structural and technological changes. The new problems brought on by unification and globalization placed increasing difficulties on an institutional system of industrial relations which had been created for a different era (Giersch *et al.*, 1992; Hassel and Schulten, 1999).

Having weathered the energy crisis and the economic decline of the 1970s experienced by other industrialized economies in the 1980s, West Germany was faced with the major hurdle of unification in 1990. A politico-economic system, which varied greatly from its own, had to be absorbed at a time when its own economy was weakening. The exercise involved the transplantation of West German institutions such as 'socially circumscribed markets, negotiated firms, enabling state intervention and market-regulating associations' to East Germany. A major task was the instituting of parity in wage and skill levels between the two, and, in fact, raising East German levels to those in the West. An estimated investment of 900 billion German Marks (DM) was transferred to the five new *Lander* to promote East German economic development and to meet the costs of social security measures. Streeck admits that the financial burden of German unification could erode the German model of social consensus and ultimately end up

affecting the 'quality-competitive "social market economy"' (Streeck, 1997b, p. 48).

Despite the claims of the German social market model, the fact that Anglo-American countries adopted neoliberal policies in response to the recession of the early 1970s gave market liberals an opportunity to oppose it. Even though the German economy continued to be internationally competitive in terms of exports and added value per worker, the momentum for reform resulted in the Kohl government announcing a series of measures in its 50 point programme in 1990. The reform targeted worker benefits like sick pay which was reduced from 100 to 80 per cent of salary for the first six weeks, then to 70 per cent for the next 78 weeks, after which the worker would be entitled to a state disability benefit. Other changes to dismissal rules, age of retirement and changes to health entitlements resulted in a saving of 2 per cent of GDP (Upchurch, 1999, p. 68).

The response was primarily an austerity measure to counter the cost of unification. The measures led to a fall by 10 per cent in unit labour costs in manufacturing in the year to February 1997, reflecting moderate pay settlements in 1996 of an average of 1.5 per cent and an increase in productivity of 8 per cent (Upchurch, 1999, p. 69). 'In achieving them both unions and employers have had to adopt a range of strategies and tactics. In doing so, the German model having shifted fundamentally as neoliberalism was becoming ascendant, the framework of co-determination has remained intact' (Upchurch, 1999, pp. 69–73; Thelen and Kume, 1999). In this changed environment of market liberalization and deregulation which sees German industrial relations to be a liability, there is likely to be direct challenge to the power of organizational labour (Upchurch, 1999, p. 87).

Consequently, the view of the German economy as a superior model of capitalism (Albert, 1993) has been challenged on grounds that it may not be sustainable. Sectors of the economy affected by the economic problems are in search of alternative solutions such as restructuring, reduction of the welfare state and alternative ways of maintaining the status quo (Kaufmann, 1998, pp. 95–6).

In the late 1990s, the German economy faced unemployment and a rising tide of strikes against the Kohl government's austerity programme. All these have raised questions about the efficacy of the German model in the face of international competition and the increasing cost of unification. Despite the post-unification problems, the social market model has been noted for its long-term consensus approach and acclaimed as an alternative to the Thatcherist laissez faire model of

deregulation. Upchurch lists the following features contained in the German model:

1. an insider system of corporate governance creating a sense of corporate solidarity not seen in Anglo-Saxon companies
2. an aversion to equity culture and a reliance on bank financing
3. a regulatory culture in the public interest
4. social partnership between employers and workers backed up by sectoral collective bargaining
5. a stability culture in monetary policy directed by the Bundesbank; and
6. an ordoliberalism whereby state intervention in the economy is confined to ensuring regulated conformity with the principle of market competition. (Upchurch, 1999, p. 60)

The post-1990s shift towards shareholder value has brought further pressure for change (Ziegler, 2000). Such pressure from capital mobility through cross-border transactions is, according to Ziegler (2000), to be viewed in the context of national institutional variations. While economies vary on the basis of how enterprises are financed, managed and organized, the diversity of German enterprises acts as an obstacle to automatic changes in form from international forces of globalization. The other difference is in the variation in concept of efficiency. The Anglo-American emphasizes rate of return on investment based on short-term, while countries such as Japan and Germany sacrifice the short-term for longer-term allocative efficiency. Fundamental to the difference between the German and the Anglo-American concept of corporate governance is the latter's 'conception of property rights and the German conception of the firm as a constitutional construction for balancing the interests of contending social groups' (Ziegler, 2000, p. 211).

Notwithstanding the accommodation between labour and capital which was intended to promote economic and social objectives like competitiveness in international quality markets, the management of such an economy at a time when capital and labour are increasingly mobile has become difficult. In the case of Germany, the shift of labour and capital has been towards Europe, with the Euro currency completing the regionalization process. 'As national boundaries wither away, and the German financial sector dissolves into a globally integrated financial services industry, the special relationship between German banks and German firms may increasingly become less "relational"

and more market-like' (Streeck, 1997b, p. 51). While the shift towards globalization is inevitable, it is yet premature to conclude that this has or will undermine the German model. In a rapidly changing economy where the emphasis of German government policy has always been on doing things better rather than on doing them first, the goal of its high-quality and high-cost manufacturing may place its economy at a disadvantage when competing with manufacturers from Asia who focus on high quality at low cost. What is becoming increasingly obvious is that Germany cannot continue to rely on traditional manufacturing industries for economic growth unless it directs its resources towards newer technologies such as semiconductors and information technology (Burton and Hanson, 1993). Moving into new areas that demand innovation is seen as problematic in the context of an institutional framework of codetermination which requires considerable consultation to arrive at a consensus in an atmosphere generally regarded as unresponsive to external pressures.

Conclusion

As we have seen in this study, Germany offers an alternative model of capitalism falling somewhere between the Anglo-American unrestrained market-type and the Japanese 'Developmental State'. In conceiving the concept of the 'social market economy', Germany's postwar leaders instituted a modified version of market with social responsibility, reflecting, on the one side, the need to restrain the power of the state, and, on the other, the prospects of effective collaboration between labour and capital. The success of this model over 50 years has to be seen in the context of the cooperative and consultative culture that developed in the process of instituting it and is a credit to the political parties and their leaders who adopted moderation as a prerequisite for success.

Rejecting the American competitive market, the German model of cooperative capitalism instituted a set of social institutions encouraged by the state which included industry associations, banks and a system of governance based on codetermination and workers' councils. Such a cooperative relationship between state, business and labour is quite distinct from either the Anglo-American adversarial model or that of state guidance of the Japanese variety. The performance of the German economy until the mid-1980s is evidence of the viability of the model particularly in comparison to the Anglo-American. That both Germany and Japan have successfully withstood crises similar to those faced by capitalist economies and handled them differently raises an important

difference and that point of difference is the role of the state. While neoliberals are strongly in favour of keeping the state out of markets, recent critics of comparative capitalism extensively cited in this study favour the social systems of production that act as restraints.

In favouring a historical view that acknowledges the social context in the development of industrial capitalism, the resilience of the German economy is strong evidence of my stance. The oil shocks of the 1970s, the repeated recessions of the 1980s, the unification of 1990 and the changes to the European Union appear to have been easily absorbed by Germany while retaining its position as a powerful actor in the region as well as the world. While there are areas that other industrialized economies can emulate, careful analysis must precede replication.

References

Albert, Michael, *Capitalism vs Capitalism* (New York: Four Walls Eight Windows, 1993).
Arrighi, Giovanni, *The Long Twentieth Century: Money, Power and the Origins of Our Times* (London: Verso, 1994).
Burton, Daniel and Kathleen M. Hanson, 'German Technology Policy: Incentives for Industrial Innovation', *Challenge*, vol. 37 (1), January–February (1993), 37–47.
Chandler Jr, Alfred, *Scale and Scope: The Dynamics of Industrial Capitalism* (Cambridge, Mass.: Harvard University Press, 1990).
Clark, Linda *et al.*, 'The Political Economy of Training: Should Britain Try to Emulate Germany', *Political Quarterly*, vol. 65 (1994), 74–92.
Coleman, James S., 'Social Capital in the Creation of Human Capital', *American Journal of Sociology*, vol. 194 (1988), Supplement S95–S120.
Cowen, M. P. and R. W. Shenton, *Doctrines of Development* (London: Routledge, 1996).
Crouch, Colin and David Marquand, *Ethics and Markets: Cooperation and Competition within Capitalist Economies* (Oxford: Blackwell, 1993).
Culpepper, C. Pepper, 'Employees, Public Policy and the Policies of Decentralized Cooperation in Germany and France', in Peter Hall and David Soskice (eds), *Varieties of Capitalism: The Institutional Foundations of Comparative Advantage* (Oxford: Oxford University Press, 2001), 275–306.
Delorme, Robert, 'Regulation as an Analytical Perspective: The French Approach', in Atle Midttun and Eirich Svindland (eds), *Approaches and Dilemmas in Economic Regulation: Politics, Economics and Dynamics* (Basingstoke: Palgrave Macmillan, 2001), 1–26.
Dyson, Kenneth, 'West Germany: The Search for a Rationalist Consensus' in Jeremy Richardson (ed.), *Policy Styles in Western Europe* (London: Allen & Unwin, 1982), 17–46.
Esser, Josef, 'Germany: Symbolic Privatization in a Social Market Economy', in Vincent Wright (ed.), *Privatization in Western Europe: Pressures, Problems and Paradoxes* (London: Pinter Publishers, 1994), 105–21.

Fear, Jeffrey R., 'Constructing Big Business: The Cultural Concept of the Firm', in Alfred J. Chandler Jr et al., (eds), *Business and the Wealth of Nations* (Cambridge: Cambridge University Press, 1997).

Gershenkron, Alexander, 'Economic Backwardness in Historical Perspective', in Mark Granovetter and Richard Swedberg (eds), *The Sociology of Economic Life* (Boulder: Westview Press, 1988).

Giersch, Herbert et al., *The Fading Miracle: Four Decades of Market Economy in Germany* (Cambridge: Cambridge University Press, 1992).

Gourevitch, Peter, *Politics in Hard Times: Comparative Responses to International Economic Crises* (Ithaca: Cornell University Press, 1986).

Granovetter, Mark and Richard Swedberg (eds), *The Sociology of Economic Life* (Boulder: Westview, 1988).

Gray, John, *False Dawn: The Delusions of Global Capitalism* (London: Granta Books,1998).

Greenfeld, Liah, *The Spirit of Capitalism: Nationalism and Economic Growth* (Cambridge, Mass.: Harvard University Press, 2001).

Hall, Peter A. and David Soskice (eds), *Varieties of Capitalism: Comparative Institutional Advantage* (Oxford: Oxford University Press, 2001).

Hallett, Graham, 'West Germany', in *Government and Economies in the Postwar World: Economic Policies and Comparative Performance 1945–85* (London: Routledge, 1990), 79–103.

Hart, Jeffrey A., 'The Effects of State–Societal Arrangements on International Competitiveness: Steel, Motor Vehicles and Semiconductors in the United States, Japan and Western Europe', *British Journal of Political Science*, vol. 22 (1992), 255–300.

Hassel, Anke and Thorstein Schulten, 'Globalization and the Future of Collective Bargaining: The Example of German Metal Industry', *Economy and Society*, vol. 27 (1999), 486–522.

Herrigel, Gary, *Industrial Constructions: The Sources of German Industrial Power* (Cambridge: Cambridge University Press, 1996).

Hirsch, Fred, *The Social Limits of Growth* (Cambridge, Mass.: Harvard University Press, 1976).

Jurgens, Ulrich et al., 'Shareholder Value in an Adverse Environment', *Economy and Society*, vol. 29 (2000), 54–79.

Katzenstein, Peter (ed.), *Policy and Politics in West Germany: The Growth of Semi-Sovereign State* (Philadelphia: Temple University Press, 1987).

Kaufmann, Franz-Xaver, 'Normative Conflicts in Germany: Basic Consensus, Changing Values, and Social Movements', in Peter L. Berger (ed.), *The Limits of Social Cohesion: Conflict and Mediation in Pluralist Societies* (Boulder: Westview Press, 1998), 84–112.

Kenworthy, Lane, 'Are Industrial Policy and Corporatism Compatible?', *Journal of Public Policy*, vol. 10 (1990), 233–65.

Kenworthy, Lane, 'Civic Engagement, Social Capital and Economic Cooperation', *American Behavioural Scientist*, vol. 40 (1997), 645–74.

Kern, Horst, 'Lack of Trust, Surfeit of Trust: Some Causes of Innovation Crisis in German Industry', in Christel Lane and Reinhard Bachmann (eds), *Trust Within and Between Organizations* (Oxford: Oxford University Press, 1998), 203–23.

Landes, David, *The Unbound Prometheus: Technological Change and Industrial Development in Western Europe from 1750 to the Present* (Cambridge: Cambridge University Press, 1969).
Lazonick, William and Mary O'Sullivan, 'Big Business and Skill Formation in the Wealthiest Nations: The Organizational Revolution in the Twentieth Century', in Alfred D. Chandler Jr *et al.* (eds), *Big Business and the Wealth of Nations* (Cambridge: Cambridge University Press, 1997), 497–521.
Leaman, Jeremy, *The Political Economy of West Germany, 1945–1985: An Introduction* (London: Palgrave Macmillan, 1988).
Moore Jr, Barrington, *Social Origins of Dictatorship and Democracy: Lord and Peasant in the Making of the Modern World* (London: Penguin, 1966).
Nutzinger, H. G. and J. Backhaus (eds), *Codetermination: A Discussion of Different Approaches* (London: Springer-Verlag, 1988).
Offe, Clause, 'The German Welfare State: Principles, Performance and Prospects after Unification', *Thesis Eleven*, no. 63 (2000), 11–37.
Olson, Mancur, *The Rise and Decline of Nations: Growth, Stagflation and Social Rigidities* (New Haven: Yale University Press, 1982).
O'Sullivan, Mary, *Contests for Corporate Control: Corporate Governance and Economic Performance in the United States and Germany* (New York: Oxford University Press, 2000).
Putnam, Robert, *Making Democracy Work* (Cambridge, Mass.: Harvard University Press, 1993).
Shonfield, Andrew, *Modern Capitalism: The Changing Balance of Public and Private Power* (Oxford: Oxford University Press, 1965).
Smith, Tony, 'The International Origins of Democracy: The American Occupation of Japan and Germany', in Theda Skocpol (ed.), *Democracy, Revolution and History* (Ithaca: Cornell University Press, 1998), 191–209.
Smyser, W. R., *The German Economy: Colossus at the Crossroads* (London: Longman, 1992).
Spulber, Nicolas, *United States: The Struggle for Supremacy in the 21st Century* (New York: Cambridge University Press, 1995).
Streeck, Wolfgang, 'Between Pluralism and Corporatism: German Business Association and the State', *Journal of Public Policy*, vol. 3 (1983), 265–84.
Streeck, Wolfgang, 'Beneficial Constraints: On the Economic Limits of Rational Voluntarism', in Rogers Hollingsworth and Robert Boyer (eds), *Contemporary Capitalism: The Embeddedness of Institutions* (Cambridge: Cambridge University Press, 1997a).
Streeck, Wolfgang, 'German Capitalism: Does it Exist? Can it Survive?', in Colin Crouch and Wolfgang Streeck (eds), *Political Economy of Modern Capitalism: Mapping Convergence and Diversity* (London: Sage, 1997b), 32–54.
Swenson, Peter, *Fair Shares: Unions, Pay, and Politics in Sweden and West Germany* (London: Adamantine Press, 1989).
Thelen, Kathleen, 'Varieties of Labor Politics in Developed Democracies', in Peter Hall and David Soskice (eds), *Varieties of Capitalism: The Institutional Foundations of Comparative Advantage* (Oxford: Oxford University Press, 2001).
Thelen, Kathleen, and Ikuo Kume, 'The Effects of Globalization on Labour revisited: Lessons from Germany and Japan', *Politics and Society*, vol. 27 (1999), 477–505.

Upchurch, Martin (ed.), *The State and Globalization: Comparative Studies of Labour and Capital in National Economies* (London: Mansell, 1999).

Vitols, Sigurt, 'Varieties of Corporate Governance: Comparing Germany and the United Kingdom', in Peter Hall and David Soskice (eds), *Varieties of Capitalism: The Institutional Foundations of Comparative Advantage* (Oxford: Oxford University Press, 2001), 337–60.

Weiss, Linda, *The Myth of the Powerless State* (Ithaca: Cornell University Press, 1998).

Wengenroth, Ulrich, 'Germany: Competition Abroad – Cooperation at Home 1870–1900', in Alfred Chandler Jr *et al.*, *Big Business and the Wealth of Nations* (Cambridge: Cambridge University Press, 1997), 139–75.

Wever, Kristen S. and Christopher S. Allen, 'Is Germany a Model for Managers?', *Harvard Business Review*, September–October (1992), 36–43.

Whitley, Richard, *Divergent Capitalism: The Social Structuring and Change of Business System* (Oxford: Oxford University Press, 1999).

Ziegler, Nicholas J., 'Corporate Governance and the Politics of Property Rights in Germany', *Politics and Society*, vol. 28 (2000), 196–211.

9
Japan: The East Asian Developmental State

Introduction

The postwar recovery programme of Germany under the Marshall Plan and Japan under General Macarthur's occupation forces contributed to their emergence as liberal industrialized democracies posing a challenge to American economic dominance (Spulber, 1995). From fascist states with nation-centred neomercantilist economic policies before the war, both became known in the postwar period for their economic liberalism. American influence in promoting a world economy sustained by local leaders willing to respect economic openness and interdependence was vital in both. Heralding the beginning of 'embedded liberalism' and postwar Japanese and German recovery, the Bretton Woods agreement was ambitious 'not simply for reworking the thinking and organization of German and Japanese economic establishment but for also actually providing a world order capable of meeting the needs and new expectations of these two countries' (Smith, 1998, p. 204). Labelled as miracles, their economic success has been identified as the Rhine model (Albert, 1993), not because of geographical location, but because they adopt similar approaches to relations between state and the economy, a relationship deemed superior to the Anglo-American adversarial model (Johnson, 1982).

This study of the comparative political economy of industrial capitalism has in previous chapters sought to examine the role of the state in industrialized economies such as Anglo-American, German and Japanese. Such comparative studies highlight both convergence and divergence between industrialized economies adopting free markets and democratic systems in which the state has played a significant role. Variations in the role of the state are seen to have been influenced by

historical, cultural, ideological or situational factors. Notwithstanding such variation, that role is, for purposes of this study, seen as fundamental to the functioning of a capitalist economy.

Accordingly, in the next section, the focus will be on the historical background to Japanese industrialization. The third section attempts an understanding of the unique characteristics of Japanese industrial organization seen as an enigma in the non-Asian context. The fourth section analyses postwar developments of Japanese industrialization, the 'Developmental State', followed by an evaluation of its economic performance. I then examine the pressures of the international economy and the Japanese response to its competitors, ending with a conclusion in the last section.

Historical background

The Meiji restoration is the watershed to understanding the start of Japan's journey towards modernization. Tabb (1995) comments that it also represents a clue to its past. As industrialization first began in the West, modernization for non-western societies was equated with westernization and was therefore a cause for discomfort. The discomfort stemmed from the awareness that efforts to modernize would entail large-scale absorption of technologies and institutions from the West. Central to this discomfort is the ambivalence involved in wanting to learn new skills and new ways of doing things while at the same time being fearful of losing one's cultural and social identity. Japan's feudal past has been seen by some historians as having eased that transition. In fact Barrington Moore Jr (1966) supports the thesis that capitalism can establish itself more easily within a feudal system than within an agrarian bureaucracy (p. 229). Of the many reforms undertaken by the Meiji government (1868–1912), two, namely the establishment of a modern centralized state and an industrialized economy, were crucial in bringing forth Japan in the image of a modern industrial society (Moore Jr, 1966, pp. 245–6). Frequent comparisons with Germany in the current literature render it appropriate for us to look for common historical antecedents. 'The survival of feudal traditions with a strong element of bureaucratic hierarchy is common to both Germany and Japan. It distinguishes them from England, France and the United States where feudalism was overcome or absent and where modernization took place both early and under democratic auspices – fundamentally and with all due qualifications those of a bourgeois revolution. In this respect, Germany and Japan differ also from both Russia and China,

which were agrarian bureaucracies rather than feudal polities' (Landes, 1965; Moore Jr, 1966, p. 253).

While feudal origins explain the ease with which Japan was able to industrialize, the process of adapting to the use of new technology is nonetheless a difficult one, if unaccompanied by certain preconditions. These preconditions require changes in traditional values and social organization and constitute a possible cause of conflict. National consensus on the importance of modern technology had been achieved by the time of the Meiji restoration. Such national consensus achieved as a result of political leadership, cultural legitimacy and a high degree of social integration was instrumental in minimizing the conflict involving the transition (Hayashi, 1990, p. 4). Although conscious of its superiority, Japan was at the same time keen and willing to learn from others. 'It accepts the status of a pupil when it is necessary, invites foreign firms which have something to teach into joint ventures, and it knows how to be satisfied with the best bargain possible' (Dore, 1989, p. 1674). In this quest, overseas experts and technicians were hired and Japanese citizens were sent to other countries to observe and learn their ways. During that learning process, they were willing to swallow their pride and accept what Dore refers to as 'teeth gritting humility' (p. 1674).

The Japanese went about the process of modernization in a systematic way by setting up a postal service, adopting new standard time and a system of public education. Both time and education were used to instil discipline, obedience, punctuality and respect for authority in the form of the Emperor.

Loyalty to nation in the form of reverence to the emperor was encouraged by having his picture in every school and 'on every national holiday, the same ritual was performed in front of this icon throughout the country *at the same time*'. Landes (1998, p. 376) observes, 'Other countries sent young people abroad to learn the new ways and lost them; Japanese expats came back home. Other countries imported foreign technicians to teach their own people, the Japanese largely taught themselves. Other countries imported foreign equipment and did their best to use it. The Japanese modified it, made it better, made it themselves' (p. 381). While this explains why Japan has succeeded in becoming a modern industrialized nation, the process of getting there has not been without pain.

Japanese enterprise is noted for its extraordinary sense of national pride, its loyalty to a national ideal which transcends private and local interests and its ability to work in close cooperation with government. Such features, singularly absent in Anglo-American capitalism, are

attributable to the early support to business from government and to the sense of reverence to authority inculcated at school in the Meiji period. Landes cites the need to resist foreign domination and protect the polity from dissolution as providing the impetus for change (Landes, 1965, p. 139). The nature of that state assistance in the case of Japan differed from that provided by other European countries which possessed abundant natural resources and strategic investments. Landes wonders how this latecomer with limited resources made such strides in such a short span (1965, pp. 100–11). Indeed, the rapidity of industrialization achieved by an Asian country has evoked particular interest in academics and policy-makers in the West.

Japanese industrial enterprise

Interest in comparative studies has grown with evidence of variation between countries adopting the capitalist mode of competitive enterprise in which the state plays different roles and where historical and cultural factors have influenced the mode of industrial organization. The relationship between and within organizations, often categorized in terms of markets or hierarchies if applicable largely to the Anglo-American corporate sector, is, in Japanese corporations of equal strength, described as 'obligated relational contracting'. 'It is the concentration of such relationships which is the dominant characteristic of the famous large enterprise groups, known to the Japanese as *grupu*, and to foreigners, usually, as *zaibatsu* or *keiretsu*' (Dore, 1983, p. 467; Lincoln et al., 1996). Such types of organizational arrangements confirm the Japanese preference for long-term commitment in business dealings. Where such cooperative relations exist, a business can rely on one's trading partner to rescue it in return for a similar deed undertaken earlier. 'It is a calculation, perhaps, which comes naturally to a population which until recently was predominantly living in tightly nucleated hamlet communities in a land ravished by earthquake and typhoon. Traditionally, you set to, to help your neighbour rebuild his house after a fire, even though it might be two or three generations before yours was burnt down and your grandson needed the help returned' (Dore, 1983, p. 470). Williamson (1996) attributes such cooperation to ethnic homogeneity and to the long experience of sharing water rights (p. 317).

Such historical and cultural foundations on which Japanese industrial enterprise has been built overlooks Adam Smith's prescription of self-interest for benevolence as a duty (Dore, 1983, p. 470). While duty and mutual obligation under relational contracting may be seen as ineffi-

cient when compared with the individualistic competitive business world, Dore (1989) lists three favourable outcomes. These are: (1) that relative security of such relations encourages investment in supplying firms, (2) the relationship of trust and mutual dependency makes for a rapid flow of information about markets, and finally (3) the general emphasis on quality (p. 475). Referred to as one of the three treasures of Japanese business practices, long-term obligation through relational contracting has become the foundation of the Japanese system of lifetime employment providing stability in employment relations (Johnson, 1982). Williamson (1996) prefers the term 'hybrid contracting', that is, 'long-term contractual relations that preserve autonomy but provide added transaction-specific safeguards, compared with the market' (p. 378). He adds that this system of contracting, neither romantic nor softheaded, has, in Japan, been raised to a higher level of refinement (p. 318).

One outcome of this employment policy is the close, cooperative relationship formed by white- and blue-collar workers on the work site. Those relationships have arisen from the joint training and the practice of hiring highly educated engineers and assigning them to production sites to work alongside blue-collar workers (Morikawa, 1997, p. 310).

O'Sullivan (2000) observes that such organizational integration was instrumental in Japan's phenomenal rise, eventually challenging American dominance in the 1960s and 70s. In making that observation, she attributes America's decline to the bifurcation between managers as insiders and workers as outsiders, causing the loss of that integration so essential to organizational learning (p. 107).

Chalmers Johnson (1982) warned against projecting Anglo-American concepts of economic behaviour in trying to understand the Japanese economic miracle (p. 7). Focusing on the special relationship between the state and business enterprise as one of state intervention of the developmental type, Chalmers Johnson coined the term 'developmental state'. Unlike the market rational model of Anglo-American adversarial government–business relations, the Japanese plan-rational gives precedence to industrial policy, adopting a strategic or goal oriented approach to the economy and involving close government–business cooperation (Johnson, 1982, pp. 18–19). Described as 'guidance', this consistent and predictable pattern of relationship is overseen by a pilot agency, the Ministry of International Trade and Industry (see later in the chapter for details).

The rapid growth of the Japanese economy in the 1970s and 1980s and the corresponding decline in American industry encouraged a

microeconomic view that stressed the internal organization of firms – that is, the distinctive properties relating to the assembly of factors of production. Of particular attention to non-Japanese observers are management practices such as *keiretsu*, *kanban* and links with suppliers and employee relations. 'The core of these process innovations lies in the microorganizational structure within firms, as well as between firms and their upwardly and downwardly linked allies. In support of this system, Japan developed a complex regulatory system linking firms, government and the market into a network of managed competition' (Gourevitch, 1998, p. 217).

While growing evidence of Japanese and German success emerges, one is starting to doubt the inflexibility or unresponsiveness of capitalist enterprise in the Anglo-American group of countries to economic change. Lazonick (1991) notes that the successful capitalist countries are ones that have moved from market coordination to planned coordination, or, according to Johnson (1982), from market rational to plan rational. Britain, the 'workshop of the world', began with an economy initially based on proprietary capitalism where market coordination was sufficient. In the early twentieth century, however, it gradually lost ground to the managerial capitalism of the US followed by Germany and Japan.

Japan emerged as an economic power by using and elaborating upon the institutions of managerial capitalism which had contributed to the success of the United States. That principle of planned coordination was extended across firms, within firms, and to business–government relations. 'The Japanese have not rejected managerial capitalism, but have elaborated it into a set of institutional relationships that I call collective capitalism' (Lazonick, 1991, p. 15). Morikawa traces the gradual influence of salaried managers in Japanese business enterprises which were once family owned. This shift towards the American model of managerial enterprise took place in the 1930s. Following United States occupation after the war, the Japanese economy underwent considerable change with the dissolution of the *zaibatsu*. Over 5,000 older managers were asked to resign and were replaced by younger (in Japanese terms) and better educated ones. The purges had other effects on Japanese enterprise, like the emergence at the top of people, largely from production and engineering, lacking experience but possessing a better understanding of blue-collar workers. 'Today Japan's large-scale industrial enterprises are, with very few exceptions, run by salaried managers. If we add the drop in the percentage of shares owned by individual shareholders, we find that Japan has almost entirely entered the age of the managerial enterprise' (Morikawa, 1997, pp. 320–1).

While Japanese business enterprise was transformed into Chandler's (1990) categorization of managerial enterprise, that transformation was and is linked to a continuing historical influence of (1) business networks (the *keiretsu*), (2) the prevalence of flexible production, and (3) distinctive organizational culture.

(a) Japanese networks

Japanese enterprise groups or networks of interrelated companies called *keiretsu* are a vital component of Japanese historical and cultural foundations. Termed 'Goodwill and the Spirit of Capitalism' by Dore (1983), they work together within a relationship seen by non-Japanese as collusive or anti-competitive: 'the main *raison d'être* of these groups is as networks of preferential, stable, obligated *bilateral* trading relationships, networks of relational contracting. They are not conglomerates because they have no central board or holding company. They are not cartels because they are all in diverse lines of business. Each group has a bank and a trading company, a steel firm, an automobile firm, a major chemical firm, a ship building and plant engineering firm and so on' (Dore, 1983, p. 468). Established with the intention of warding off market adversity, such networks are based on the principle of mutual obligation and support. While economic sociologists recognize the importance of non-economic factors such as social embeddedness (Granovettor, 1985) in economic activities, it must also be recognized that some of the social and economic embedding in non-western economies has been eroded during the development of modern market capitalist economies (Gerlach, 1992, p. 39):

> Financial and business analysts coming from the individualistic and universalistic orientation see such business networks purely in contractual terms, which are adversarial and thus characterise them as anti-competitive. Recent studies by sociologists attribute the *keiretsu* as enhancing the viability of the group as a whole by realigning its members' prospects and resources. The *keiretsu*, it appears, equalize the fortunes of their members, smoothing inequality in financial returns across participating firms at any given time, and perhaps over time as well, for any given company. These adjustments also described as 'alliance capitalism' (Gerlach, 1992) amount to 'taxing' prosperous members to guarantee the survival and hasten the recovery of financially troubled affiliates.
>
> (Lincoln *et al.*, 1996, p. 68).

Morikawa (1997) distinguishes *keiretsu* into two types: brethren and parent–child. Brethren-type are formed by corporations with international shareholdings with each member enjoying independent decision-making powers. The parent–child type arises when a corporation pursues vertical integration or diversification strategy and spins off business units as subsidiaries. As holding company, the parent company has considerable decision-making powers over such subsidiaries (pp. 328–9).

In 1977 the six largest *keiretsu* accounted for 16 per cent of all sales, 27 per cent of profits and 6 per cent of employment. With the rapid growth of the Japanese economy, however, their power has waned. Unlike the 1950s and 60s, individual firms are today less dependent on a single bank for their finance. *Keiretsu* generally avoid having a stake in more than one firm in a given industry and are therefore called 'one-setism', although the more recently formed Fuyo, Sanwa and Daichi-Kangin have chosen to deviate from that principle (Hart, 1992, p. 45). *Keiretsu* linkages across firms are, according to Hart (1992), a feature of the historical evolution of the Japanese economy. In the absence of a formal structure which defines the roles and responsibilities of member corporations the *keiretsu* is faced with an organizational problem. Monthly meetings of the presidential committee, the *schacho-kai*, bring together the various chief executives for informal discussions and exchange of information. While the president's council organizes group interests, the interaction between firms involving flow of resources represents the concrete manifestation of *keiretsu* interests (Gerlach, 1989; Gerlach, 1992). As in Germany but unlike the United States, a close relationship exists between firms and banks. 'Japanese firms have long had among the highest ratios of debt to equity of any developed country' (Gerlach, 1989, p. 153). Each *keiretsu* is linked to a bank, a practice that dates back to early *zaibatsu* days. As its number-one lending institution and the company's 'main bank', the bank provides a significant proportion of its capital and looks after its interests in several ways.

In their capacity as major shareholders, banks play a vital role in the financial control of Japanese business. While several may own stock, it is the *main bank* which closely monitors the business affairs of the company. With banks as major shareholders, Japanese business is ensured stability and protection from takeover threats. A bank's monitoring role only arises if a business is poorly run. In a well-run firm, the top management is internally selected and employee interests remain a prime concern (Aoki, 1990). In the financial system of Japanese business in which banks play a vital role, the 'voice' mechanism is more likely to be used instead of the 'exit' associated with Anglo-American business en-

terprise (Hirschman, 1970). According to Lincoln *et al.* (1996), 'There are some analysts for whom no *"keiretsu* network" exists: only sets of stable financial transactions between an array of corporations and the large banks on whose financing they depend.... In our view, the main-bank model is an extreme simplification that molds reality to the stark and simplistically dyadic agency-theoretic perspectives of corporate finance economics.' They view *keiretsu* groupings as a 'far-flung web of overlapping financial, commercial, and governance relations issuing from a central core to pull in large segments of the Japanese economy' (p. 72). The above differences in views indicate growing interest in Japanese business organizations from various disciplinary perspectives.

Following the 1997 Asian financial crisis when leading banks such as Credit Bank of Japan and Nippon Credit Bank faced bankruptcy as a result of adopting principles of market competition, the *keiretsu* have become a target for reform. Institutions burdened with excessive bad debt were allowed to go bankrupt, while other institutions have received public capital to regenerate and strengthen themselves. As a result, Japan's 20 large financial institutions have now been reorganized into four main banking groups. 'As a matter of course, the consolidation has led to the demise of the vertical "keiretsu" structure centred around the nation's top banks' (Sakaiya, 2000, p. 5).

Like other industrialized countries, Japan was hit by oil price hikes in the 1970s and exchange rate fluctuations in the 1980s. 'Yet despite these pressures, Japan's business system has proved itself both resilient (where change was not necessary) and adaptable where it was' (Gerlach, 1992, p. 248). A major source of resilience is the existence of intercorporate alliances which stabilize critical business relationships, while leaving individual companies to make adjustments in costs, new products or quality improvements (Gerlach, 1992, p. 248).

Gerlach introduces a significant element in understanding the functioning of systems, and their functional reliability, and identifies Hirschman (1970) as an exception who recognizes the need to tolerate repairable losses. Gerlach comments that there is surprisingly little consideration in economic theory to the connection between reliability and uncertainty. In the present climate of shareholder value, 'the leading sources of uncertainty in the contemporary American economy result from the challenges to the basic operations and integrity of the large corporation' (1992, p. 249). 'The result has been a radical restructuring of US industry – both as a result of takeovers and takeover attempts and a pre-emptive defense gainst them.' (pp. 250–1). The stockmarket-induced restructuring has been hotly debated. There are those who believe it has led to organizational

efficiencies, while others believe that, in this preoccupation with buying and selling assets, investments that would have promoted long-term competitive viability have been ignored. In addition, some social costs such as employee layoffs have been overlooked. 'Direct costs to these layoffs are borne by society through lost income-tax revenue and the payment of government unemployment benefits' (Gerlach, 1992, p. 251).

The Japanese market has historically been known for less reliance on stockmarkets for funds as the state plays a critical role in industrial credit allocation. 'Zysman, for example, views the financial system centred on credit relationships as "the eyes and hands of state's industrial brain"' (Calder, 1993, p. 7). Many companies in the 1980s sought external funds from the stockmarkets with none of the signs of stockmarket volatility seen in the United States. 'Reliance on stable, outside business partners buffers Japanese firms from the normal fluctuations of the business-cycle, as banks provide a steady source of capital to their close affiliates and external subcontractors provide a reliable source of production to buffer firms from economic swings' (Gerlach, 1992, p. 252). Such stable external relations have an automatic effect on internal relationships, allowing firms to concentrate efforts on 'product market competition, technological innovation and the development of employee skills' (Gerlach, 1992, p. 253).

(b) Flexible production

The second special characteristic of Japanese enterprise is the continued use of sub-contracting and the growing importance of flexible production. This helps firms to coordinate their operations flexibly and to respond quickly to technological and environmental changes (Aoki, 1990, p. 3). Japan's ability to combine flexibility with rigidity as well as quality and price competitiveness within mass production has been seen as a post-Fordist solution. According to Amin, Japan offers scale economies and institutional advantages of 'mass production and corporatist regulation, and the flexibility of scale and scope generated through subcontracting, loose independence within organizations, cultures of consensus and cooperation and so on' (Amin, 1994, pp. 22–3).

The Japanese system of multilayered sub-contracting had by the 1970s become transnational. It differed from other systems in the following ways:

1. the adoption of a decentralized structure of productive activities through a multilayered contract system which was more extensive than that adopted by other capitalist countries

2. it was a more stable and effective instrument of inter-enterprise cooperation than its counterparts in the US and Western Europe with a long-term perspective assisted by lead banks and powerful leading companies, the *sogo shosha*.
3. the multilayered contracting system was 'but one aspect of a more general management strategy of inter-enterprise cooperation aimed at minimizing competition between small and larger enterprises in the labour market' (Arrighi, 1994, p. 344).

Adaptation requires flexibility and can be achieved when operations are limited in size and require smaller amounts of investment. Studying this evidence of Japanese manufacturing practices, Friedman (1988) rejected the convergence idea (pp. 12–15). Continuous product development as witnessed in the Japanese automobile industry can be achieved only when products are made on a flexible basis. While encouraging domestic competition, it clearly differentiates Japanese flexible production from the American system of cost reduction through standardized mass production. Competition, then, does not have to lead to a common pattern of industrial development, that is, a single efficient outcome. Instead a 'complex political process determines what form of production a given industry or country will adopt' (Friedman, 1988, pp. 13–14).

Flexible production is the ability to produce an ever-changing range of goods tailored to different tastes. In creating specialized products to meet consumer demand, the producer works for a premium return. 'Mass production and flexible production require different skills in the factory, different strategies of using labour and machines, and different ways of integrating other firms into the manufacturing process' (Friedman, 1988, p. 15).

Friedman (1988) attributes Japan's economic success to the greater diffusion of flexible manufacturing strategies. The adoption of flexible production has enabled Japanese business to compete through product and price differentiation, to launch new products more easily than its competitors and to create a demand for unique goods. 'The Japanese political economy developed a network of financial and organizational practices that supported the continuous creation of small, flexible firms throughout the high-growth period' (Friedman, 1988, p. 21). Japan was thus in a better position to adjust to demand changes, material shortages and price fluctuations during business cycles and periods of economic crisis. The advantages achieved through flexibility resulted in competitive advantage and accounted directly for Japan's rapid industrial expansion (Friedman, 1988, pp. 20–4).

When combined with manufacturing flexibility, sub-contracting offers Japanese business ample opportunity to adjust to business fluctuations caused by recessions. Some critics view the use of sub-contractors as a way of safeguarding larger companies at the expense of the smaller. They also point to the resulting two-tier structure with its differential wages as exploitative. For Japan, however, the overall outcome has been the postwar success of the economy and the emergence of a flexible workforce which functions within an environment of loyalty and co-operation.

While flexible production is now widely prevalent in most industrialized countries, the reason for its predominance in Japan can be seen in the contextual politics of the country's industrial development. Affirming this, Friedman (1988) rejects both the bureaucratic and market regulation thesis which assumes that Japanese industry is the same as elsewhere, albeit more efficient (p. 25). It seems appropriate here to conclude this sub-section with a quote from Dore (1992): 'There are today, however, far more Japanese who would say, rather, we just have a basically different – and better – way of conceiving the nature of the business firm' (p. 17).

(c) Organizational characteristics

Japanese business is characterized by the existence of certain institutionalized 'shared set of norms and behavioural expectations' such as lifetime employment, seniority and enterprise union. Associated with the Confucian ethic and referred to as the 'three sacred treasures' (Johnson, 1982), these unique characteristics contribute to the sense of loyalty and belonging that one observes in Japanese business enterprise. Until recently it was quite usual for employees to spend their entire working life within a single firm. Young university graduates work alongside blue-collar workers as part of their early shop-floor experience. The commitment of Japanese workers is demonstrated by employees at Toyota who, on their way home after work, stop to reset windscreen wipers on cars parked in the factory yard awaiting movement to the dealers. Unusual as this may seem to non-Japanese readers, this is quite the norm in the distinctive Japanese work culture. Such a cooperative environment has developed as a result of the way employees are treated. Employees enjoy a special status, their stake being seen as paramount (Aoki, 1990). Amicable industrial relations and the ensuing sense of harmony have enabled Japanese industry to create an economic miracle. Dominant employee interest indicates that Japan is closer to postwar Germany than to the Anglo-American system of capitalism.

While many institutions were adversely affected following Japan's defeat in the Second World War, the one that survived postwar decades and in fact expanded its functions was the 'Japanese system of corporate governance'. Systems such as enterprise unions which strengthened workers' rights had an indirect effect on workers' sense of belonging to their companies. High economic growth caused a labour shortage in Japan and reinforced management's supportive attitude towards workers, causing it to institutionalize lifelong employment practice. 'As a result, the Japanese style of corporate governance has expanded its role as a mediating institution of normative conflicts to a still greater extent in postwar Japan' (Sato, 1998, pp. 307–8).

Interestingly, both Germany and Japan have been commended for their amicable industrial relations. In both, shop-floor control is in the hands of labour unions. While the German system relies on a high degree of coordination among firms within and across sectors, the Japanese system is based on strong plant-based labour markets (Thelen and Kume, 1999).

The advantage of Japanese companies relative to the German competitors 'seems to be their capacity for cross-functional integration on the shop floor as well as in management structures. German enterprises like their Japanese counterparts and in contrast to most American companies, have in the postwar period, attained considerable success in organizing the hierarchical integration of technical skills. However, two key features of the German system that facilitated hierarchical integration – specialized skills among production workers and functional divisions within managerial organization impeded cross-functional integration' (O'Sullivan, 2000, p. 268). This failure to achieve cooperation across functions renders Germany vulnerable to international competition, especially when introducing new products.

While globalization has brought increasing pressure for reform on employers, it appears unlikely that employers will implement measures that will hurt their own long-term interests of stability and quality. Both countries invest in training of workers without the fear often expressed in other industrialized economies of worker poaching by other employers. In fact, 'together, seniority wage and lifetime employment provided incentives for workers to stay with the company that trained them, which in turn made them safe for the firm to invest heavily in skills without fear of workers absconding with these skills to other firms' (Thelen and Kume, 1999, p. 485).

Although globalization is seen as shifting power towards employers with capital mobility and options of exit, the response is different when

firms are competing on the basis of quality and reliability in the context of just-in-time production. As it demands stable and cooperative relations with labour at the plant level, employers are reluctant to move beyond a point because they are averse to upsetting relations with unions.

As a consequence of the three sacred treasures – lifelong employment, salary on the basis of seniority and the company union – Japan enjoys 'greater labor commitment, loses fewer days to strikes, can innovate more easily, has better quality control, and in general produces more of the right things sooner than its international competitors' (Johnson, 1982, p. 11). Suggesting that Japan's economic policy has to be seen in totality of several and not just these three unique institutions, Johnson questions the impact of these institutions, citing several other equally important factors which have been overlooked such as the personal savings system, the 'descent from heaven' (*amakudari*) movement of retired bureaucrats into management positions in private enterprise, industrial groupings (*keiretsu*), elaborate system of sub-contracting, limited influence of shareholders and financial institutions like the Japan Development Bank, and so on.

According to Aoki (1990), lifetime employment and promotion on the basis of seniority only tell half-truths. The real explanation is that incentives are linked to rank and not to specific jobs: that is, people of a rank can work at several jobs and compete for promotion on the basis of merit. Administered by a personnel department developed specially by Japanese firms, the rank-hierarchy incentive system is well integrated with a horizontal coordination system rendering it organizationally effective (pp. 13–14). 'There is thus a clear higher – lower relationship, but there is also a pervasive sense of the classless membership of all in one organization where everyone puts its welfare uppermost' (Ketcham, 1990, p. 105).

Another practice that helps to explain the close working relationship between government and business in Japan is the *amakudari* or descent from heaven. On retirement at the age of 55, bureaucrats from government departments move to jobs in private corporations or government agencies or may even assume high positions in the Liberal Democratic Party (LDP). According to Perkin (1996), 'the bureaucrats and their *amakudari* ex-colleagues have a foot in all three camps of the administrative ruling elite. They are the leading thread in the tapestry, the reinforcing rods in the concrete, the hard drive in the computer of the Japanese system' (p. 156).

Tabb (1995) attributes Japanese economic success to (1) powerful national consensus implemented by a cohesive elite, (2) the institutionalization of entrepreneurship in a governance system extending to both

corporate entities and the development state, (3) embeddedness of the economy in supporting cultural institutions, and (4) the most effective systems of work organization, labour control, human capital development, and incentive structures yet developed (p. 30).

While loyalty and a sense of belonging have been inculcated over a period of time their sustenance however depends on ongoing practices. Japanese businesses avoid practices that differentiate between management and employees. All staff, whether white or blue collar, wear the same uniform and share common dining and toilet facilities. Another significant departure from western corporations is the low differential between salaries of top managers and workers. The feelings of togetherness generated by the egalitarian atmosphere and efficient outcomes has become central to the culture of Japanese business.

Japanese business culture is characterized by hard work, business ethics and a healthy respect for one's employer, for co-workers, and customers. Deeply indoctrinated in Japanese corporate life, this departure from the traditional specialized demarcation witnessed in other industrialized economies accounts for the fast, efficient, high-quality production of the Japanese work force (Tabb, 1995). 'Here team spirit, loyalty to the group, plant and firm, collective bonuses, "single status" for workers and managers, and, at a remoter level, the "three treasures" of life-long employment, wages rising with seniority, and the enterprise union, all play their part. That depends less on organization than on attitude to work and the corporation, which means high-trust industrial relations, in a word, a culture of cooperation' (Perkin, 1996, p. 164).

Recent setbacks to the Japanese economy have led to questions being raised as to whether the sacred treasures have outlived their usefulness and become an obstacle to change. Following restructuring undertaken in 1999, this vestige of postwar Japanese recovery is now under stress. Sakaiya (2000) explains that 'the way of thinking of the Japanese people is also changing. For decades, Japanese white-collar salaried workers have identified themselves not with their families, not with their local societies, not even with their religions or hobbies, but based on a powerful sense of affiliation with their work place. I call this phenomenon the "work place society," that is, a society that is dominated by work relationships' (p. 8).

Role of the state

Interest in the role of the state in the economy has generated interest in the political economy approach which essentially recognizes the

interdependence of economics and politics. According to Johnson (1982), the role of the Japanese state in the economy has led to a resurgent interest in 'political economy' in the twentieth century (p. 18). Termed 'plan rational' to distinguish it from market rational, the role of the state in the economy in Japan differs from the plan ideological of the Soviet type. 'At the most basic level the distinction between market and plan refers to differing conceptions of the functions of the state in economic affairs.... In states that were late to industrialize, the state itself led the industrialization drive, that is, it took on developmental functions... setting of such substantive social and economic goals' (Johnson, 1982, pp. 18–19). Characteristics identified with a developmental state are (1) precedence given to industrial policy by promoting a structure of domestic industry that is internationally competitive, (2) the adoption of a strategic, goal-oriented approach to the economy, (3) the appointment of economic bureaucrats to important positions in the economic ministries which make important economic decisions in accordance with government's strategic direction, (4) the move of such bureaucrats to private sector business in top management positions following retirement, (5) close collaboration between government and private enterprises encouraging the adoption of new technology and promoting the national goals of economic development, and most important of all, (6) the subordination of economic interests to political objectives (Johnson, 1982, pp. 19–24).

Weiss (1998) cites characteristics such as the quality and prestige of its bureaucrats, strong in-house capacity for information gathering and the existence of the Ministry of International Trade and Industry (MITI) as features which have contributed significantly to Japan's growth. These features by themselves are insufficient to explain the success of the developmental state. What is essential is the operation of an appropriate relationship with the political system, and this, in the case of Japan, is the role played by the Liberal Democratic Party (LDP) over the years (pp. 49–54). However, Japan's current economic woes are being attributed to the faction-ridden old guard of the LDP which appears to be out of tune with the demands of a modern capitalist economy.

Although industrial policy in Japan has enjoyed prominence since the late-nineteenth-century Meiji period, it was not until the 1970s that it attracted attention. Monitored by the 'pilot agency', the Ministry of International Trade and Industry (MITI), such policy is comprised of two basic components: 'industrial rationalization policy' and 'industrial structure policy'. Industrial rationalization has to do with state intrusion into detailed operations of individual enterprises with the intention of

improving operations. In general terms, this is old style 'scientific management'. Industrial structure policy has to do with different sectors of the economy with government focusing on the differing proportions in the context of the overall economy (Johnson, 1982, pp. 26–7).

Okimoto (1989) defines industry policy in Japan as 'government's use of its authority and resources to administer policies that address the needs of specific sectors and industries (and if necessary, those of individual companies) with the aim of raising the productivity of factor inputs' (p. 8). In seeking to use its authority and resources towards specific industrial objectives, government acknowledges that such outcomes cannot be achieved through the market mechanism.

While the developmental state plays an active role in promoting industry in Japan, one cannot conclude that the state is a dominant actor in the economy. In terms of revenue, outlay, and equity ownership, the Japanese state is smaller than most capitalist countries (Okimoto, 1989, p. 2). With national priorities and political objectives playing such a significant part in the Japanese way of thinking, it appears unlikely that Japan will rely solely on market forces to achieve these objectives. Since Meiji Japan, that line of thought linking economic vitality with national security has been dictated by three principles: (1) that control over credit and non-financial resource allocation should be retained by the industrial planner eliminating the banker, (2) that adequately directed growth is attainable only through an alliance of the state with emerging, non-establishment economic forces, and (3) that coherent, planned economic growth can be achieved efficiently only in an environment devoid of pluralist politics (Calder, 1993, p. 50). 'To derive optimal outcomes, the visible hand of the state must work in conjunction with the invisible hand of the market' (Okimoto, 1989, p. 12). Okimoto (1989) offers two other explanations: (1) the need for a compensatory role to correct market deficiencies like imperfect information, narrow short-term pursuits, primacy of individual company interests, opportunistic behaviour and free-rider approach to public goods; and (2) multiple entry points for state intervention offered by Japanese market structure. Here Okimoto cites 'extra-market institutions like the *keiretsu* structure, inter-corporate stockholding, close banking–business ties, subsidiary and sub-contracting networks, specialized trading companies and industrial associations (pp. 12–17). While Okimoto's reasoning is sound, unlike Johnson (1982) he fails to distinguish state intervention from state role in the economy. While the former is a reactive response to market malfunctioning, the latter lays down the broad parameters of the state's role. In Japan the latter is

explicitly spelt out and is not the set of haphazard ad hoc reactions that one often observes in Anglo-American economies.

While such distinctions are possible at an analytical level, they often get blurred in day-to-day functioning. In the 1950s and 1960s Japanese governments intervened to (1) establish sectoral priorities, (2) mobilize resources for development, (3) protect infant industries, (4) issue guidance on investment levels, (5) organize rationalization and anti-recession cartels, (6) allocate foreign exchange credits, (7) regulate technology flows inside and outside Japan, (8) control foreign direct investment, (9) issue administrative guidance, and (10) publish white papers on the long-term future of the economy (Okimoto, 1989, p. 23).

Okimoto (1989) equates the Japanese concept of market to their aesthetic approach to nature. In the traditional Japanese garden one respects and works with nature but one can also enhance nature by using human capacity for adaptation and thus blend man-made with natural beauty (p. 49). It is this blending that MITI set out to achieve by the year 2000 by (1) shifting from energy-intensive heavy manufacturing to knowledge-intensive high technology, (2) creating a stable and supportive business environment, (3) reaching state-of-the-art frontiers in high-technology research and development, (4) improving economic efficiency and productivity, (5) improving the quality of life, (6) ensuring economic security, and (7) integrating Japan's industrial economy into the international economic system (p. 49).

Freeman (1988) attributes Japanese postwar technological performance to the management of technical change by Japanese enterprises combined with the social and institutional changes promoted by MITI. Perkin (1996) considers this relationship between the state and market in Japan to be unique because it is based neither on the free market model nor on bureaucratic dominance. 'It is the belief system of a partnership between bureaucrats, politicians and *zaikai*, the top business functionaries. They operate without any blueprint other than the flexible goal of economic growth, but with the tacit agreement and collaboration of men who, in whatever sector, know each other's mind because they are the same kind of people from the same educational and social background, who have fought their way up the same career ladders with the same competitive spirit and determination.' In the Japanese system the distinction between public and private hardly exists, the three sectors – politicians, bureaucrats and business executives – are so closely intermeshed that it is impossible to know who pulls which strings. 'It derives from the Confucian tradition that Japan took over from China and "naturalized" with infusions of Buddhism and

Shinto, to create the ideal of the "golden mean", social harmony, and mutual responsibility within the group (family, clan, firm, nation) that explains the unity of the Japanese against outsiders' (Perkin, 1996, pp. 160–1). Within a historically determined culture combining individual ambition with group loyalty, the Japanese build close cooperation between politicians, bureaucrats and business. Corporate managers respond to informal suggestions from bureaucrats on various aspects of industrial policy knowing full well that it is likely to benefit them in the form of subsidies, loans, contracts, cheap capital and even new markets. Such collaboration between public and private sectors, not practised elsewhere, is responsible for Japan's phenomenal growth (Perkin, 1996, p. 162). Johnson (1982) terms this 'administrative guidance', the 'coordination of plant and equipment investment for each strategic industry' (p. 29). By adopting an industrial policy which encourages private sector investment, it is possible to encourage the growth potential of the economy at a rapid rate of development.

Three institutional conditions are necessary for effective state involvement in the economy: (1) a well-trained bureaucracy capable of formulating policy; (2) the ability of that bureaucracy to implement such policy; and (3) capability of forging a consensus on the goals of such policy. While Japan's bureaucracy has played a vital role, the dominance of MITI has overshadowed other departments. In the implementation of policy, MITI, with the support of various ministries and businesses, has played a prominent role, particularly through its control over allocation of foreign exchange and technology imports. The third condition, achieving a consensus on goals of policy, has been easily achieved because all groups share in the objectives of policy.

Japanese postwar policy of state involvement in industrial development has been classified into four stages: (1) the reconstruction period (1945–59) when priority was given to renewing key industries such as electric power, coal, iron and steel and chemical fertilizers, (2) the period of rapid growth (1960–9) when Japan opened its economy to foreign competition by liberalizing trade and flow of international capital, (3) the period of qualitative consolidation (1970–9) following the oil crisis when the economy was able to overcome adverse conditions caused by the crisis, and (4) the period of promoting creative and knowledge-intensive industries (1980s) when MITI drew up a long-term plan for research and development of new industries. 'Throughout these four stages, the basic philosophy of Japan's industrial policy has been to achieve optimal resource allocation from a long term, dynamic viewpoint, which cannot be accomplished by the market mechanism alone,

although the principle of free competition in the marketplace has been to a very high degree respected' (Koshiro, 1986, pp. 162–3).

While Japan is committed to a free enterprise capitalist economy, there is also an awareness of the limits of markets to direct resources into areas favourable to the economy. That position has been made explicit in the form of an industrial policy. While some countries who support the market have failed to clarify that role on the assumption that government should have no role in the formation of industrial policy in an open capitalist system (Johnson, 1982, p. 28), other countries have intervened, albeit in an ad hoc manner.

During the rapid growth period of the 1960s, Japan adopted two types of tools, the protective and the developmental. Protective devices included discriminatory tariffs, preferential commodity taxes on domestic products and import restrictions based on foreign currency allocations and controls. The developmental tools offered low interest funds to certain targeted industries through government financial institutions, subsidies, exclusion from import duties of designated critical equipment, licensing of import for technology, developing the infrastructure and providing administrative guidance. After due consultation reflecting the nature of government–business relations, MITI, acccording to Johnson (1982), arrived at a proper mix of tools which 'enabled the government to achieve genuine industrial policy and also preserved competition and private enterprise in the business world' (pp. 28–9).

It is difficult to establish if Japan's economic performance can be attributed to its industrial policy alone. In understanding Japan and its superior postwar economic performance, one has to adopt a holistic view and consider the contribution of several factors which have together combined to bring about a total concept of the economy. This then is a timely warning to those who think that Japanese industrial policy can be adopted with ease elsewhere (Johnson, 1982, p. 30).

Critics of Japanese industrial policy falter because they begin with a unified model of capitalism associated with the Anglo-American model. That initial model of capitalism which owes its origin to Adam Smith's concept of market has gradually evolved to what now fits the concept of divergent capitalism shaped by national systems based on culture, history and their respective political economies. The differences are becoming increasingly recognizable with the demise of centrally planned economies, described by Perkin (1996) as the 'great arch'. While my study builds on the assumption that there can be no market without a proper system of government, a successful capitalist system is built on an appropriate mix derived by each country from crucial characteristics

during different periods of its political and economic history. Currently experiencing a serious setback with 'triple recession', Japan is questioning whether its model of capitalism dating back to the Meiji Restoration is appropriate to meet the needs of the transition from a growing to a mature economy. Its modern industrial state which fostered industry under bureaucratic guidance has perhaps created social systems too centralized for an era of diverse knowledge, thus necessitating major reform of the administrative system. In promoting major rationalization of the ministries and agencies from 21 to 13, the objective now is to shift power from the elite bureaucracy which had partitioned budgeting and government administration between them to the Prime Minister whose office is to exercise greater control in future (Sakaiya, 2000).

In a recent study, Porter and Takeachi (1999) claim that the problems now faced by Japan arise from state intervention which adopted selective strategies of targeting certain industries for development and in the process failed to encourage market competition throughout the economy (p. 71).

Evaluation of economic performance

That Japan's postwar economic performance, described as a miracle, has become the subject of serious analysis by outsiders is in itself a resounding verdict. While the pacesetters of modern industrial capitalism became more market-oriented, adopting traditional criteria of economic performance based on competition, growth, expansion and ultimately profit as reflected in sharemarkets, the Japanese, arriving late on the scene, worked hard to catch up, mastering new technology, expanding into markets by increasing market share and enhancing their operational and organizational efficiency to compensate for lack of natural resources.

Economic devastation following the war had left the Japanese per capita GNP at $380 (in terms of 1980 US dollars). Rapid growth of the economy took place between 1960 and 1970 when the annual rate was recorded at 10 per cent. This soon grew to $12,750 in 1987 and to $35,000 in 1996. The production index of mining and manufacturing grew 8.2 times its 1955 figure; exports grew tenfold and wages grew 3.5 times as much. The 1960–70 boom was followed by the shocks of the 1970s caused by changes in American policy, falling exchange value of the yen and two oil shocks. Initially the oil shocks halved the growth rate and accelerated the inflation rate, but the eventual outcome for Japan was its emergence as the most energy-efficient economy in the world,

rendering its exports competitive and resulting in a balance of payments surplus.

Japan's extraordinary postwar industrial development in the 1950s and 1960s was spearheaded by MITI. In 1960 Japan's share of world automobile production was 2 per cent, but by 1980 this had increased to 29 per cent. By transforming the way in which products were developed in a range of industries, Japan was able to gain competitive advantage, in particular market segments through high-quality low-cost products (O'Sullivan, 2000, p. 148). Japanese industrial development when compared with its competitors was helped by the higher productivity of its workers, in industries such as steel, metal working, autos and consumer electronics. The average annual rate of change in output per hour for 1960–86 was 7.6 per cent, compared with 3.0 per cent for the United States (Spulber, 1995, p. 89). Crucial to Japan's success in industrial development, according to O'Sullivan (2000), was the organizational integration achieved within and across business organizations through the adoption of innovative management practices such as total quality control, concurrent engineering and close links with suppliers and customers (p. 151).

The oil shocks of the 1970s severely affected the 10 per cent annual growth that had characterized the period 1960–70. Prior to the oil price hikes Japan's economy had been moving towards second place behind the United States. But then it had to face the 'Nixon shocks' – American policies to counter inflation and balance of payments problems. Anticipating a decline in exports and a recession in the domestic economy, the Japanese government adopted a policy of stimulating the domestic economy by easing monetary conditions and increasing the level of public investment. This however resulted in land speculation with the price of land increasing by 58 per cent between 1972 and 1974. Prices of general commodities then rose, leading to panic buying, fuelling inflation. Tight monetary and fiscal policies were introduced to stem these trends. The industrial slowdown and the resulting idle capacity in production brought about by declining domestic demand was handled through major rationalization drives and improved financial efficiency. 'Operation scaledown' combined with the response of the government led to a recovery by the late 1970s.

The eventual outcome of the two oil shocks was Japan's ability to become energy efficient by cutting down energy consumption (Nakamura, 1995). By overcoming the impact of the oil crisis, Japan emerged as the world's leading creditor nation with the largest trade surplus, giving its people a new sense of confidence and a desire to play an

international role. Although that confidence was somewhat moderated by the collapse of the 'bubble economy' in 1983 and rising unemployment caused by international competition and the continued flow of investment overseas, Japan did sustain its economic growth (Sato, 1998, pp. 312–13). During the 1970s and 1980s issues such as the quality of life, various religious activities, poverty and problems of urban living emerged as major concerns.

When the price of land sky-rocketed during the '1980s bubble economy', excessive population concentrated on limited land in urban centres led critics of Japan to describe it as a 'rich country poor man' (Hartcher, 1998, p. 81).

The 1997 Asian financial crisis resulted in a prolonged and deep recession, the repercussions of which are still being felt. Poor performance on the part of financial institutions starved small and medium-sized businesses of working capital. Manufacturing suffered from excess capacity, excessive debt and excess employment, while operating at a loss due to decline in demand and sales prices. This was reflected in a 25 per cent downturn in share prices over the year and a depreciation of 83 per cent in the value of the yen against the American dollar between 1995 and 1998. In other words, the effect of the 'bubble' has continued to affect the Japanese economy despite a short-term recovery in the mid-1990s. According to some analysts, the 'bubble' represents failure on the part of Japan to make the transition from a growing to a mature economy. Japanese society had worked hard to become a modern industrial state. While such an achievement was instrumental in transforming Japan into a leading industrialized economy, it did not prepare it to meet the demands of diverse knowledge. 'Not only was the Japanese economy suffering from the constitutional defects of heart disease, excess fat cholesterol build-up, the organizational structures that had been painstakingly established turned into shackles, and the skills that the nation had acquired were no longer of any use' (Sakaiya, 2000, pp. 4–5).

The postwar Japanese model of development based on export-driven pursuit of market share experienced a major setback with the burst of the bubble in the 1980s. While the crisis was clearly a case of poor governance of banks and other financial institutions, Japanese corporations were equally guilty of lack of oversight and accountability in the interim period between freedom from bank discipline and the subjection of stockmarket discipline. Owing to its nature, Japan's financial system did not lend itself to such market adjustment (Zysman, 1983) while its banking system, on which business largely relied for funds, lacked a proper monitoring system and competition. The shortage of

capital faced by Japanese business was caused by non-performing loans given to new ventures in tourism, housing, entertainment and resorts. 'In this wild orgy of lending and buying by Japanese entrepreneurs, both Okurasho (Finance Ministry) and the Bank of Japan failed in their role of guardians of monetary policy. Unlike the US and Germany, where independent central banks managed the 1987 crash, the Japanese Ministry of Finance failed' (Hartcher, 1998, pp. 87–8).

Several other factors need to be explored further to understand the banking crisis of the 1980s which impacted severely on Japanese economic performance in the 1990s. The first is the concept of the safety net as a social system of dealing with distressed banks – that is, distributing social costs associated with bank failures among related parties. The government provides the safety net in order to minimize the spillover effects of failure of banks and other financial institutions. This is an extension of the mutual obligation of the community model of business as distinct from the company law model.

The other factor noted by critics of Japan's financial system is that monitoring is carried out through the *amakudari* system. Poor performance as monitors by incumbents is likely to result in failure to obtain good jobs on retirement. The converse of this is the chance of collusion resulting in an undermining of the monitoring role and engaging in unsound practices at the cost of shareholders (Osano and Tachibanaki, 2001, pp. 151–2). That collusion was in fact instrumental for poor monitoring is confirmed by Hartcher (1998) who states that the *amakudari* was misused when ex-finance ministry officials colluded with bank officials and corrupt businesses (pp. 87–9).

Similar failure to monitor banks arising from conflict of interest has been seen recently in the case of Arthur Andersen vis-à-vis Enron. In its desire to enter into consulting assignments with the latter, the former compromised its independent auditing role, failing to alert regulatory agencies of the impending collapse of the energy giant.

Although associated with the 'developmental state, Japan's economy appeared inflexible when faced with rapidly changing information technology, decentralized industrial structure and growing internationalization. The culprit, according to O'Riain (2000), was the increasingly powerful and inflexible bureaucracy. Characterized as 'embedded autonomy', the developmental state is now seen to be 'embedded in local capital through close social ties between state bureaucrats and domestic business owners and managers' (O'Riain, 2000, p. 158). To extricate itself from this bureaucratic stranglehold, the Japanese government has announced a major shakeup of the bureaucracy, thus upsetting the

harmony or 'wa' of the Japanese system of government. The intention is to shift power from bureaucrats to politicians by creating a Cabinet Office for the development of policies. Ministries will be reduced from 23 to 13 with a 25 per cent reduction in the civil service (currently numbering 540,000) in ten years. Credited with Japan's postwar success, the bureaucracy has shown itself incapable of coping with the effects of the bubble, resulting in a decision to induct private sector personnel on contracts to develop policy (*The Australian*, 8 January 2001).

Conclusion

Like Germany, Japan made a remarkable recovery after the Second World War and took its place among other industrialized economies possessing democratic political systems and market economies. Notwithstanding assistance from the United States and its allies, Japan relied on its cultural, historical and technological foundations dating back to the Meiji Restoration that appear to shape its new capitalist system with the state playing a unique role.

While generating much interest in political economy, the central issue of interest to this study is the role played by the state in Japan's economy. Studies such as this increase our understanding of modern industrialized economies to a point where academics and policy-makers can recognize the scope for multiple types of market economies, similar to pluralistic democratic political systems. Japan's experience and success until the 1980s has been instrumental in the recognition of such variation. The importance of that experience and its impact on comparative political economy is discussed in the concluding chapter.

References

Albert, Michael, *Capitalism vs Capitalism* (New York: Four Walls and Eight Windows, 1993).
Amin, Ash (ed.), *Post-Fordism: A Reader* (Oxford: Basil Blackwell, 1994).
Aoki, Masohiko, 'Towards an Economic Model of the Japanese Firm', *Journal of Economic Literature*, vol. 28 (1990), 1–27.
Arrighi, Giovanni, *The Long Twentieth Century: Money, Power and the Origins of Our Times* (London: Verso, 1994).
Calder, Kent A., *Strategic Capitalism: Private Business and Public Purpose in Japanese Industrial Finance* (Princeton: Princeton University Press, 1993).
Chandler Jr, Alfred D., *Scale and Scope: The Dynamics of Industrial Capitalism* (Cambridge: Belknap Press, 1990).
Chandler Jr, Alfred D *et al.* (eds), *Big Business and the Wealth of Nations* (Cambridge: Cambridge University Press, 1997).

Dore, Ronald, 'Goodwill and the Spirit of Capitalism: Hobhouse Memorial Lecture', *British Journal of Sociology*, vol. 34 (1983), 459–82.

Dore, Ronald, 'Technology in a World of National Frontiers', *World Development*, vol. 17 (1989), 1666–75.

Dore, Ronald, 'Japan's Version of Managerial Capitalism', in Thomas A. Kochan and Michael Useem (eds), *Transforming Organizaitions* (New York: Oxford University Press, 1992), 17–27.

Freeman, Christopher, 'Japan: A New National System of Innovation', in Giovanni Dosi *et al.* (eds), *Technical Change and Economic Theory* (London: Pinter Publishers, 1988), 330–48.

Friedman, David, *The Misunderstood Miracle: Industrial Development and Political Change in Japan* (Ithaca: Cornell University Press, 1988).

Gerlach, Michael, 'Kieretsu Organization in the Japanese Economy: Analysis and Trade Implications', in Chalmers Johnson *et al.* (eds), *Politics and Productivity: How Japan's Development Strategy Works* (New York: Harper Business, 1989), 141–74.

Gerlach, Michael, *Alliance Capitalism: The Social Organization of Japanese Business* (Berkeley: University of California Press, 1992).

Gourevitch, Peter, 'The Political Sources of Democracy: The Macropolitics of Microeconomic Policy Disputes', in Theda Skocpol (ed.), *Democracy, Revolution and History* (Ithaca: Cornell University Press, 1998).

Granovetter, Mark, 'Economic Action and Social Structure: The Problem of Embeddedness', *American Journal of Sociology*, vol. 91 (1985), 481–510.

Hart, Jeffrey A., *Rival Capitalists: International Competitiveness in the United States, Japan and Western Europe* (Ithaca: Cornell University Press, 1992).

Hartcher, Peter, *The Ministry: How Japan's Most Powerful Institution Endangers World Markets* (Boston: Harvard Business School Press, 1998).

Hayashi, Takeshi, *The Japanese Experience in Technology: From Transfer to Self-Reliance* (Tokyo: United Nations University Press, 1990).

Hirschman, Albert O., *Exit, Voice and Loyalty: Response to Decline in Firms, Organization and States* (New York: Free Press, 1970).

Johnson, Chalmers, *MITI and the Japanese Miracle: The Growth of Industrial Policy 1925–1975* (Stanford: Stanford University Press, 1982).

Ketcham, Ralph, *Individualism and Public Life: A Modern Dilemma* (Oxford: Basil Blackwell, 1990).

Koshiro, Kazutoshi, 'Japan's Industrial Policy for New Technologies', *Journal of Institutional and Theoretical Economics*, vol. 142 (1986), 163–77.

Landes, David S., 'Japan and Europe: Contrasts in Industrialization', in William Lockwood (ed.), *The State and Economic Enterprise in Japan: Essays in the Political Economy of Growth* (Princeton: Princeton University Press, 1965), 93–182.

Landes, David S., *The Wealth and Poverty of Nations: Why Some Are So Rich and Some So Poor* (New York: W. W. Norton & Company, 1998).

Lazonick, William, *Business Organization: The Myth of the Market Economy* (Cambridge: Cambridge University Press, 1991).

Lincoln, James R., Michael L. Gerlach and Christina L. Ahmedjian, 'Keiretsu Networks and Corporate Performance in Japan', *American Sociological Review*, vol. 61 (1996), 67–88.

Moore Jr, Barrington, *Social Origins of Dictatorship and Democracy: Lord and Peasant in the Making of the Modern World* (New York: Penguin, 1966).

Morikawa, Hidemasa, 'Japan: Increasing Organizational Capabilities of Large Industrial Enterprises', in Alfred D. Chandler Jr *et al.* (eds), *Big Business and the Wealth of Nations* (Cambridge: Cambridge University Press, 1997), 307–35.
Nakamura, Takafusa, *The Postwar Japanese Economy: Its Development and Structure, 1937–1994*, 2nd edn (Tokyo: Tokyo University Press, 1995).
Okimoto, Daniel L., *Between MITI and the Market* (Stanford: Stanford University Press, 1989).
O'Riain, Sean, 'The Flexible Developmental State: Globalization, Information Technology, and the Celtic Tiger', *Politics and Society*, vol. 28 (2000), 157–93.
Osano, Hiroshi and Toshiaki Tachibanaki, *Bankers, Capital Markets and Corporate Governance* (Basingstoke: Palgrave, 2001).
O'Sullivan, Mary, *Contests for Corporate Control: Corporate Governance and Economic Performance in the United States and Germany* (New York: Oxford University Press, 2000).
Perkin, Harold, *The Third Revolution: Professional Elites in the Modern World* (London: Routledge, 1996).
Porter, Michael E. and Hirotaka Takeachi, 'Fixing What Really Ails Japan', *Foreign Affairs*, vol. 79 (1999), 66–81.
Sakaiya, Taichi, 'The Present and Future of the Japanese Economy', Speech at Yale University, New Haven (2000), http//www5.cao.go.jp/2000/b/0505b-daijin-kouen-e.html 11/3/01.
Sato, Seizaburo, 'Japan: Normative Conflicts in Japan', in Peter L. Berger (ed.), *The Limits of Social Cohesion: Conflict and Mediation in Pluralist Societies* (Boulder: Westview Press, 1998), 293–319.
Smith, Tony, 'The International Origin of Democracy: The American Occupation of Japan and Germany', in Theda Skocpol (ed.), *Democracy, Revolution and History* (Ithaca: Cornell University Press, 1998).
Spulber, Nicolas, *United States: The Struggle for Supremacy in the 21st Century* (Cambridge: Cambridge University Press, 1995).
Tabb, William K., *The Postwar Japanese System: Cultural Economy and Economic Transformation* (New York: Oxford University Press, 1995).
Thelen, Kathleen, 'Varieties of Labor Politics in Developed Democracies', in Peter Hall and David Soskice (eds), *Varieties of Capitalism: The Institutional Foundations of Comparative Advantage* (Oxford: Oxford University Press, 2001), 71–103.
Thelen, Kathleen and Ikuo Kume, 'The Effects of Globalization on Labor Revisited: Lessons from Germany and Japan', *Politics and Society*, vol. 27 (1999), 477–505.
Weiss, Linda, *The Myth of the Powerless State* (Cornell: Cornell University Press, 1998).
Williamson, Oliver, *The Mechanisms of Governance* (New York: Oxford University Press, 1996).
Zysman, John, *Governments, Markets and Growth: Financial Systems and the Politics of Industrial Change* (Ithaca: Cornell University Press, 1983).

10
Comparative Perspective of Industrial Capitalism

Industrialized economies such as the Anglo-American, German and Japanese have adopted market capitalism within which different types of socio-economic and political institutions have evolved. Such embeddedness within socio-economic and political institutions has varied over three industrial revolutions, dictated by factors unique to each but operating within the framework of the market. In this era of the third industrial revolution, we witness the growing integration of markets through globalization, impelled by evolving communication and information technology.

While neoliberals hoped for the emergence of a globalized market economy as the ultimate outcome of economic liberalization, they failed to notice that the Fordist model, its centrepiece, was in decline. Perceived as inefficient in comparison with flexible production systems, it was unable to adjust to changing markets and technologies. Led by the influential French regulationist school, critics have noted a movement away from mass production to new production regimes that rely on collective institutions at regional, sectoral and national levels (Whitley, 1999; Hall and Soskice, 2001). Such studies have, according to Hall and Soskice, extended their analysis to a wide range of institutions that generate trust or enhance learning within economic communities.

The persistence of distinct forms of economic organization as variants of industrial capitalism has prompted Whitley (1999) to suggest that it would be productive to understand the processes underlying such divergence (Whitley, 1999; Hall and Soskice, 2001). While historical analysis is helpful in understanding such variation in the development of industrial capitalism and the divergent ways of coordinating and controlling economic activities in different institutional contexts, it is equally important to recognize the importance of the history of ideas. That Smith,

Marx, List and Weber with analysts of modern capitalism such as Schumpeter, Polanyi, Hirschman, Shonfield and Galbraith continue to be significant sources of ideas has been confirmed by Greenfeld's *Spirit of Capitalism* (2001). This study has focused on the postwar role of the state in industrialized capitalist economies while acknowledging historical and institutional influences.

The era of postwar economic recovery and sustained growth of capitalist economies witnessed the evolution of unique models of capitalism that succeeded in transforming the economies of Japan and Germany. In this recovery the state played a decisive role in promoting and supporting the private sector of the economy categorized as 'mixed economy'.

Characterized by close understanding between the public and private sectors of the economy which resulted in stability and sustained growth, the golden age came to an end with the economic crisis of the early 1970s, resulting in serious economic decline brought on by stagflation, high levels of unemployment, adverse balance of payments and declining economic growth.

In rejecting the *supply-side* theories which attribute the downturn to pressures on profits from workers, Brennen (1998) regards the unplanned, uncoordinated and competitive nature of capitalist production as the cause of the crisis. The fall in aggregate profitability was 'not so much an autonomous vertical squeeze by labour on capital, as of the overcapacity and over-production which resulted from intensified, horizontal inter-capitalist competition' (p. 8).

In reaction to the economic crisis of the 1970s, western industrialized economies reverted to neoliberal policies of unfettered free enterprise. Harking back to the 'invisible hand' of Adam Smith and severely curtailing the state's role in the economy, this era of new laissez faire marked the start of a growing divergence between capitalist economies. The neoliberal resurgence in the form of economic liberalization, deregulation and privatization was basically a response to political activism and to ideas emanating from monetarist and public choice schools and overlooked the growing evidence of successful organized capitalism.

The occurrence of such trends about the time when the fruits of state intervention were appearing in the form of the 'third industrial revolution' in information and communication technology has resulted in two distinct developments. The first is the internationalization and globalization of economies, raising questions as to the relevance of the role of the state in a borderless world economy where capital can freely move across countries. The second is the survival of small-scale and medium

type enterprises adopting flexible systems of production in industrial districts identified with craft-based skills. If such developments strike at the fundamental assumptions of the Fordist-type of capitalism, another and more significant development is seen since the late 1990s, in the upsurge of the 'new economy' centred primarily around information technology resulting in a phenomenal revival of the United States economy in sustained growth and a stockmarket boom.

Differences between countries, while reflected in different organizational forms and performance, can be linked to national institutions. It is important to recognize institutional embeddedness such as the nature of the political system, the links between industry and finance and the nature of the educational system which contribute to relative differences in the performance of different industrial sectors (Chandler Jr et al., 1997). To understand such influences, I have adopted the 'new institutionalist' approach to compare modern industrial economies. For example, one views concentration of power in narrowly focused institutions quite differently from widespread distribution of such power. The Japanese enterprise system allows for relatively greater consultation and involvement in day-to-day operations, unlike the political and administrative system which is more bureaucratic if not authoritarian. Contrast this with the German model which, both at the political and enterprise levels, allows for considerable participation and consultation. Described as contested organizational control at enterprise level, the system provides for wide-ranging analysis of the German economy undertaken by five institutions and the Konjunkturrat (or business-cycle council) comprising federal, regional and municipal levels of government, the Bundesbank, industry associations and labour to confer on issues affecting the two industrial orders (Herrigel, 1995).

If differences in national types are a product of specific institutions identified with a particular national type of capitalism, crucial to such differences is the way firms or industries organize their productive resources. Their ability to produce higher-quality goods at low cost and compete with other producers rests on the way organizational control is exercised.

The nature of state–business relations has a bearing on the functioning of industrial enterprises. In the Anglo-American model, short-term objectives based on the profit motive dictate internal structure and organization. The internal organizational structure of an enterprise has to constantly adapt to fluctuations dictated by extraneous factors which are then reflected in the value of shares on the stock exchange. The German model seeks to combine business success with the promotion

of values of the welfare state, recognition of the role of workers and the allocation of a monitoring role to banks. Despite changes in government, Germany has largely retained this model and avoided taking new policy initiatives. Apart from the institutional structure of the German political system, two important factors account for the incremental nature of economic policy-making. The first is a distinct neoliberal economic policy in which the state distances itself, assuming it is not the government's task to cope with structural change, and the second is a consensus approach to policy-making which discourages abrupt shifts in policy. Overall, West German policy-makers have continued to display cautious, step-by-step orthodoxy in their efforts to defend stability through incremental policy change in a rapidly changing global economy (Katzenstein, 1987, pp. 93–4). In the Japanese system, long-term national interest is promoted by harmonious government–business relations.

The policy of reducing the role of the state and encouraging the private sector has met with mixed responses across countries with mixed results. The response and the results in a volatile share market and a booming new economy of communication and computer technology have transformed the content of such economies from investment in long-term productive capital to investment in short-term speculative capital in globalized markets. Thus the economic boom of the 1990s particularly in the United States is difficult to compare with the pre-1970s economic performance, as the structure of the economy has changed dramatically, leaving overworked Americans with 'plenty of nothing' (Palley, 1998). The setback to Enron, the largest energy trading company in 2002, and the tremors faced by internet companies serve to confirm the growing uncertainty of the shareholder value approach to assessment of business success. We are now witnessing a change from 'retain and invest' policies to those of 'downsize and distribute', an outcome of changes in thinking brought about by the economic theories of organization where managers are now seen as agents of principals, the shareholders (Lazonick and O'Sullivan, 2000). The stockmarket boom and the growth of the 'new economy' in the 1990s, particularly in the United States, has led to pressure from investors to focus on shareholder value: that is, a shift from managerial control to shareholder control.

In the extraordinary revival witnessed in the US and Britain in the mid and late 1990s, the doctrine of shareholder value emerged pre-eminent. The performance of the corporation was centred on capital investment alone, while other factors of production such as employees, suppliers and consumers slid into insignificance. Central to this new view of the

corporation is the role of corporate governance where shareholders, board members, and managers are best equipped to promote and achieve the primary objective – that is, profit. The approach to corporate performance identified with the financial conception of the firm has encouraged mergers and acquisitions and is being suggested as a model for both Germany and Japan whose economies in the 1990s had experienced a slowdown.

While this study has focused on the role of the state, it is important too to acknowledge that the performance of the economy relies essentially on the success of business which, while dependent on innumerable factors of production, is also dependent on the changing economic and political environment. For example, Germany and Japan rose from the ravages of the war with Allied assistance. Intent on erasing the immediate past that had led to two world wars, they carved unique institutional models drawing from past historical, religious and cultural experience. The outcome of such efforts were the German 'social market' and the Japanese 'developmental state' and the adoption of a market economy on the lines of western industrialized economies in which government plays an active role of guidance. Differing from the orthodox neoliberal view of seeking autonomy for business from government interference, the German and Japanese approach seeks to establish linkages between government and business, with the expectation that it will promote economic transformation. That hope has eventuated for most of the post-Second World War period and has worked well, with the exception of unexpected occurrences such as the unification of East and West Germany, or the bubble period recently experienced in Japan.

Critics have identified the Japanese crisis of the late 1990s with the 1980s bubble. Government command over trade and industrial policy that existed in the 1970s was lost when Japan adopted the floating exchange rate, forcing a shift towards fiscal and monetary issues. Undertaken at the initiative of the US and Britain, the liberalization of finance created a new environment of free flowing capital in which the Japanese government found it difficult to maintain a balanced mix in its fiscal and monetary policy, thus triggering the bubble. Facing international pressure, Japan however went down the path of liberalization, deregulation and privatization, while continuing to provide social protection under domestic pressures. While the Japanese state struggled between these two agendas (Bai Gao, 2001), the notable losers from the changes were the bureaucrats, once instrumental in turning on the miracle.

The turbulence that advanced capitalist economies faced with the beginning of the energy crisis and subsequent economic cycles has had lesser impact on Germany when compared with the Anglo-American and, more recently, the Japanese economies. Germany survived such economic setbacks and proceeded successfully with the unification with East Germany in the 1990s, as well as membership of the European Union. Unlike Japan whose political system has not kept pace with its status as an economic power, Germany's strength lies in its political system.

Essentially, the foundation of the German and Japanese capitalist systems is based on effective social systems of production, somewhat akin to the postwar consensus of embedded liberalism or bounded capitalism when governments, business and labour combined to work within the framework of rules and regulations laying the foundation of the modern welfare state. Moreover, owing to the extensive linkages built into their social systems of production, Germany and Japan, unlike the Anglo-American countries, have shown less vulnerability to economic fluctuations.

The adoption by industrialized economies of different types of government–business relations has, according to Fear (1997), to be seen in the context of 'notions about the role of business in society'. Relating this to the importance of values that underlie the notions of competition or cooperation, Fear (1997) cites the acceptance of cartels in Germany and Japan which are not allowed in the United States. 'The Anglo-Saxon notion that cartels inevitably lead to disastrous economic performance may need to be differentiated. It is quite paradoxical that in most fields of human endeavour – except modernist economics – cooperation is considered "good"' (p. 553).

As late industrializers, both Japan and Germany tolerated cartels, emphasized the role of banks and encouraged greater worker incorporation in shop-floor management. Viewed as major contributors to the performance of both Japan and Germany, these are being discussed extensively and, in some cases, adopted selectively. However, the macro view still holds to a position that internal structure is the business of the firm and this is strongly supported by business in the Anglo-American countries. In taking such a position, corporations cloud out deficiencies of their internal structure which become known only through share markets which are unpredictable and do not often reflect the true functioning of industrial enterprises. The extraordinary power of information and the widespread use of institutional funds can lead to unexpected outcomes like that of the Enron crisis in the United States.

The volatility and dramatic upturns and downturns witnessed in postwar capitalist economies renders any conclusion tentative. This study is not intended to be a verdict on any of the types of capitalism discussed. Instead, by identifying the importance of the state in the functioning of advanced capitalist economies, I focus on the variations between them. Frequent changes in technology and markets are leading towards greater reliance on institutions such as unions, industry associations, banks, and political and administrative institutions. If one acknowledges the presence or absence of such institutions as a product of the historical developments of individual capital systems, then, according to this comparative study, one must also acknowledge that Germany and Japan are better endowed to respond to a change of demands than their Anglo-American counterparts; indeed, better equipped to respond to the larger environment, although perhaps discouraging for individual initiative and autonomous decision-making. At a micro-level, enterprises strive for greater independence and autonomy but prefer greater stability and certainty at the economy-wide level. Globalization and financial volatility have rendered the attainment of stability and certainty with the demands of international interdependence increasingly impossible. That lesson appears to have dawned on Japan in particular, on Germany to some extent and, to a lesser extent, on the Anglo-American group.

The changes witnessed in the recent past demonstrate that policy-makers need to anticipate demand and to adopt a different way of thinking. In particular, the economic crises of the 1990s highlight the need for stronger coordination in economic policy-making. Another cause for concern is the disregard for ethical values in the current neoliberal market environment.

My hope therefore is that this study will encourage further interdisciplinary research, daunting though such a task may appear with the emergence of a constant stream of research and literature in the field.

References

Brennen, Robert, 'The Economics of Global Turbulence', *New Left Review*, vol. 229 (1998), 1–262.

Chandler Jr, Alfred D. *et al.* (eds), *Big Business and the Wealth of Nations* (Cambridge: Cambridge University Press, 1997).

Fear, Jeffrey R., 'Constructing Big Business: The Cultural Concept of the Firm', in Alfred D. Chandler Jr *et al.* (eds), *Big Business and the Wealth of Nations* (Cambridge: Cambridge University Press, 1997), 546–74.

Gao, Bai, *Japan's Economic Dilemma: The Institutional Origins of Prosperity and Stagnation* (Cambridge: Cambridge University Press, 2001).

Greenfeld, Liah, *The Spirit of Capitalism: Nationalism and Economic Growth* (Cambridge, Mass.: Harvard University Press, 2001).
Hall, Peter A. and David Soskice (eds), *Varieties of Capitalism: The Institutional Foundations of Comparative Advantage* (Oxford: Oxford University Press, 2001).
Herrigel, Gary, *Industrial Constructions: The Sources of German Industrial Power* (Cambridge: Cambridge University Press, 1996).
Katzenstein, Peter (ed.), *Policy and Politics in West Germany: The Growth of the Semi-Sovereign State* (Philadelphia: Temple University Press, 1987).
Lazonick, William and Mary O'Sullivan, 'Maximizing Shareholder Value: A New Ideology for Corporate Governance', *Economy and Society*, vol. 29 (2000), 13–35.
Palley, Thomas I., *Plenty of Nothing: The Downsizing of the American Dream and the Case for Structural Keynesianism* (Princeton: Princeton University Press, 1998).
Whitley, Richard, *Divergent Capitalism: The Social Structure and Change of Business Systems* (Oxford: Oxford University Press, 1999).

Bibliography

Aglietta, Michel, *A Theory of Capitalist Regulation* (London, NLB, 1979).
Albert, Michael, *Capitalism vs. Capitalism* (New York: Four Walls Eight Windows, 1993).
Amin, Ash (ed.), *Post-Fordism: A Reader* (Oxford, Blackwell, 1994).
Aoki, Masahiko and Ronald Dore (eds), *The Japanese Firm: The Sources of Competitive Strength* (New York, Oxford University Press, 1994).
Arrighi, Giovanni, *The Long Twentieth Century: Money, Power and the Origins of our Times* (London: Verso, 1994).
Ashford, Douglas E., *History and Context in Comparative Policy* (Pittsburgh: Pittsburgh University Press, 1992).
Berle Jr, A. A., *The Corporation in Modern Society* (New York: Atheneum, 1973).
Bottomore, Tom, *Theories of Modern Capitalism* (London: Allen & Unwin, 1985).
Chandler Jr, Alfred D., *Scale and Scope: The Dynamics of Industrial Capitalism* (Cambridge: Belknap Press, 1990).
Chandler Jr, Alfred et al. (eds), *Big Business and the Wealth of Nations* (Cambridge: Cambridge University Press, 1997).
Crouch, Colin and David Marquand (eds), *Ethics and Markets: Co-operation and Competition Within Capitalist Economies* (London: Basil Blackwell, 1993).
Crouch, Colin and Wolfgang Streeck (eds), *Political Economy of Modern Capitalism: Mapping Convergence and Diversity* (London: Sage, 1997).
Dore, Ronald, *Taking Japan Seriously: A Confucian Perspective on Leading Economic Issues* (Stanford: Stanford University Press, 1990).
Evans, Peter, *Embedded Autonomy: States and Industrial Transformation* (Princeton: Princeton University Press, 1995).
Evans, Peter et al. (eds), *Bringing the State Back In* (Cambridge: Cambridge University Press, 1985).
Fligstein, Neil, *The Transformation of Corporate Control* (Cambridge: Harvard University Press, 1995).
Fligstein, Neil, *The Architecture of Markets: An Economic Sociology of Twenty-First Century Capitalist Societies* (Princeton: Princeton University Press, 2001).
Friedman, David, *The Misunderstood Miracle: Industrial Development and Political Change in Japan* (Ithaca: Cornell University Press, 1988).
Galbraith, John Kenneth, *The New Industrial State* (Harmondsworth: Penguin, 1967).
Gerlach, Michael, *Alliance Capitalism: The Social Organization of Japanese Business* (Berkeley: University of California Press, 1992).
Gershenkron, Alexander, *Economic Backwardness in Historical Perspective* (Cambridge, Mass.: Harvard University Press, 1956).
Giersch, Herbert et al., *The Fading Miracle: Four Decades of Market Economy in Germany* (Cambridge: Cambridge University Press, 1992).
Gourevitch, Peter, *Politics in Hard Times: Comparative Responses to International Economic Crisis* (Ithaca: Cornell University Press, 1986).

Gray, John, *False Dawn: The Delusions of Global Capitalism* (London: Grant Books, 1998).
Greenfeld, Liah, *The Spirirt of Capitalism: Nationalism and Economic Growth* (Cambridge: Harvard University Press, 2001).
Hall, Peter A., *Governing the Economy: The Politics of State Intervention in Britain and France* (Oxford: Polity Press, 1986).
Hall, Peter A. and David Soskice (eds), *Varieties of Capitalism: The Institutional Foundations of Comparative Advantage* (Oxford: Oxford University Press, 2001).
Hart, Jeffrey A., *Rival Capitalists: International Competitiveness in the United States, Japan and Western Europe* (Ithaca: Cornell University Press, 1992).
Hartz, Louis, *The Liberal Tradition in America* (New York: Harcourt Brace, 1955).
Harvey, David, *The Condition of Postmodernity: An Enquiry into the Origins of Cultural Change* (Oxford, Blackwell, 1990).
Held, David, *Democracy and the Global Order: From the Modern State to Cosmopolitan Governance* (Stanford: Stanford University Press, 1995).
Herrigel, Gary, *Industrial Reconstructions: The Sources of German Industrial Power* (Cambridge: Cambridge University Press, 1996).
Hirschman, Albert O., *Exit, Voice and Loyalty: Response to Decline in Firms, Organizations and States* (New York: Free Press, 1970).
Hirschman, Albert O., *Rival Views of Market Society and Other Recent Essays* (New York: Viking, 1986).
Hollingsworth, Rogers J. and Robert Boyer, *Contemporary Capitalism: The Embeddedness of Institutions* (Cambridge: Cambridge University Press, 1997).
Hutton, Will, *The State We're In* (London: Jonathan Cape, 1995).
Jessop, Bob *et al.* (eds), *The Politics of Flexibility: Restructuring State and Industry in Britain, Germany and Scandanavia* (London: Edward Elgar, 1991).
Johnson, Chalmers, *MITI and the Japanese Miracle* (Stanford: Stanford University Press, 1982).
Katzenstein, Peter (ed.), *Policy and Politics in West Germany: The Growth of Semi-Sovereign State* (Philadelphia: Temple University Press, 1987).
Kitschelt, Herbert *et al.* (eds), *Continuity and Change in Contemporary Capitalism* (Cambridge: Cambridge University Press, 1999).
Lane, Robert, *The Loss of Happiness in Market Societies* (New Haven: Yale University Press, 2000).
Lazonick, William, *Business Organization and the Myth of the Market Economy* (Cambridge: Cambridge University Press, 1991).
Leaman, Jeremy, *The Political Economy of West Germany: 1945–1985* (London: Palgrave Macmillan, 1988).
Lindblom, Charles E., *Politics and Markets* (New York: Free Press, 1977).
Lodge, George C. and Ezra F. Vogel, *Ideology and National Competitiveness: An Analysis of Nine Countries* (Boston: Harvard Business School Press, 1987).
Maddison, Angus, *Dynamic Forces in Capitalist Development: A Long-Run Comparative View* (Oxford: Oxford University Press, 1991).
Maier, Charles, *In Search of Stability: Explorations in Historical Political Economy* (Cambridge: Cambridge University Press, 1987).
Marglin, Stephen and Juliet B. Schor, *The Golden Age of Capitalism: Reinterpreting Postwar Experience* (London: Clarendon, 1990).
Marsh, James G. and Johan P. Olsen, *Rediscovering Institutions: The Organizational Basis of Politics* (New York: Free Press, 1989).

Mascarenhas, Reginald C., 'State Intervention in the Economy: Why is the United States Different from other Mixed-Economies', *Australian Journal of Public Administration*, vol. 52 (1992), 385–97.

Mascarenhas, Reginald C., *Government and the Economy in Australia and New Zealand: The Politics of Economic Policy Making* (San Francisco: Austin & Winfield, 1996).

Mascarenhas, Reginald C., *Comparative Political Economy of East and South Asia: A Critique of Development Policy and Management* (London: Palgrave Macmillan, 1999).

Moore Jr, Barrington, *Social Origins of Dictatorship and Democracy: Lord and Peasant in the Making of the Modern World* (London: Penguin, 1966).

Okimoto, Daniel L., *Between MITI and the Market* (Stanford: Stanford University Press, 1989).

Olson, Mancur, *The Rise and Decline of Nations: Economic Growth, Stagflation, and Social Rigidities* (New Haven: Yale University Press, 1982).

O'Sullivan, Mary, *Contests for Corporate Control: Corporate Governance and Economic Performance in the United States and Germany* (New York: Oxford University Press, 2000).

Piore, Michael J. and Charles Sabel, *The Second Industrial Divide: Possibilities for Prosperity* (New York: Basic Books, 1984).

Ruggie, John Gerard, 'International Regimes, Transactions and Change: Embedded Liberalism in Postwar Economic Order', *International Organization*, vol. 36 (1982), 379–415.

Sabel, Charles and Jonathan Zeitlin, *World of Possibilities: Flexibility and Mass Production in Western Production* (New York: Cambridge University Press, 1997).

Shonfield, Andrew, *Modern Capitalism: The Changing Balance of Public and Private Power* (Oxford: Oxford University Press, 1965).

Spulber, Nicolas, *United States: The Struggle for Supremacy in the 21st Century* (New York: Cambridge University Press, 1995).

Steinmo, Sven *et al.* (eds), *Structuring Politics: Historical Institutionalism in Comparative Analysis* (New York: Cambridge University Press, 1992).

Strange, Susan, *The Retreat of the State: The Diffusion of Power in the World Economy* (Cambridge: Cambridge University Press, 1996).

Tabb, William K., *The Postwar Japanese System: Cultural Economy and Economic Transformation* (New York: Oxford University Press, 1995).

Thurow, Lester, *Head to Head: The Coming Economic Battle Among Japan, Europe and America* (New York: William Morrow & Co., 1992).

Vogel, David, *Kindred Strangers: The Uneasy Relationship Between Politics and Business* (Princeton: Princeton University Press, 1996).

Weaver, Kent and Bert Rockman, *Do Institutions Matter? Government Capabilities in the United States and Abroad* (Washington, DC: Brookings Institution, 1993).

Weiss, Linda, *The Myth of the Powerless State* (Ithaca: Cornell University Press, 1998).

Weiss, Linda and John W. Hobson, *States and Economic Development: A Comparative Historical Analysis* (London: Polity Press, 1995).

Whitley, Richard, *Divergent Capitalism: The Social Structure and Change of Business Systems* (Oxford: Oxford University Press, 1999).

Williamson, Oliver, *The Mechanism of Governance* (New York: Oxford University Press, 1996).

Zysman, John, *Governments, Markets and Growth: Financial Systems and the Politics of Industrial Change* (Ithaca: Cornell University Press, 1983).

Index

Aglietta, Michel, 25, 155
Albert, Michael, 175, 179, 199
alternative capitalism (*see also* industrial districts), 2–3, 74, 113–30
  counter to liberal vision of the economy, 127
Anglo-American capitalism, 86, 108, 135–61
  challenged by German and Japanese capitalism, 137–8
  different from other types of capitalism, 137–8
  economic performance of, 150–4
  effect of neoliberal policies on, 90, 108
  government and business in, 147–50
  institutions of, 76
  market, 82
  phases in the process of diversification in, 148–50
  reasons for mass production in, 138
  response to decline of, 159–62
  role of the state in, 100
  shift to shareholder value in, 135–6, 229
Arrighi, Giovanni, 88, 99, 142, 155, 208–9

beneficial constraint, 80–1
British model of personal capitalism, 138–42
Bendix, Reinhard, 10, 11
Boyer, Robert, 88, 158
bounded capitalism, 3, 9, 30, 50–1, 71, 83–4, 105, 108, 231

capitalism (*see also alternative models*)
  alliance (*see also keiretsu*) 205
  collective, 74, 110, 204
  comparative, 47
  competitive, 30, 47, 185
  critics of, 37–40
  definition of, 34, 42
  developments in modern industrial, 30–44, 72
  difference from market, 13
  difference in academic studies of, 19
  disorganized, 103, 105
  emergence of types of, 3, 37, 110, 139
  family or personal, 139
  German cooperative, 185
  golden age of, 3, 9, 10, 71, 77, 83–5
  micro, 128–9
  philosophical foundations of, 31–40
  reasons for decline of, 40
  role of the state in capitalist economies, 5, 77, 150
  Schumpeter on, 39
  Smith on, 31–2
  Weber, 33–4, 37
Chandler, Jr, Alfred, 45, 69, 70, 77, 78, 138
comparative political economy, 1, 9, 10, 13
  classical political economy, 4
  institutional approach, 17, 20–1, 22, 103
comparative studies, 15, 20–1
  importance of, 17
  of industrial capitalism, 16, 17, 97, 113, 150
  purpose of, 11
corporate device, 141–7
  in Japan, 211
  power of American corporations, 141
  in USA, 230
corporatist, 22, 107, 179, 183, 87, 114, 154
  arrangements in Germany, 179, 194
  distributional coalitions, 107
  Panitch critique of, 83
  policy-making in, 83

Crouch, Colin, and Wolfgang Streech, 10, 45, 77–8

developmental state (*see also* Japan), 1, 47, 51, 105, 106, 136, 213–19, 222, 230
  as administrative guidance, 217
  characteristics of the, 214
  Johnson's view of, 203
discomfort index, 85
Dore, Ronald, 79, 81–2, 125, 126, 201, 202, 205, 210

embedded liberalism, 3, 9, 25, 49–50, 71, 84,108, 199, 231
Etzioni, Amitai, 55
Evans, Peter, 14, 15, 52, 102, 104–5, 108

flexible specialization, 25, 79–80, 87, 88, 128
  as a characteristic of industrial districts, 115
  importance of trust and cooperation for, 127
  reasons for adopting, 118
  response to limitations of mass production, US experience with, 157–8
Fligstein, Neil, 24–6, 86–9, 113–14, 148, 160
Fordism, 24–6, 86–9, 113–14, 228
  and flexible production, 25, 120
  crisis of, 88
  critique of, 25, 86–9, 226
  post-Fordism, 24–6
  response to the crisis of, 154–9
  reasons for Fordist-type production in US, 120
  Second Industrial Divide, 74, 114, 125
Frieburg school, 172
Friedman, David, 209–10

Galbraith, John Kenneth, 40, 67, 72
Gerlach, Michael, 205, 206, 208
Germany (*see also* social market), 85, 103, 106, 136
  apprentice system, 81, 184–5
  as a heterogenous system of industrial capitalism, 169
  characterized by unique institutions, 168, 169
  co-determination, 177–82, 183, 194
  Herrigel's interpretation of industrial constructions, 169
  industry associations, 174–6
  Ordoliberalism, 171, 173
  marriage of iron and rye, 171
  performance of the economy, 185–91
  role of the state in, 100
  role of banks, 176–7
  semi-sovereign state, 189
  subsidiary right, 174
  works councils, 178, 179–80,
Gershenkron, Alexander, 36, 76–7, 117, 176
Giersch, Herbert *et al.*, 180, 189, 191
globalization, 4, 46, 96–109
  as a free market promoted by World Bank, 98–9
  as voluntary or involuntary, 107–9
  changing nature of, 101–2
  declining role of state with, 97, 102–5
  Lowi's concept of, 106–7
  role of credit rating agencies, 108–9
  seen as deregulation and privatization, 98
Goldthorpe, John, 13, 19, 58, 85, 160
Gourevitch, Peter, 71, 79, 83–4, 144, 204
  government and the economy, 56, 77
  neoliberal view of government, 57
  role in the development of modern capitalism, 77, 150
government and business, 53–5, 60, 72, 74, 78, 79, 83
  in American capitalism, 147, 150
  as adversarial in Anglo-American, 125, 144–5, 147
  appropriate role for government, 56, 125, 228
  as distinctive regulatory approach in US, 53, 78

as mutual obligation in Japan, 125, 126, 203
as planned coordination in Japan, 204
power of business, 55
Gray, John, 98, 99, 101, 109, 110, 190

Hall, Peter, 20, 22, 23
Hall, Peter, and David Soskice, 10, 22, 24, 45, 75, 78, 78, 96, 97
Hart, Jeffrey, 80, 179, 206
Herrigel, Gary, 77, 117–18, 168, 177–8, 179, 189
Hirsch, Fred, 38, 39, 82
Hirschman, Albert O., 12, 15, 19, 37–8, 75, 77, 144, 206–7
Hirst, Paul, and Graham Thompson, 96, 101, 106
Hollingsworth, Rogers, 115, 120, 138, 158
Hollingsworth, Rogers, and Robert Boyer, 10, 75, 78, 80, 88, 96, 116, 135

industrial districts, 4, 30, 72, 74, 113–30
  as arenas of action, 123
  Baden Wurttemberg, 120–1
  characteristics of, 115, 122
  definition of, 116
  functioning of, 125–7
  in Germany, 117
  its distinct social environment, 126
  importance of trust in the functioning of, 122–3
  Marshall, Alfred, on, 115–17
  role of Christian Democrats in Italy and Germany in promoting, 128–30
  social embeddedness of, 122, 124
  survival of pressure from mass production, 124
  the regional character of, 118–19
  'Third Italy', 120–1
  unique or universal, 127–30
institutional approach, 2, 21, 22, 23–4, 103, 228
interdisciplinary studies, 15

Japan, 85, 88 (*see also* developmental state)
  alliance capitalism (*see also* keiretsu), 205
  amakudari (descent from heaven), 212, 222
  approach to modernization, 200–1
  bubble economy, 221, 230
  critique of Toyotaism, 158
  economic performance, 219–3
  flexible production in, 208–10
  industrial enterprise in, 202–13
  industrial policy, 217–19
  influence of Confucian tradition, 216–17
  Japanese business culture, 210–13
  keiretsu, 202, 204, 205–8, 215
  kanban, 204
  Meiji reforms on the development of, 200–1
  Ministry of International Trade and Industry, 203, 214, 216, 217
  relational contracting, 81–2, 202–3, 205
  role of the state, 100, 213–19
  state intervention as distinct from state role in the economy, 217–19
Jessop, Bob, 87, 88, 155, 156
Johnson, Chalmers, 199, 203, 210, 212, 214, 217

Katzenstein, Peter, 172, 174, 180–1, 87, 188, 189

Landes, David, 184, 201,202
Lane, Robert, 82, 144
large-scale organization, 68, 70, 73, 125, 138, 142–7, 154
  in American business, 70, 120
  and the corporate device, 141–7
  distinct from small and craft type, 118
  as a form of organizing production, 119–20, 138, 139, 154
  increasing power of, 69–70
  its effect on capitalism, 69, 74
  its effects on markets, 69
  relationship of railroads and, 121

large-scale organization (*cont.*)
  studying the governance structure of, 70
Lindblom, Charles, 12, 15, 55–6, 69, 77, 82, 83
List, Frederich, 32–3, 48–9, 77, 167–8
Lowi, Theodore, 106–7

Maddison, Angus, 84
market, 72, 83
  advocacy of agency theory of, 145
  as distinguished from authority system, 83, 155
  broader than capitalism, 13
  competitive market economy, 14, 72, 171
  coordinated market economy, 80, 113
  distinguish coordinated from liberal market economy, 22, 75, 77, 115, 182
  embedded, 74–5
  government role in the functioning of, 51, 71–2 73–4, 89–90, 167
  increased role of state in, 13, 72, 73, 148
  prospects for ideal market, 16–7
  public choice approach, 14, 46, 57
  state role in taming the, 41–2, 60, 77, 82
  state as victim of market with globalization, 104
  system of managed competition in Japan, 204
Marshall, Alfred, 115–17
Marsh, James, and Johan Olsen, 21, 22, 23, 24
Mascarenhas, Reginald, 14, 22, 45, 48, 71–2
Marx, Karl, 32–3, 156–7
mixed economy, 51–3, 71, 83, 227
  bounded capitalism, 30
  development of industrial capitalism within a, 45–9
  a product of state role in markets, 13–14
  role of the state in, 23, 47, 52–3, 67, 100
moral economy, 36, 53

Moore, Jr, Barrington, 17, 18–19, 36, 117, 200–1
Morikawa, Hidemasa, 203, 204, 206

Nelson, Richard, 56–7

Okimoto, Daniel, 215
Ordoliberalism, 171, 172
O'Sullivan, Mary, 12, 70, 76, 90, 138–9, 152, 153, 183, 187, 203, 211, 220

Piore, Michael, 122–3, 124, 127
Piore, Michael, and Charles Sabel, 74, 87, 88, 113, 115, 117, 120, 121, 123, 124, 130, 155
Polanyi, Karl, 35–6, 72, 74
policies, neoliberal, 45–6, 58–9, 76, 86, 89, 90, 98, 152, 159–62, 227
  as conservative ressurgence in Anglo-American, 160
  constraints in adopting neoliberal policies in Germany, 190
  differences in countries adopting, 231
  effects on the performance of the economy adopting, 90
  effect of policies on globalization, 98
  effect of the role of the state with, 46
political economy, 12–13, 15–16, 47, 76
  definition of, 10
  of industrial development, 76
  Maier's distinction, 14–5
  new political economy, 14, 45–6, 57
  problems of adopting an interdisciplinary approach, 15
  purpose of the interrelationship between the polity and the economy, 12
  revival of interest in, 12–13, 21, 213–14
  utility of the comparative institutional approach to, 21
private enterprise, 48, 72–3
  contributed to growth of state sector, 73–4
  dislike of state intervention, 56
  influenced by values of individualism, 143

and the public interest, 71–6
operates within a set of rules, 83
power and influence of, 55–6, 143
role of state in regard to, 59
shift in the role of private enterprise with globalization, 105
public choice, 14, 46, 57, 59, 76
Putnam, Robert, 129–30, 181

regulation (*see also* Fordism) 25, 87–9, 155–56, 158
Rhenish model (*see also* social market), 5, 36, 74, 106, 173, 199
Ruggie, John Gerard, 49–50, 71

Sabel, Charles, and Jonathan Zeitlin, 115, 116, 117, 119, 130, 131, 157
Schumpeter, Joseph, 39–40
Shonfield, Andrew, 42, 76, 77, 175
social market, 5, 74, 106, 167, 171, 173, 190, 191, 192–3, 194, 230
state and the economy, x, 2, 3, 20, 45, 48, 54, 59, 60, 71, 108–9, 148, 150, 199, 200, 213–19
state intervention, x, 2, 3, 20, 45, 48, 54, 59, 60, 71–2, 110, 159
Streeck, Wolfgang, 80–1, 175, 185, 186, 187, 188

Tabb, William, 200, 212–13

Thelen, Kathleen, 182
Thelen, Kathleen, and Ikuo Kume, 181, 211

United States, 72, 76
distinctive approach to government–business relations, 53, 150
new economy and shareholder value, 76, 145, 158
power of business groups, 55
prefer regulation of private enterprise, 145
reasons for economic decline, 151–3
response to economic decline, 159–62

Vogel, David, 78, 145

Weber, Max, 10, 11–12, 33–5, 55
Weiss, Linda, 105, 123, 128–9, 131, 175, 214
Weiss, Linda, and John Hobson, 75–6, 151, 152
Whitley, Richard, 226
Williamson, Oliver, 72, 202, 203

Ziegler, Nicholas, 193
Zysman, John, 78–9, 105, 106